D0875488

EARLY MODERN LITERATURE IN HISTORY

General Editor: Cedric C. Brown
Professor of English and Head of Department, University of Reading

Within the period 1520–1740 this series discusses many kinds of writing, both within and outside the established canon. The volumes may employ different theoretical perspectives, but they share an historical awareness and an interest in seeing their texts in lively negotiation with their own and successive cultures.

Titles include:

Pauline Kiernan
STAGING SHAKESPEARE AT THE NEW GLOBE

Ronald Knowles (*editor*)
SHAKESPEARE AND CARNIVAL
After Bakhtin

James Loxley
ROYALISM AND POETRY IN THE ENGLISH CIVIL WARS
The Drawn Sword

Arthur F. Marotti (*editor*)
CATHOLICISM AND ANTI-CATHOLICISM IN EARLY
MODERN ENGLISH TEXTS

Mark Thornton Burnett
MASTERS AND SERVANTS IN ENGLISH RENAISSANCE
DRAMA AND CULTURE
Authority and Obedience

The series Early Modern Literature in History is published in association with the Renaissance Texts Research Centre at the University of Reading.

Poetic Occasion from Milton to Wordsworth

John Dolan
Senior Lecturer
University of Otago
New Zealand

Published by PALGRAVE
Houndmills, Basingstoke, Hampshire RG21 6XS and
175 Fifth Avenue, New York, N. Y. 10010
Companies and representatives throughout the world

PALGRAVE is the new global academic imprint of
St. Martin's Press LLC Scholarly and Reference Division and
Palgrave Publishers Ltd (formerly Macmillan Press Ltd).

Outside North America
ISBN 0–333–73358–4

In North America
ISBN 0–312–22094–4

This book is printed on paper suitable for recycling and made from fully managed and sustained forest sources.

A catalogue record for this book is available from the British Library.

Library of Congress Cataloging-in-Publication Data
Dolan, John (John Carroll)
Poetic occasion from Milton to Wordsworth / John Dolan
p. cm.— (Early modern literature in history)
Includes bibliographical references and index.
ISBN 0–312–22094–4
1. Occasional verse, English—History and criticism.   2. Literature and history—Great Britain—History.   3. English poetry—History and criticism.   I. Title.   II. Series.
PR509.O24D65   1999
821.009—dc21   98–54305
                                                                          CIP

10   9   8   7   6   5   4   3   2
08   07   06   05   04   03   02   01

Printed and bound in Great Britain by
Antony Rowe Ltd, Chippenham, Wiltshire

PR
509
.O24
D65
2000

For my parents, John F. and
Mary Anne Dolan

Contents

1

Occasional Poetics in the Early Modern Lyric

Occasional poetics as a factor in the evolution of the modern English lyric has been relatively little studied. In this work I argue that the demands of poetic occasion played a major role in shaping the evolution of an important strain of English lyric poetry from Milton's time through to the mid-eighteenth century. I consider first the reasons for and ramifications of the narrowing scope for poetic invention which was one of the socio-literary consequences of the English Reformation. I then examine several successive generation of poets' ingenious responses to the problem of narrowing invention, which climax in the work of what I consider a greatly underrated generation of technically innovative poets of the early 1740s, who produced poems which created occasional pathos without a public occasion. These works showed later poets like Wordsworth how they could evade readers' infinitely troublesome demand for a truthful event grounding the poem by shifting from public occasions to a private, unquestionable 'mental occasion'.

Since this work covers the evolution of occasional poetics from Milton's time to Wordsworth's, it may be useful to begin with a comparison of the two poets at the beginning of their careers. Milton's best-known early poem, 'Lycidas', came into existence as an entry in a poetic funeral-games: as an entry in a memorial volume in which young poets strove against one another for fame, and in turn strove to make their university's memorial volume for a recently-deceased alumnus, Edward King, outshine that being produced in memory of Ben Jonson, who had also recently died, by Cambridge's rival, Oxford. Milton, coming to maturity at a time in which occasional poetry was one of the few genres open to the aspiring poet, accepted the opportunity to commemorate King, probably not a close acquaintance, and in doing so produced 'Lycidas'.

By contrast, Wordsworth, attending the same university a century-and-a-half later, refused, in an epochal step, to take advantage of a similar opportunity:

> The Master of the college died in March 1789. As was the custom of the day, literary-minded students from the college pinned on the coffin some nicely composed verses of appreciation. William [Wordsworth], however, refused, saying he had had no connection with the dead man, nor any interest in him, so why should he write something. His uncle couldn't understand it. Here was his nephew ... not taking an opportunity to distinguish himself by having his verse read by the Cambridge public. (Davies, 36)[1]

Milton, an ambitious and intelligent young poet of the 1630s, accepted the occasional/funereal tourney as a necessary venue for his poetic career; Wordsworth, coming of age at the end of the eighteenth century, refused a strikingly similar opportunity. In a sense, this work attempts, by analysing the evolution of occasional poetics from the time of 'Lycidas' to that of the *Lyrical Ballads*, to answer the question: what made it possible for Wordsworth to refuse the occasional début on which so many earlier poets had relied? What had changed about the occasional grounding of English poetry between Milton's time and his?

The precise boundaries of what readers and writers might consider to be occasional poetry changed many times between the early seventeenth and late eighteenth centuries – the period covered in this work. But there is a simple definition which covers the central meaning of the term, the one which determined the success or failure of individual poems: occasional poetry is poetry which relies on a verifiable event as its genesis. Occasional poems are not in any simple sense meant to be taken as works of the imagination. They are instead what Aristotle called 'epideictic' rhetoric, ostensibly produced by community-approved speakers who celebrate community values at a time when these values require commemoration, as after the death of a prominent person or a critical battle. (A discussion of epideictic rhetoric in seventeenth-century English literature, is given in Sloane, T. O. *Donne, Milton, and the End of Humanist Rhetoric*, pp. 93–4 and 130–44.) As I will argue in this work, the confluence of an ever-increasing number of literary aspirants in early-modern English literary culture, combined with a post-Reformation emphasis on 'truthful'

– that is, largely occasional – poetry produces a tricky interaction between literary ambition and epideictic function, and the ways in which successive generations of English poets dealt with this uneasy coexistence of ambition and piety helped to shape the influence of occasional poetics on the modern lyric.

The key element of occasional poetry is that the reader must believe it to originate with an actual event in order to accept the pathos-claims of the text. Occasional poetry, then, is not grounded in the author/audience compact known as 'fiction.' But here a suggestive and little-studied parallel between the development of reader belief in early-modern prose and poetry occurs. Scholars have accepted for some time that the novel, most successful of modern genres, depended heavily, at the beginning of its seventeenth-century revival, on gaining the reader's literal belief. Philip Stewart emphasizes, in a study of the revived novel, that early novelists wanted to deceive their readers into accepting their novels as real memoirs. Stewart makes a vital distinction between the two fundamental ways an audience can believe a literary narrative: 'Belief, as defined at the outset of this study, is of two kinds: literal and imaginative'.[2] Stewart is at pains to emphasize, in the face of the long critical emphasis on 'suspension of disbelief', that 'literal belief', for the early modern novelists, was a phenomenon distinct from and more extreme than 'verisimilitude':

> There are … two distinct levels of 'illusion.' First, the kind of absorption we have all experienced when reading a spellbinding work, where we temporarily forget that the work is fiction, as we can forget that a stage is really just a stage, a movie screen no more than a two-dimensional image. In the second, more literal illusion, the reader sincerely believes that the story is factual – that the novel in his hands is authentically something other than a novel....
>
> The technical matter which concerns us is not just verisimilitude but *illusion:* the writer was not only striving to be realistic, but to suggest to his reader that the story was not an invention at all – not even a 'realistic' one. (Stewart, 5)

The 'technical matter' identified by Stewart – hiding invention under the claim of literal truth – constitutes the 'poetic licence' under which one important strain of the modern lyric arose. The reader belief which the occasional poet wants to inspire is, in Stewart's terms, 'literal', not imaginative.

The importance of the grounding of occasional poetry in a true, verifiable event is closely related to its epideictic function and its resultant sanction to arouse intense pathos. As a catalyst for shared grief, it is legitimate; as a vehicle for poetic ambition masquerading as such a catalyst, it is – and was, even at the time of 'Lycidas' – highly suspect. 'I like not tears in tune', said Cleveland of his own and his colleagues' contributions to the memorial volume in which Milton's 'Lycidas' appeared, and over a century later, Samuel Johnson made essentially the same criticism of 'Lycidas' itself. This sort of uneasiness about elegiac ethics is an old problem. The formal claim of most first-person, elegiac poems throughout the history of the English elegy is that they arise out of grief; but the fact that these poems have been, for many centuries, collected, published, used to establish literary careers, has always been a cause of anxiety in English literary culture. Uneasiness about the 'sincere grief' hypothesis crops up again and again in discussion of the elegy, most famously in Johnson's oft-quoted (and oft-attacked) remark about 'Lycidas': 'Where there is leisure for fiction, there is little grief'. (Chalmers, 7: 302) 'Lycidas' exemplifies the way in which the conditions of production of elegy, when investigated, simply do not support the possibility of 'sincere' grief as a motive power for the elegy (a question which is quite distinct from that of the actual state of mind of the elegiac poet – a question beyond the present study).

One popular manner of 'periodizing' the topic of motive in elegiac poetry is to grant that before Wordsworth, before the Romantics, poets under the influence of an older poetics may have had no qualms about elegizing people who meant nothing to them, simply to further poetic ambition; but, as Wordsworth's refusal signals, with the inauguration of Romantic aesthetics, with its emphasis on the genesis of the poem in the individual's 'sincere' feelings, this sort of insincere elegizing ceased to be a legitimate part of poetic practice. As Dennis Kay says of Wordsworth's refusal to write an elegy of the occasion of a college official's death, 'This anecdote shows Wordsworth and his uncle standing on opposite sides of the chasm that separates us from the culture of Spenser, Donne and Milton'. (Kay, 232).[3] Wordsworth's famous refusal of the occasion was indeed epochal, signalling a change in the poetics of occasionality. But Wordsworth's scorn for the exploitation of such occasions is not what is new; distaste for occasional poetry as career-vehicle was felt, as the next chapters of the present work will show, by every generation from Milton's onward. Wordsworth's refusal heralds, rather, a technical innovation in poetic occasioning-devices, an innovation which affords avant-garde poets in the late eighteenth century the luxury of refusing such troubling occasions as the death of a scarcely-known college official. Wordsworth's decision to decline a funereal opportunity of precisely the sort Milton accepted in 'Lycidas' must be seen as a career decision, and as such it is rather like a promising young talent's refusal to take a poor job offer. Wordsworth's refusal implies a great deal about the climate of the poetic profession circa 1790: it implies that the profession, at least to its younger, avant-garde members, offered brighter opportunities. Wordsworth's refusal is the wise decision of a man with a future, a poet who realized that in the coming poetics, ethos is all.

Wordsworth was in a position to decline the occasion because, synthesizing several trends in poem-grounding technique developed during the late-seventeenth and early-eighteenth centuries, he had found a way to occasionalize the first-person lyric without requiring an actual, verifiable death. The most crucial fact about the autobiographical-narrative strain in modern English poetry is contained in this remark casually reported by a biographer: '[Wordsworth] used to say that every observation and incident [narrated in his poems] was true, and that if necessary he could name the date and place'. (Davies, xii). This assertion has an extra-ordinary implication: that Wordsworth, the prototypical modern poet in English, found it necessary to offer documentation for every incident narrated in his supposedly 'imaginative' art, implying that his work would somehow be vitiated if a hint of 'fiction' crept in.

Wordsworth's synthesizing achievement lay in the extension of the rules of epideictic/occasional rhetoric into the unlimited realm of mental events. If the pathos-benefits of occasionality could be extended to every reported event (e.g. 'I wandered lonely as a cloud'), then what need had Wordsworth to soil himself – and, most of all, compromise his readers' trust in his ethos, the all-important factor in occasionalized autobiographical lyric – by writing a sordid, openly competitive elegy on the death of a functionary whom he hardly knew?

The history of this particular first-person/occasional genealogy runs from 'Lycidas' to the *Lyrical Ballads* of Wordsworth and Coleridge – from the beginning of the post-Jacobean famine in literary invention, circa 1700, to the mid-eighteenth-century's paradigmatic solutions to the problem of legitimate invention, solutions which contemporary poets of the first-person lyric strain still employ. When the scope of possible poetic occasion broadens, as it was doing in Wordsworth's youth, the strictly-defined funereal occasion (e.g. the death of a college official) declines in importance; when the scope of acceptable occasion is constricted, as it was for most of the latter part of the seventeenth century, strict occasion-ality is what is left. Inventive drought and occasionality are always linked, because the drought in poetic invention is driven by a distrust of invented narrative – a distrust which, as Russell Fraser has demonstrated,[4] intensifies in English literary culture through-out the seventeenth century. Occasional poetry (which tends to be funereal poetry above all) along with poetry grounded in the authority of Scripture, is the genre which can best survive the audi-ence distrust of invented stories; after all, it rises from a confirmable event – a battle, a coronation, a death. Such strictly occasional poems are not the poet's 'invention' (and thus, to an anti-inventive culture like Interregnum England, the poet's *fault)* in a way that obviously invented poems are. The careers of Milton and Dryden were launched in mid-seventeenth-century England – a period of constriction of invention. Poets' reliance on occasion for a living could be, in this environment, very strong indeed. For example, Dryden's most acrimonious trade rival, Elkanah Settle, ended his life

> … in … carrying an elegy or epithalamium, of which the begin-ning and end were occasionally [i.e. according to the occasion] varied, but the intermediate parts always were the same, to every house where there was a funeral or a wedding [in the hope of selling it]. (Chalmers, 8: 442)[5]

Struggle to claim a corpse is in fact the defining action of the occasional poet. This struggle was not motivated simply by literary aims. It was often careerist and even straightforwardly commercial. The unscrupulous London bookseller Edmund Curll (1683–1747), always tried to be the first to place on sale memorial volumes – cornering the market, as it were, on the occasion:

> If a great man died, Curll announced immediately that his 'Life' was in the press and would be speedily published. This might be true, but usually … Curll would then invite the public to make the proposed publication complete by contributing any

biographical bits they might have. The result was usually a strange concoction.... But it was between covers and selling long before the grieving family or friends could publish anything at all.... Curll played variations on this technique. A few verses might appear by an anonymous writer. Some weeks later there would be a 'biography' of the supposed writer. Then the two pamphlets would be issued together as 'Poems on Several Occasions, with Some Account, etc.' (Pinkus, 55)[6]

Curll's primary impulse is to make it into print in as timely fashion as possible after the death he intends to exploit. His attempt to corner the occasional market was a serious and even dangerous business; '[Curll] was imprisoned, stood in the pillory and on one memorable occasion tossed in a blanket by the Westminster school-boys for printing a funeral oration without permission'. (Pinkus, 70). Curll and the poets of the occasion-centred poetics which predominated roughly from the mid-seventeenth to the mid-eighteenth century are primarily concerned with the timely production of poetry in a highly competitive environment ruled by occasionality.

Dryden, eager to make a career in this difficult environment, could never have afforded to turn down an opportunity like the one Wordsworth rejected. In fact, Dryden took the one he was given, gaining his first publication, in 1649, precisely as Milton had in 1638: as a contributor to (and competitor in) a memorial volume on the death of a member of his academic community ('Upon the Death of the Lord Hastings'). These early careers are linked by the theme of scarcity, what today we might call writer's block; Milton speaks of little else in the poems and letters of his youth, while Dryden had managed to publish only three poems – all occasional – by the age of 27. In Milton's, and even more in Dryden's time, the primary moment of opportunity for an aspiring poet was entry in a highly competitive (but ostensibly grief-stricken) volume of memorial verse for a dead schoolmate or master. Poetic careers were often begun, in seventeenth- and eighteenth-century England, with a poem in this sort of memorial volume.

The social function of this genre as a provider of consolation in moments of public grief has led, understandably, to the conflation of the effects of the genre on its auditors with the conditions of its production by poets. The tendency to confuse the state of mind of artist and audience is perennial (that is, it cannot be dismissed simply as a product of Modern/Romantic aesthetics). One of its more succinct modern expressions is the debate between Johnson and Gibbon about whether an actor feels the grief he mimes:

> GIBBON: But you will allow, however, that this sensibility, those fine feelings, made [Garrick] the great actor he was.
> JOHNSON: That is all cant, fit only for kitchen wenches and chambermaids. Garrick's trade was to represent passion, not to feel it. Ask Reynolds whether he felt the distress of Count Ugolino when he drew it.
> GIBBON: But surely he feels the passion at the moment he is representing it.
> JOHNSON: About as much as Punch feels. That Garrick himself gave in to this foppery of feelings I can easily believe; but he knew at the same time he lied. He might think it right, as far as I know, to have what fools imagined he ought to have. But it is amazing that any one should be so ignorant as to think that an actor will risk his reputation by depending on . . . [his] feelings.
> (Hillis, 118–19)[7]

This exchange sums up a long-standing cultural anxiety about the 'representation' of passion, which anxiety in turn had much to do with the intense suspicion and hatred many English consumers felt for invented ('feigned') passion, especially on the stage. It was inevitable that the elegy would be the focus of greatest anxiety about the sincerity of the artist when representing passion; an 'insincere' love poem might be merely contemptible, but an 'insincere' elegy implies a sort of exploitation of a tragic epideictic occasion. The 'insincere' elegist resembles the tragic actor in that his job is to represent, in a troublingly professional, careerist manner, a moment of communal emotion; thus the corollary of the extra rewards awaiting the successful epideictic poet is the more severe censure awaiting the elegist found to be 'insincere.'

The intense suspicion of literary invention held by the seventeenth-century intellectual is typified by the well-known aversions of Hobbes for any sort of synthetic, fancified histories. But the problem faced by the poet was often that of the less cerebral, religiously grounded dislike of false stories. Hundreds of seventeenth-century pamphlets and sermons testify to the intensity and duration of the hostility the poet faced in sixteenth- and seventeenth-century England. One petition, delivered to the King only four years after 'Lycidas', condemns 'the swarming of lascivi-ous, idle, and unprofitable books and pamphlets, playbooks and ballads'. (Fraser, 165). The hatred of literature tends to focus on poetry as the most mannered of the arts, but involves a hatred of all 'fancy' or invention: 'Wee have nowe long inough played with our owne fancies' asserts one anti-poet, joined by another anonymous pamphleteer, writing only a few years before the appearance of 'Lycidas', in condemning 'Love-songes, amorous books, filthy ballads, [and] Enterludes ....' The hatred of poets often displays a violent turn, as in a gloating description of the violent death of the 'braine-sicke and prophane poet', Marlowe, or even more blood-thirsty satisfaction at the collapse of a theatre with the loss of many lives in 1652. (Fraser, 23–4)

The hatred of literature cannot be dated in any simple fashion:

> The identification [of poetry with dissembling] is not new in the sixteenth and seventeenth centuries. Early in the twelfth century, a Scholastic philosopher wishes to know how the soul is profited by 'the strife of Hector, the arguments of Plato, the poems of Vergil or the elegies of Ovid'. The same question occurs in Plato himself, in attacking poetry as the father of lies. Only it is urged more insistently [in Reformation England] .... (Fraser, 6)

As the objections to literature are 'urged more insistently', the strategy of restricting oneself to forms grounded in something the English audience accepts as true becomes more and more charac-teristic of the poetry; occasionality, along with Scripture, becomes a crowded and dangerous haven for poets. In taking refuge there, however, poets have made a huge strategic concession: they have accepted the premise of poetic sincerity, and the corollary that 'insincere' poems (at least insincere poems grounded in epideictic contexts) are of dubious value. Poets of Reformation England had to accept, or at least work within or around, the criterion of sincer-ity; but, strangely enough, many of the more conservative twentieth-century critics of English elegy seem to have accepted the criterion as well. Eric Smith's *By Mourning Tongues* (London, 1977) is typical of this tendency. Other works within this tendency include John Jump's *The Ode* (London, 1974), Karen Mills-Courts's *Poetry as Epitaph: Representation and Poetic Language* (Baton Rouge, 1990), and Dennis Kay's *Melodious Tears: The English Funeral Elegy from Spenser to Milton* (Oxford, 1990). The field of interpretation –

specifically the restriction of that field to 'sincere' intellectual/ commemorative motives – defines this approach to occasional poetry. For example, in this passage dealing with the self-evident 'insincerity' of elegiac hyperbole, Smith, a representative critic of this school, attempts to distinguish a 'sincere' core within clearly hyperbolic verses:

> It is obvious, I think, that no one ever believed all this about a sudden devastation [of all nature] following on a sad death.... Yet, if the [elegaic hyperbole] was not believed, it could only spring from a deep ... kinship between man and Nature for whom alike the fact of death did not appear to make sense. 'Fallacy' of this sort springs out of basic human needs. The feeling of kinship may or may not linger with us from a more primitive stage of existence, but what it does powerfully suggest is what appears to the bereaved (and to others at times) as the essential loneliness of man in the face of forces which appear to make a mockery of all that he holds valuable. (Smith, 7)

The passage grants the unlikeliness of pure expression of grief as the motive force of elegiac poetry, but then, oddly, reasserts the expressive motive as grounded in larger – and more vague – issues like 'the loneliness of man'. This sort of movement, in which the critic nervously grants the inadequacy of 'sincere' reading of elegy and then goes on as if the concession had never been made, is oddly common. It seems to me to be founded in anxiety at an anomalous tropic feature of the genre – that is, a clearly unbeliev- able level of hyperbole which cannot be accounted for according to the notion of elegy as 'sincere' expression of grief. As Smith notes, meadows and forests do not grieve – and no seventeenth-century English poet or reader really thought they did. If the poem claims, then, something patently false (grieving Nature), its 'sincerity' becomes problematic. Yet this sort of hyperbole is one of the most fundamental characteristics of the elegiac genre, and virtually comes to define it during the mid-seventeenth century in England. Thus, hyperbole poses a problem for the sincerity hypothesis.

Smith's resolution of the anxiety depends, as does much of the criticism of elegiac anomalies, on a projection of the form backwards, out of its actual conditions of production in seven- teenth-century schoolrooms to 'a more primitive stage of existence' – presumably intended to be the time when the first elegy to employ hyperbole based on the seasons was created. 'From a resemblance of spring to human joy, and of autumn to human woe, the sense of analogy was fancifully extended until Nature was animated.' This hypothesis may or may not account for the original employment of elegiac hyperbole, but it does not account for the retention of the trope in cultural contexts like the one in which Milton and Dryden began their careers, which showed a violent hostility to 'fancies' far less patently false than the notion of animate, grieving seasons. Explaining the possible cognitive connections which may allow readers to see the link between autumn and sorrow does not illuminate the rhetorical considerations which led the contributors to *Justa Edovardo King*, writing for an anti-fanciful climate, to employ so much of precisely the sort of elegiac hyperbole which ought to have remained in that 'more primitive stage of existence' in which such things could be believed.

'"Fallacy" such as this springs out of basic human needs', Smith asserts. The human needs Smith posits as allowing for the implausibilities of elegiac hyperbole are 'the feeling of kinship [with Nature] which may or may not linger with us from a more primitive stage of existence' and/or 'the essential loneliness of man in the face of forces which appear to make a mockery of all that he holds valuable'. These excellent sentiments may well have been the primary concern of some elegists; but consideration of the typical English elegy as it actually came into being in Milton's or Dryden's time suggests that other needs, of a sort likely to be slighted by critics, might also have played a role. Such a poem would often have been written in a hurry – to meet a deadline, please a master, grace a family gathering or adorn a coffin (as in the case of Wordsworth's classmates, thronging to paste an elegy to the college official's coffin). And it would have been written, in many cases, by an ambitious schoolboy or young literary contender, seizing the opportunity of a Royal birth or a classmate's death to distinguish himself as literary aspirant.

A catalogue of the work produced by Edward King – who, as will be discussed in the next chapter, changed from occasional poet to poetic occasion when he died in a shipwreck – shows the importance of public occasions in generating poems for young writers of Milton's day. Ten poems by King have been found. All were written in Latin and nine of the ten are grounded in royal occasions:

> Of the ten poems ..., seven were written in celebration of the birth of royal children: poems 1–4 celebrate the birth of Prince Charles and Princess Mary, poem 8 the birth of Prince James, poem 9 the birth of Princess Elizabeth, and poem 10 the birth of the short-lived Princess Anne.... Poem 5 celebrates the recovery of King Charles from smallpox in the winter of 1632, and poem 6 is a thanksgiving for his safe return from his coronation in Scotland in 1633. (Postlethwaite, Norman and Gordon Campbell, eds. *Edward King, Milton's 'Lycidas': Poems and Documents*, 81–2)

Grief and empathy played a role in many of the poems produced in this context. Indeed, the unexpected death of Princess Diana in 1997 brought a wild rush of occasional response which may make it easier to understand the power of royal occasions, especially royal death, in seventeenth-century elegy. But not every royal marriage, departure, return, victory, defeat, birth or death was likely to attract such intense pathos. They inspired the writing of occasional verse because they sanctioned the act of literary creation and thus satisfied other 'human needs' which critics have been wary of acknowledging – above all that 'human need' which traditional literary critics would rather not consider at all: literary ambition. Like it or not, literary ambition is a major factor in the production of early-modern poetry. Richard Helgerson in *Self-Crowned Laureates* (Berkeley, 1986) stresses the importance of ambition in the early work of three of the most important early-modern English poets:

> 'I take it for a rule', Thomas Mann wrote ..., 'that the greatest works were those of the most modest purpose. Ambition may not stand at the beginning[...]'. This book is about three English Renaissance poets who broke Mann's rule...three poets who strove to achieve a major literary career and who said so[:] ... Edmund Spenser ... Ben Jonson ... [and] John Milton. (Helgerson, 1)

Many recent studies of literary invention in the seventeenth century have helped to redefine the question by shifting focus from vague, ahistorical 'human needs' to what one critic has usefully termed 'the literary system' or enterprise as it shaped the early modern English poem. Among recent work central to the thesis of the present work are Helgerson's *Self-Crowned Laureates*, John Guillory's *Poetic Authority: Spenser, Milton and Literary History* (New York: Columbia University Press, 1983) and Joshua Scodel's *The English Poetic Epitaph: Commemoration and Conflict from Jonson to Wordsworth* (Ithaca, NY, 1991). Of the many somewhat older works which bear strongly on the argument, central is W. J. Bate's *The Burden of the Past and the English Poet* (Cambridge, MA, 1970). Bate's view of the pressure of invention on poetic careers, rather than the Freudian psychodrama of the author, makes him a much closer ancestor of my approach than his better-known pupil, Harold Bloom. For consideration of the place of Classical and Renaissance rhetorical theory and pedagogy in seventeenth-century English literary culture, I have relied on Tom Sloane's *Donne, Milton, and the End of Humanist Rhetoric* (Berkeley/Los Angeles 1985). Paul Fry's work has also been crucial, particularly *The Poet's Calling in the English Ode* (New Haven, 1980) and the more theoretical *The Reach of Criticism: Method and Perception in Literary Theory* (New Haven, 1983). While Helgerson presents a detailed picture of the way that poets went about creating literary careers for themselves in early-modern English literary culture, Guillory's work defines the moment at which the Miltonic stance toward poetic invention assumed its shape, and offers a convincing explanation of the forces which gave it that shape. Briefly, Guillory investigates the problem of 'authority' in poetic invention – that is, how poets derive their right to make poems. Guillory tracks, during the crucial period from Spenser to Milton, 'those manoeuvres of invocation and recognition by which an author becomes an *auctor*' [*sic*] (Guillory, x) – that is, the ways in which an author acquires the right to write. Building on the work of E. R. Curtius's *European Literature and the Latin Middle Ages* (New York, 1963) and Russell Fraser's *The War against Poetry* (Princeton, 1970), Guillory argues that the period from Spenser to Milton is crucial to the history of poetic authority and invention because the Jacobean explosion of literary imagination was a legacy viewed by Milton and other mid-seventeenth-century figures with ambivalence (admiration mixed with theologically-grounded guilt at the flowering of 'imagination'). Guillory thus examines in detail the development of the literary climate which, in its hostility to invention, enforced reliance on strict occasionality and thus began the long process leading, I argue, to the creation of the first-person narrative/epiphanic poem.

Explanations of the actual mechanism of the hatred of literary invention in seventeenth-century England vary, encompassing religious, sociological, intellectual and other factors. The violent suspicion of literature displayed by many seventeenth-century English people has often seemed almost excessive or inexplicable: '[The Reformation anti-poetic pamphleteer] has (apparently) no legitimate target.... His extraordinary ferocity seems almost as puzzling as repellent'. (Fraser, 22). Guillory offers a convincing explanation grounded in Protestant theology, arguing that Reformation England came to regard the literary imagination as a 'usurper' of the ground which ought to have been left reverently vacant so as to allow God's word to suffuse it:

> The reduction of the supernal vision to the mere image, denounced by the Counter-Reformation Tasso, means even more to the Protestant poet: it means the usurpation of vision, the displacement of God's word by the fallen word of man, and the substitution of a human authority and a human origin for that of the divine author. (Guillory, 14)

In this climate, the poem must find a way to justify itself, ground itself. Milton's solution, Guillory argues, is to renounce the imagination in its 'wild' Jacobean form, represented for Milton by Shakespeare in general and *Midsummer Night's Dream* in particular, in favour of grounding within the sacred texts – within which strategic context tactical invention may be seen as 'inspired'. Reading Milton's 'On Shakespeare', (Guillory, 19) Guillory treats the text as an epochal dissociation of himself by Milton from the free, wild 'fancy' of the Jacobean poet, an elegy to a wide-ranging poetic invention to which Protestant poets can no longer aspire: 'The elegiac lines take an ironic turn when the reader discovers that "our fancy" is the object of which we are bereaved'. Guillory's summary of the situation implied by Milton's generation's renunciation of the inventive faculty emphasizes the defensive, restricted posture adopted by mid-seventeenth-century poets:

> The 'imagination' names for the post-Miltonic poet an 'internal vision,' a source of poetry, but it does not name the sacred text so much as the desire for such a text. As a name for poetic power, the word preserves both the visionary longing, and the failure of

that longing. The authority of the poet is henceforth more problematic, and requires an ever more complex defense. (Guillory, 22)

The salient characteristic of the rhetorical situation facing the mid-seventeenth-century literary aspirant, as developed in Helgerson's, Fraser's and Guillory's accounts, is its oxymoronic combination of intense literary competition with a deep suspicion of poetic invention. In this climate, poetic invention 'requires an ever more complex defense'. This is the landscape of 'Lycidas', and of the ambitious beginning of Milton's literary career, which form the topic of the following chapter.

Considering a revered figure like Milton as literary aspirant, treating his elegiac works as rhetorical texts, goes against the grain of more reverent criticism. It means, as Paul Fry says, considering 'poets as poets' (*The Poet's Calling*, 7)[8] rather than as oracles – and above all, taking seriously the notion of poetry as a career. A career-centred critical strategy has been adumbrated by Lawrence Lipking:

We have heard too much about the lives of the poets.... Yet the life of the poet – the shape of his life *as a poet* – has not been exhausted. Indeed, it has hardly been studied. We know far more about the facts of poets' lives, their quirks and torments, their singularities, than we do about the life that all poets share: their vocation as poets. (Lipking, vii–viii)[9]

The question is a vital one, especially if one accepts (as I do) Richard Helgerson's assertion that 'style follows genre, but both follow career-type'. (Helgerson, 34) Lipking's and Helgerson's central question: *How does a poet forge a career?* then assumes great importance in the analysis of the role of poetic occasion in the evolution of English poetry. Lipking, writing in 1981, claimed that this question had been largely ignored by critics. Thanks to several more recent studies of the literary career, we now have a clearer view of the development of the concept of the literary professional in early modern England. The period with which this study begins, the period in which Milton made his début as a poet, was not only an exciting but also a desperate time for the literary aspirant: more school-bred rivals, more professionalism – and all this, just at the moment that the literary imagination itself is under attack. No wonder that in Milton's youth, many poets felt a newly urgent need to develop ever more complex defences for the very existence of each new poem.

The defences poets developed led to widespread generic reper-cussions in Milton's time, some of them so fundamental that they are hard for us to see – precisely because they continue to operate in the definition of poetry in our own culture. The most basic of the consequences of the constriction of invention in early-modern English poetics is that English poetry from the mid-seventeenth century onwards became fixed in the status of a *reactive* art. By 'reactive' I mean that post-Miltonic poetry in English, even when not strictly occasional, tends to ground its origin in some 'real' event. By 'real' I imply no judgement about the ontological status of the grounding event but rather designate the traces of rhetorical effort by the poet to make the event appear to have been real. I do not mean to imply that the actual generative process of a post-Reformation poem in the mind of its author is necessarily different from that of a novel, essay, or screenplay, but rather that the authors of a text in those other genres would be likely to hide the fact that the genesis of their text occurred in an overheard remark, a childhood incident, or a newspaper article, whereas the twen-tieth-century poet would be likely to ground the poem as clearly as possible in whatever incident led to its invention. Indeed, poets have, for well over two centuries, gone to considerable lengths to fabricate such grounding occasions when the real genesis of an invented text was too private, too obscure, too purely *imaginative* to use. This is counter to the practice of most arts which describe themselves as 'imaginative'. Thus the reactive/imaginative distinc-tion centres on the manner in which invention occurs within the literary representation: modern lyric poems of the first-person/narrative strain on which this study focuses tend to hide their inventedness, while other literary genres tend to emphasize the imaginative results, rather than the original material which produced those results.

Wordsworth's offer to document 'date and place' of every inci-dent narrated in his verse is simply the most dramatic instance of this general tendency. Wordsworth could refuse to write an elegy because he had managed to synthesize a way to get elegiac (occasional) pathos out of mental events which required no embarrassing jostling around a literal corpse.

This fact, I argue, is the genesis of the contemporary first-person narrative poem: an epideictic, elegiac poem *without a corpse.* 'Reactive' poetry of this particular strain – that is, first-person narrative grounded in claimed autobiographical truth – first develops in the seventeenth century. In the literary reaction to this demand, two main streams can be distinguished: one grounded in Scriptural narrative, and another grounded in public, secular occasion. Both supplied the foundations for huge amounts of verse; but they were useful to aspiring poets in different ways. The supply of scriptural raw material was fixed, the material already well combed by generations of poetic glosses; this limited the extent to which most poets could exploit it. Occasions (deaths, battles, coronations, elevations) were by comparison 'fresh', and thus attracted more interest from aspiring poets. Occasional competition had profound implications in the way poets began forging their careers. Poetry, for an aspiring poet – Milton circa 'Lycidas', or Dryden, a decade later – was tending to become a career path, and the entrance examination for this career was coming to consist of a public rhetorical competition staged over the corpse of some public figure. (This is why budding English translators of the *Iliad* in the seventeenth and early eighteenth century almost always choose as their showpiece the scene in which glory-seeking warriors fight over Patroclus's body.)

This strange spectacle is the stage on which evolved one important strain of the modern English lyric: the ostensibly-autobiographical, first-person epiphanic narrative.

2

'Pardon, Blest Soul, the Slow Pac'd Elegies': Ambition and Occasion in *Justa Edovardo King*

1. MILTONIC CONTEXT: PIETY, SCHOOLING AND THE DRYING UP OF INVENTION

> If Milton had spared some of his learning, his muse would have gained more glory than he would have lost by it.
>
> Edward Young, *Conjectures on Original Composition*

Schooling, belatedness and ambition define the early career of John Milton. Belatedness is evident everywhere in Milton's early work; indeed, he uses the term himself: '"I do notice a certain belatedness in me".... The young Milton was ... always aware of his superior abilities but also aware of his slow development'. (Schiffhorst, 18); 'His was a "slow-endeavouring art";... It was his destiny to be slow in development.' (Parker, W. R. *Milton: a Biography* [ed. Gordon Campbell] Oxford, 1996, 145)

The antinomian partner of this feeling of belatedness is ambition. R. B. Jenkins has demonstrated at length in his study of fame in Milton's works that 'Milton's interest in fame began when he was quite young and continued during every period of his life'. (Jenkins, 9).[1] Milton is sometimes wary of disclosing the full intensity of his lust for fame; but when he is excited, as in this 1637 letter to Diodati, one can see the force of this hunger for celebrity:

> Listen, Diodati, but in secret, lest I blush; and let me talk to you grandiloquently for a while. You ask what I am thinking of? So

help me God, an immortality of fame. (Milton, *Prose Works*, 1: 327)[2]

Starting with his earliest remaining works and letters, Milton talks about fame incessantly, inevitably associating it with the notion of immortality:

> ... [P]leasure with which none can compare – to be the oracle of many nations, to find one's home regarded as a kind of temple, to be a man whom kings and states invite to come to them, whom men from near and far flock to visit, while to others it is a matter of pride if they have but set eyes upon him once. These are the rewards of study, these are the prizes which learning can and often does bestow upon her votaries in private life. (Milton, 1: 297)

With such blunt evidence in Milton's own words that literary fame meant a great deal to him, one would expect that critics would long have recognized the drive to celebrity as one of Milton's basic motives. But, as Jenkins goes on to point out, 'This theme [of literary ambition] has been left relatively unexplored by scholars ...'. (Jenkins, 9) Most traditional Milton critics – like Merritt Hughes, Irene Samuel and Eric Smith – have in the past attempted to divide the notion of fame, as it occurs in Milton, into two sorts. One kind of fame, the kind they admit Milton sought, is virtuous. The other is ignoble, and seems to resemble the modern hunger for literary celebrity. These critics then prove that Milton desired only the virtuous sort of fame. Smith, for example, while conceding the presence of a longing for fame in 'Lycidas', says that '... fame [in 'Lycidas'] is not vaingloriously defined'. (Eric Smith, 11)[3] This antithesis between 'good' and 'bad' types of literary ambition is peculiarly well-suited to Milton criticism, since it was developed by Milton himself ('Lycidas', lines 78–84: '"Fame is no plant that grows on mortall soil ..."')

Yet it is difficult to accept Milton's division of fame into noble and ignoble subspecies as a stable solution to the problem of ambition in seventeenth-century poetry (and especially in a pathetically-charged genre as elegy). Milton, and the literary culture in which he worked, worried deeply about the ethics of the search for literary fame. The structure of his famous sentence to Diodati reveals anxiety about the legitimacy of the hunger for fame; why else would the young Milton direct his confession to Diodati 'in secret'? The very existence of the many spirited denials of any interest in fame which occur in mid-seventeenth-century occasional poetry suggests that the lust for fame ('fame' as a hopelessly mixed-up, troubling concept, not safely divided into good and bad) was a major concern of the occasional poet in Milton's time.

Of course notions of fame change through time, according to changes in genre, technology and economic structure. As Leo Braudy notes,

> In every era and culture of the West since the Classical age, fame has been a complex word into which is loaded much that is deeply believed about the nature of the individual, the social world, and whatever exists beyond both. (Braudy, 585)[4]

The particular shape of Milton's longing for fame is important in considering the way literary aspirants of the early modern period conceived of literary celebrity. The particular stresses in Milton's notion of fame are three: schooling, international erudition-tournaments, and occasional poetics. These are the ways to fame pursued by the young Milton. Helgerson's detailed discussion of Milton's career-strategy in *Self-Crowned Laureates* has established that Milton not only desired but worked toward literary fame from an early age. In this, Milton was a modern figure; for while it may be true that literary ambition, broadly conceived, has been a constant since the beginning of literary narrative, literary ambition in its Modern poetic form (what Helgerson figures as the tournament for the 'laureateship')[5] develops in its modern form in England in the early seventeenth century, and the youthful Milton is at once example and chronicler of the phenomenon.

The change in the nature of ambition from Renaissance to post-Miltonic form is related to the dissemination of the idea of 'literature' and its institutionalization in the seventeenth-century public school. In the early seventeenth century, England began to produce increasing numbers of highly-educated young men. As the idea of a literary career emerges – newly tempting, public, and risqué – and as the newly cosmopolitan public schools focus on training the young English élite for the Continental literary rivalries, there is a change, exemplified by Milton's early literary career, in the way literary fame is pursued and imagined.

Milton was a product of this new-modelled schooling. Education was revered in his family: '[Milton's parents] had the good sense to instil in their son an enduring love of learning'. (Parker, 7) He worked first with a private tutor (Parker, 11–12) and thus prepared, received 'the best education that [his] family could provide ...' (Schiffhorst, l6) at St Paul's School in London. The educational system employed there and at Cambridge represented the fruition of efforts by reforming pedagogues to reintegrate England into mainstream European culture. (See Patrides, C. A. and R. B. Waddington, eds *The Age of Milton* [Manchester, 1980]; Clark, Donald L. *Milton and St. Paul's School* [New York, 1948]; *Poetry and Politics in the English Renaissance* [London 1985].)[6] This system directly created Milton as poet in a way that no earlier English educational system could claim to have done in creating the poetry of the Jacobeans or Elizabethans. The institutionalization of English education coinciding with Milton's youth has everything to do with his writer's block, his lust for fame, and finally his involvement in occasional poetics.

Formal schooling and occasional poetics are very strongly linked in Reformation literary culture. John Guillory shows in his analysis of Milton's poem to Shakespeare how strongly the young Milton associates the uneducated, freeranging Jacobean playwright with a fecund imaginative power now lost. (Guillory, Chapter 1)[7] But Guillory argues that the power of free invention was lost, as it were, in church (that is, through the influence of Reformation theology); it seems to me that it also was lost at school. Milton's belatedness, paralysis, and fear of invention is representative of a generation of literary aspirants who define themselves as students, and who continue to do so well into what a literary freebooter like Marlowe would have thought middle age. Milton's well-known capsule autobiography stresses the identity of student:

My father destined me from childhood to the study of humane letters, and I took to those studies with such ardor that, from the time I was twelve, I hardly ever gave up reading for bed until midnight.... My father had me daily instructed in the grammar-school, and by other masters at home. He then ... sent me to the university of Cambridge. Here I passed seven years in the usual course of instruction and study ... till I took the degree of Master of Arts. (Milton, *Areopagitica* ... 290–91)[8]

Milton's first poetic efforts are 'schoolwork' in a manner which is unprecedented in English poetry of the generations which reached adulthood before the new-modelling of the educational system: 'John [Milton]'s earliest efforts at versifying were ... aimed at pleasing his teachers and a few friends ...'. (Parker, 14); it was by shining in the composition of poetry that the best student could '... occupy the small desk, higher than the other benches, in which the "President" or best scholar of each form sat by way of eminence'. (Parker, 13)

These school poems can be conveniently divided into three categories: paraphrases of sacred texts, notably the psalms; strict funereal elegies; and school-work, practice-poems. The common denominator of these early works is the total absence of what Classical rhetoric would have defined as 'Invention' and a corresponding, compensatory flowering of figurative elaboration – that is, the capacity to elaborate a given topic as dramatized in many of Milton's youthful works such as 'Sonnet VII'.

Invention has always been the largest, most ambitious and most problematical of the aspects of Rhetorical pedagogy. Most classically-derived handbooks divided Rhetoric into five parts: Invention, Memory, Arrangement, Style and Delivery. Invention tended to become first among these equals, since the other four depend on the generation of a topic and an argument, which are the responsibility of the Invention. Invention is defined by Aristotle at the very beginning of the *Rhetoric* as 'the faculty of observing in any given case the available means of persuasion'. (Aristotle, 24) In a real rhetorical context this would mean the formulation of whatever arguments can be discovered to help one's cause; for example, in a forensic context, one would seek helpful arguments which might be grounded in the character of the defendant or the plaintiff, the circumstances of the crime, or the basic prejudices of the auditors about motivation or general psychology.

Aristotle divides Invention in the *Rhetoric* into three contexts: Deliberative (political), Forensic (courtroom), and Epideictic (ceremonial). Of the three major divisions of Rhetoric, the one which most closely concerns the poet is epideictic. Invention could be adjusted downward from strategic (that is, coming up with basic arguments or story-lines) to tactical (embroidering impressively on a given argument or scene). The Classical tradition, with the significant exclusion of Aristotle, had always been suspicious of pure invention and had preferred the latter, merely tactical sort of invention, as practiced in pedagogical techniques like *ethopoeia*. Classical texts often display the results of training of school-rhetoric in much the same way that Reformation poems do; when Tacitus, for example, makes a barbarian chief deliver a Roman-sounding anti-Roman oration ('[The Romans] make a wasteland and call it peace') in the *Agricola,* he is displaying the sort of second-order inventive oratorical skills he learned at school, when he would have been asked to compose many such speeches as part of a day's assignment.

Aristotle defines epideictic rhetoric as the rhetoric of praise and blame, amplification and diminution, with which the poetry of funereal or martial occasions is invariably concerned. Both the *Rhetoric* and the *Poetics* are involved in training the Aristotelian orator, for the distinction between Aristotle's two writing-hand-books is not always clear. As a modern Aristotelian scholar puts it:

The main province of the *Rhetoric* is the art of persuasive oratory. The *Poetics* deals primarily with the art of fiction – more particularly with the art of storytelling in the form of the drama and the epic. But in each of these treatises, there are implicit and explicit cross references to the other ... thus confirming the interrelationship of these arts of language.

There have been times, however, when the lines of demarcation between these allied but distinctive provinces have become blurred. The distinctions between the provinces of rhetoric and poetics have been especially liable to being confused. Starting with the Italian Renaissance in the sixteenth century, it was frequently difficult to tell whether a particular creative writer or literary critic was operating in the realm of rhetoric or the realm of poetics. (Corbett, v)[9]

The revival of classical practice, filtered through largely rhetorical perspective, made such training in impromptu elaboration-tournaments the basis for Milton's education:

Teaching [at Cambridge] consisted of lectures, mostly in Latin, and public disputations or debates (Milton's Prolusions) in which the student had to defend a standard proposition ('Whether day or night is more excellent') to display his rhetorical skills. (Schiffhorst, 19)

The Reformation school-poet was given intensive instruction in Aristotelian epideictic rhetoric. Rhetorical training is always (within

and across periodic and cultural boundaries) re-falling into disre-
pute, and always being relegated to epideictic (occasional) rhetoric,
with its more dangerous inventive (dialectical) aspects being reas-
signed to more respectable faculties (philosophy under Plato;
theology in medieval Europe; law and social science today).
Milton's place and time – in particular, his Puritan background –
coincided with one such detachment of Invention from rhetoric: its
reassignment to Philosophy proper . The very placement of *inven-
tio* within the sphere of rhetoric (as opposed to transferring it to
some more reputable field like logic) was at risk from the beginning
of the seventeenth century (Sloane, 60–2 and 279–89), in a radical
Protestant campaign led by Ramus, whom Milton admired and
translated. (Sloane, 137–44) This philosophical redivision of borders
parallels the reassignment of invention away from the Reformation
poet. What is left is 'the flowers of rhetoric' – the rhetoric of
epideictic embroidery.

Until recently, Milton's biographers have tended to be unsympa-
thetic to the rhetorical tradition in English pedagogy and its
implications for Milton's writings. Often the word 'rhetoric' is listed
without elaboration as part of Milton's youthful preparation:
'… the curriculum [at St Paul's] was largely the conventional
trivium – grammar, rhetoric, and logic –'. (Schiffhorst, 17). But even
in the anti-rhetorical accounts of Milton's education at St. Paul's
can be discerned a suggestion of the degree to which literary
competition on a given topic was the basis of the curriculum. To an
extent that many commentators are loath to admit, poetry was
schoolwork and schoolwork was poetry in Milton's environment:

> On four days each week [at St Paul's] a written exercise based on
> the readings was required, such as 'a Psalm to turn into Latin
> verse', 'a story in Heathen Gods to be turned into Latin', 'a Divine
> Theme', 'a Morall Theme'. According to tradition, when Alexander
> Gill [Senior], the headmaster [during Milton's tenure] … assigned
> a verse theme to write on the miracle at Cana, Milton wrote, 'The
> conscious water saw its God and blushed'. The assignment itself
> shows that originality of poetic expression was cherished in the
> school; every boy was expected to write verse …. (Wolfe, 7)[10]

The reverent tone here obscures an important distinction in the
way that verse was employed within the curriculum. When Wolfe
says that 'poetic expression' was valued at St Paul's, he is right to

the degree he means, by 'expression', 'Style' as a distinct aspect of the rhetorical pentad; if he means that such a system encouraged basic poetic *invention,* there is a body of evidence which suggests otherwise. Milton was rewarded for brilliant elaboration on a given story. He comes up with the novel trope 'conscious water', which turns the darkening of water into wine into a reaction of coy pride (much like the feeling experienced, perhaps, by a pupil torn between literary ambition and reverence for a sacred 'assigned' theme) – and wins the competition. The legitimacy of the story rests outside him, in the Scripture itself, and next in the fact that the topic was assigned by the Headmaster. Students were praised or blamed, elevated or not (literally – to '… the small desk, higher than the other benches …' granted the leading scholar) according to their ability to elaborate, not invent.

Elaboration was also fostered by focus on copiousness, which spawned an entire pedagogical genre including a textbook written by Erasmus himself (Sloane, 82–3) in which students were given a situation – a letter of thanks, a formal compliment – and required to compete to produce the most extended, most elaborate amplification. In these exercises in copiousness, as in those requiring impromptu poetry, the invention is given from above, not chosen by the student.

The *kind* of poem students were told to write also diminished the need for invention. The first of the three student genres, paraphrase of sacred text, is removed twice over from the taint of basic invention via the reattribution which was to yield Milton's greatest work: reattribution not merely to an earlier poet but to God himself. The second category, the elegies proper, and the genre to which 'Lycidas', Milton's contribution to *Justa Edovardo King,* belongs, avoids invention by grounding the poem in a public occasion – usually a death. The third category, the school exercises, was the broadest, and often resulted in poems which had to be identified as exercises in a subtitle – a device which diminished the invention the reader would impute to them, but which would also remove the taint of invention from the student-poet.

Milton and Cowley were the shining lights of the first large generation to emerge from these first-rate, Continental-model English schools, and their ability to excel in the production of competitive literary products pleased English literati like an unexpected Olympic victory by a nation hitherto unrenowned for athletic prowess. As Samuel Johnson, not usually sympathetic to Milton, writes,

At the same time were produced, from the same university, the two great poets, Cowley and Milton, of dissimilar genius, of opposite principles, but concurring in the cultivation of Latin poetry, in which the English, till their works and May's poem appeared, seemed unable to contest the palm with any other of the lettered nations. (Chalmers, 7: 9)

As often in Johnson's writings, a part of his argument is made via syntax: the passive construction *'were produced'*, by which Johnson suggests the degree to which poets like Milton and Cowley were the products of the school system, dependent on it and on the rules they learned there for their literary inventions. Johnson identifies the genesis of the new poetics in the school exercise in this passage from the 'Life of Cowley':

The metaphysical poets were men of learning, and to show their learning was their whole endeavour; but, unluckily [they] resolv[ed] to show it in rhyme. (Chalmers, 7: 12)

Many explanations have been offered for the flowering of bizarre, elaborate, 'Metaphysical' conceits in mid-seventeenth-century English verse, but the simplest explanation is that this sort of lush metaphorical invention is what products of the schools had been trained to do. Specifically, school-bred poets were trained to compose clever tropes *in the attempt to differentiate their work from that of many rivals writing at the same time on the same theme.* 'The conscious water saw its God and blushed'; this is school-bred, 'metaphysical' verse at its best – metaphorical invention in a rigid narrative context.

As a recent biographer asserts, 'It is important to remember that in various ways, at school and university, Milton was bred to competitive performance'. (Brown, *John Milton: a Literary Life*, Basingstoke & London, 1995, p. 2) From his first days in school, Milton would have aspired to the child-scale laureateship of the 'small desk, higher than the other benches' which would be occupied by the finest composer of verses. And as he passed through the educational system, he would have been reminded of the rewards of success: at St Paul's, he was befriended by Alexander Gill, Jr, son of the High Master of the school. Gill Jr was himself a successful competitor in occasional tournaments: 'Doubtless [Milton] was shown the Greek verses which Gill had contributed to the *Academiae Oxoniensis Funebria Sacra* (1619) and he may have seen in manuscript ... the [poem] which Gill wrote in celebration of his father's sixtieth birthday ...'. (Parker, 15) Charles Diodati, Milton's closest friend, was another successful competitor in occasional tourneys: '... In 1624 there appeared a ... volume which gave [Milton] especial pleasure. This was a collection of Oxford verses on the recent death of William Camden; it contained a Latin poem signed "Carolus Deotatus"'. (Parker, 21)

The system which produced Milton operated at every level, from classroom to world. In the classroom, the clever poet sat at the higher desk; at university, he would be asked to contribute verses to occasionally-generated collections; and when he went abroad, he would take on all comers in verse competitions (usually in Latin). Milton's tour of the Continent (1638–9) was a tournament in which he competed for the honour of England and was seen as such not just by Milton and his backers, but by the Italians whom he met in literary competition, and even by Johnson, describing it over a century later:

> [When Milton visited Rome] Selvaggi praised him in a distich, and Salsilli in a tetrastic; neither of them of much value ... the encomiums with which Milton repaid Salsilli, though not secure against a stern grammarian, turn the balance indisputably in Milton's favour. (Chalmers, 7: 275)

But this system, so successful at training literary athletes for formal competition, exercised a malign influence on the student's ability to invent outside the classroom or tournament situation. In fact, Milton's years of training in literary competition in public-school context led to the second distinguishing feature of the new hunger for fame: in Milton's case, for the first time, can be seen what we now call writer's block.

The gap between the desire to obtain literary fame and the desire to complete a particular piece of writing leads to this novel phenomenon, the most remarkable symptom of the modern form of the hunger for literary fame. The public-school-trained poet, accustomed to engaging in classroom literary competition out of the desire to impress a schoolmaster rather than a broad audience, and used to having his theme (the *inventio*) set by the Master, experiences the desire to shine in that competition prior to, and distinct from, any invention – he can, like the youthful Milton, 'only stand and wait' for inspiration, once removed from the classroom. By contrast, Marlowe and other young Jacobean poets wrote, and definitely wanted recognition for their skill in writing; but had they not written, they would not have dreamed of wanting but being unable to do so. Literary fecundity is typical of young poets in Marlowe's era – just as Milton's slow, self-conscious, difficult beginning as a writer will become increasingly typical as the seventeenth century progresses. As the paradigm of literature and literary fame becomes known, the desire to be a poet is *prior to and detached from* the work itself.

Of course in Marlowe's literary culture poets had difficult moments, moments when they could not finish a project; but Milton's block is uniquely modern in that it is not the interruption of a project in progress by a technical difficulty or loss of confidence but rather the suffering of a young man whose determination to be a literary celebrity predates any idea of writing anything in particular. This is 'writer's block' in the modern form – the urge for celebrity detached from devotion to any particular composition. Milton has actually left us, in his early poems, dramatizations of the state of mind of the youthful literary-aspirant schoolboy, waiting eagerly to be assigned a topic. The famous 'Sonnet VII' is a poignant depiction of this moment, complete with metaphor of God as schoolmaster:

> How soon hath time the subtle thief of youth,
>   Stol'n on his wing my three and twentieth year!
>   My hasting days fly on with full career,
>   But my late spring no bud or blossom sheweth.
> Perhaps my semblance might deceive the truth,
>   That I to manhood am arrived so near,
>   And inward ripeness doth much less appear,
>   That some more timely-happy spirits endueth.
> Yet be it less or more, or soon or slow,
>   It shall be still in strictest measure even
>   To that same lot, however mean or high,
> Toward which time leads me, and the will of heaven;
>   All is, if I have grace to use it so,
>   As ever in my great task-master's eye.
>   (*Poems of John Milton*, 147)[11]

Read as the work of an ambitious young school-bred seventeenth-century poet, the theme of this poem is a longing for literary glory complicated by the problem of having to wait for the topic. The basic situation depicted in the poem is the student attempting to please the schoolmaster/God in the last line. This is the point of the crucial metaphor deployed in the sextet, which dramatizes the shift from *pursuing* to *awaiting* invention. Here Guillory's stress on the impact of Protestant theology on Reformation poetics comes into play: the sinner must wait for Grace, which cannot be pursued, and the poet, once out of school, must wait for an occasion or a task from outside.

The most solemn occasion was always a death. Thus there tends to be crowding, of various kinds, around the grave. In fact, the grave, in seventeenth-century English literary culture, was not really quite as private a place as Marvell's famous line claimed – more like Donne's three-deep burial. Some poetically-promising graves could become the scene of considerable jostling. Many poets not only produced elegies on the deaths of friends, but, eager to take advantage of the one poetic occasion which was, after all, their own by rights, produced poems of the 'Epitaph for himself' genre. Jonson and Herbert both wrote such auto-elegies. Other poets simply wrote several elegies on a single death; eight years before *JEK* was printed, Carew showed the extremes to which a poet's eagerness to exploit a suitable elegiac occasion could go by producing three elegies on the child Mary Villiers. A comparison of Carew's three epitaphs for Villiers demonstrates the way in which poets attempted to satisfy community (epideictic) demands and private poetic ambition. Carew's first essay in elegy is properly severe:

Epitaph on the Lady Mary Villiers

The lady *Mary Villiers* lyes
Under this stone; with weeping eyes
The Parents that first gave her birth,
And their sad friends, lay'd her in earth:
If any of them (Reader) were
Knowne unto thee, shed a teare,
Or if thyself possesse a gemme,
As dear to thee, as this to them;
Though a stranger to this place,
Bewayle in theirs, thine owne hard case;
For thou perhaps at thy returne
Mayest find thy Darling in an Urne.
(*The Poems of Thomas Carew*, 53)[12]

The poem is starkly simple in diction and moral in tone. There are no ostentatious tropes in the first ten lines to cause the reader to focus on the poet's skill. Except for the metaphor 'gem', which is familiar and utilitarian in this context, there is little poetic display at all. Carew avoids any such display of virtuosity in order to fulfil his ostensible function: the epideictic poet decorously conveying the sorrow felt by a great family. Only the final couplet, in which the apostrophe to the reader acquires a sting, introduces anything particularly surprising; yet the sudden turn of the apostrophe is not particularly elaborate, and can still be placed in the context of the poet as preacher on mortality.

Yet Carew is evidently not satisfied; it is as if the first epitaph comprised the fulfilment of his public, epideictic duty, and left unfulfilled the other, hidden motive of the elegiac/occasional poet: the opportunity to display literary skill. To satisfy this ambition, Carew produced two more poems on the same death – three elegies to one corpse, a technical violation of the one-to-one poem–corpse requirement of the *habeas corpus* rule. Here is the second, simply titled 'An other':

> The purest Soule that e're was sent
> Into a clayie tenement
> Inform'd this dust, but the weake mold
> Could the great guest no longer hold,
> The substance was too pure, the flame
> Too glorious that thither came:
> Ten thousand *Cupids* brought along
> A Grace on each wing, that did throng
> For place there, till they all opprest
> The seat in which they sought to rest;
> So the faire Modell broke, for want
> Of roome to lodge th'Inhabitant.
>   (*The Poems of Thomas Carew*, 54)

The difference between the first and second poems is remarkable. The first fulfilled a social duty by its focus on the *corpus*; this one displays the poet's skill by a wild effusion of metaphorical play. Not only does he abandon the lonely graveside scene created in the first epitaph to paint a roccocco romp of cupids, but he instinctively turns, as do so many seventeenth-century poets, to images of *overcrowding and competition* in doing so. The Cupids and Graces are portrayed as 'throng[ing] for place' until they ruin everything. In a world where occasions for effectual poetry were becoming scarcer, the notion of throngs fighting over a corpse was to become an ever-more-common feature of occasional verse.

Carew's third epitaph for 'the Lady Mary Villiers' moves even further toward self-advertising poetic display. In this version, Carew seems to throw together all the remaining metaphorical dazzle he felt honour-bound to exclude from version 1 (and was not able to fit into version 2):

An other

This little Vault, this narrow roome,
Of Love, and Beautie is the tombe;
The dawning beame that 'gan to cleare
Our clouded skie, lyes darkned here,
For ever set to us, by death
Sent to enflame the world beneath;
'Twas but a bud, yet did containe
More sweetnesse then shall spring againe,
A budding starre that might have growne
Into a Sun, when it had blowne.
This hopefull beautie, did create
New life in Loves declining state;
But now his empire ends, and we
From fire, and wounding darts are free:
His brand, his bow, let no man feare,
The flames, the arrowes, all lie here.

(*The Poems of Thomas Carew*, 54)

Carew clearly felt this material to be too good to waste, but might have saved it for the third variant out of a half-felt impression that it would have been more suitable on the death of a somewhat older woman; after all, Mary Villiers was *two years old* at the time of her death! Her beauty must have been 'hopefull' indeed.

Still, good funereal occasions were not to be allowed to go to waste; and by the use of a metonymy stressing her grave itself rather than its contents, leading to an elaborate play on the Love-as-Conqueror theme, Carew manages to eulogize this toddler as the beauty she would have been – and thus display his skill at amorous, as well as funereal verse – maximum use of a single occasion. Carew's three efforts demonstrate not only the hunger with which poets of Milton's time seized on a promising corpse, but also the repertoire of latent possibilities which mid-eighteenth-century innovators like Blair and Gray would use to escape from the *habeas corpus* rule of occasional poetics. The *subjunctive elegy* – the commemoration of what the infant Mary Villiers might have become (an ancient topos) – was to prove important as the basis of Gray's 'Elegy Written in a Country Churchyard', which is the most important single poem in the development of elegiac poetic occasion, while Blair's famous 'The Grave', climax of the 'Graveyard School's' work, is constructed almost entirely out of the metonymy grave:body (container:contained) which Carew deploys in the third Villiers elegy.

Carew displays, in this remarkable series of variations on an infant's death, the rhetorical functions of the elegy circa l630: in the first elegy he crafted a sober, socially-useful poem on grief and mortality, representing a duty fulfilled; in a second elegy, he developed a clever conceit on death as overcrowding; and in the outrageous creation of a third, he abandoned restraint and the ostensible occasion – the death of a toddler – to demonstrate his skill in the Praise-of-Mistress genre, wisely bracketed in the future-subjunctive tense but still protected by the undoubted truth of the occasion. A death is the ground of all three poems, no matter how fanciful they become. Mary Villiers really did die, and in so doing legitimized these three poems (and any others Carew's rivals might choose to write). This is how occasional poetics leads to 'Metaphysical' tropic excess; once the *habeas corpus* requirement is satisfied, the poet can write with all the pent-up imagination which has collected since the last useable occasion.

It is in this posture, eager for a chance to display their power and accustomed since childhood to writing on the same theme, at the same time, for the same judges, that the poets of *Justa Edovardo King* encounter the occasion.

2. THE MEMORIAL VOLUME AS COMPETITIVE GENRE

Justa Edovardo King, now largely remembered as the original venue of 'Lycidas', is a typical memorial volume of the mid-seventeenth century, often dismissed as 'a volume of singularly undistinguished work'. (Sloane, 20) Its occasion is the recent death by drowning of Edward King, who as alumnus of the college is the poetic property – the inheritance, as it were – of those of his fellow Cambridge men who wish to remember him in verse.

This right to commemorate was a part of literary culture; when students of Westminster School tossed the hack publisher Curll in a blanket (cited above), they were punishing him as a lower-class intruder who had been caught poaching on their elegiac territory. When King died, his erstwhile school acquaintances knew that they could expect to play their part in an important commemorative occasion. In doing so – probably by invitation from their *alma mater* – the contributors would have balanced many factors, including genuine grief, political agendas, responsibilities to their old school and the family of the deceased, and religious conventions concerning funereal rhetoric.

In the seventeenth-century literary context, the best elegy was one which would satisfy both the desire to shine and the need to fulfil one's social obligations: 'a poem or a speech … [which would] outlive its moment and audience and yet remain within its occasion as well'. (Sloane, 57) A poem which transcended its occasion too obviously would be seen as a mere vehicle of ambition. Were the poets who contributed to memorial volumes of the mid-seventeenth century aware of this problem? Did they worry about it?

A persistent accusation about 'Lycidas' (the only poem of *JEK II* which is still widely read) touches on this question. The accusation is that in 'Lycidas' Milton unscrupulously exploited the death of Edward King, for whom he really cared little. Samuel Johnson, in an oft-quoted passage from his *Life of Milton*, seems to accuse Milton of exploiting an acquaintance's death:

> ['Lycidas'] is not to be considered as the effusion of real passion; for passion runs not after remote allusions and obscure opinions. Passion plucks no berries from the myrtle and ivy, nor calls on Arethuse and Mincius, nor tells of rough *satyrs* and *fauns with cloven heel*. Where there is leisure for fiction there is little grief. (Chalmers, 7: 302)

Johnson's accusation of insincerity has been many times repeated, and as many times dismissed as unfair and anachronistic. Defenders of the poem have either tried to prove that Milton and King really were friends, or have argued that the rules governing elegy in seventeenth-century English literary culture did not require that the poet feel anything like 'sincere' grief.

Both arguments are alive and well. A recent edition of works related to *Justa Edovardo King* argues for Milton's sincerity, devoting considerable effort to proving that Milton and King really were friends. Examining the poems in *JEK* for evidence of King's character, the authors concede that though it is true that 'Commemorative poetry routinely exaggerates the virtues of the deceased', 'the repeated and extravagant praise of King's learning in *Justa* suggests that his learning was indeed remarkable'. (Postlethwaite and Gordon Campbell, 79) But the difficulty of attempting to find biographical fact in seventeenth-century epideictic poetry is shown when the editors who have just argued that poetic references to King's scholarship prove that he really was a distinguished scholar turn to the elegists' treatment of King's death-scene. Three of the poems in *JEK* describe King's death in detail, all portraying him as dying with a display of piety. If elegies offer biographical evidence about the deceased, this ought to be useful data. But there is no indication that there were any survivors of the shipwreck which drowned King. This raises a problem:

> [I]t is hard to judge statements about the shipwreck made by the poets represented in *Justa*.... The poems of William More and Isaac Oliver [say] that King knelt in prayer while other passengers panicked, and John Pullen's poem [claims] that King died with a Bible in his hand.... In fact, both the kneeling and the book are standard topoi; even Shelley went down with copies of Sophocles and Keats. The shipwreck remains mysterious.... (Postlethwaite and Gordon Campbell, 81)

But if these elements are 'standard topoi' of epideictic rhetoric, may not the hyperbolic praise of King's learning in the poems of *JEK* also be a standard *topos*? Poets who have used such topoi in one place are likely to use them in another. Texts like Erasmus' *De Copia* were designed, after all, to give students formal practice in exaggeration. King's erudition was the best available material, given the conditions of the assignment. The poets used it as they were trained to do. Beyond this it is very difficult to derive any biographical information from elegy, and still more difficult to call seventeenth-century elegies 'sincere'.

The key question is not whether King was a great scholar or not but why we feel that we need to know. This is the most important, and least-studied, aspect of occasional poetics. It assumes its greatest importance when critics argue about Milton's relationship with King. After arguing that King truly was learned, Postlethwaite and Campbell argue that King and Milton were truly friends, basing their argument on a rather intricate reading of the 'Vacation Exercise,' and concluding:

> If the introduction of [the character called] Substance in the 'Vacation Exercise' is ... an affectionate description of Edward King, then this passage implies that Milton and King were indeed friends, and that Milton was using the occasion to praise King's 'worth and excellence'.... (Postlethwaite and Campbell, 80)

The tenuousness of the proof and the way the authors use it to prove Milton's unselfish commemorative purpose begs the question: why do we worry so much about whether Milton and King were friends? Behind all the enthymemes generated about the Milton–King relationship lurks a major premise about the relation of intimacy to elegy. It is this premise which really needs to be questioned. To the extent that we need to verify Milton's friendship for King before being able to read 'Lycidas' with pleasure, we demonstrate the degree to which the rules of Reformation literary world still operate – unnoticed and unquestioned – in our own.

The alternative way of getting around the problem of elegiac sincerity in reading 'Lycidas' has been a sort of pseudo-historicized cynicism, which asserts that things were different then and our rules don't apply. The argument goes that memorial volumes like *Justa Edovardo King* were understood to be poetic miscellanies, not effusions of true sorrow. A. N. Wilson, in a recent biography of Milton, blandly asserts that, in the mid-seventeenth century, 'You did not have to feel personally the death of a public figure in order to write elegiac or commendatory poetry about him'. (Wilson, 24)[13]

This would settle the problem nicely, if only it were true. This assertion is in fact the sort of oversimplification which might be expected of a popularizer like Wilson; but until recently, scholars of more repute, unable to find biographical proof of a Milton–King friendship and emotionally involved in 'defending' Milton, have also seemed to accept this notion. More recent scholarship has shown that the ethical problem facing seventeenth-century elegists was more complex than either position indicates. Barbara Johnson, in her article 'Fiction and Grief'[14] recharacterizes the relation of literary and personal mourning, while Griffin attempts to redefine authorship in Milton's time as the way 'writers negotiated a balance among the claims of occasion, audience ... and long-term career'.[15]

A close look at certain poems in *Justa Edovardo King II*, the volume in which 'Lycidas' appeared, suggests that those English poets who appear therein, including Milton, *were* in fact uneasy about the ethics of the memorial volume. Examination of these lesser-known poems from King's funeral volume seems to show that the keen competition to sing the deceased's praises resulted in poetry which was composed of antinomian elements: guilt and ambition. The most common device employed to deal with this antinomian load was a typical elegiac feature: praeteritic reattribution, the attempt to shift the weight of blame to *other* poets – those 'bad', carrion-crow poets who would exploit the dead. By using *praeteritio*, a classical trope defined as 'a dismissal which nonetheless echoes in the minds of the audience' (Sloane, 14), poets could not only exonerate their own elegies of the charge of exploiting the dead but – by providing well-wrought samples of 'bad', exploitative elegy – praeteritically display their skill in the very sort of attention-getting devices they were ostensibly condemning. All of the poems in the volume – including 'Lycidas' – have some crucial aspects in common: an uneasiness about the ethics of funereal poetry; an acute sensitivity to rival poets; and a dramatized attempt to resolve the moral/cultural problem by poetic means.

The death of a Cambridge man (especially one like King – a pious and promising student lost at sea) – would have caused real sorrow at his former university, but it would also have signalled that a memorial volume was coming. Such a venue offered a rare and exciting opportunity for poets to display their poetic accomplishments; so any private grief they felt for King would have been in tension, in an aspiring Cambridge poet, with this feeling of opportunity.

Memorial volumes were optimal places for a poet to make his mark for several reasons. First, the memorial volume did not rest on an invented narrative. Even the most hostile Protestant critics of literary invention had no quarrel with commemorating the real death of a real person, especially if the commemorative poem could be (ostensibly) turned to a homily on the lessons of mortality. Another secret of its appeal was *Pathos*. It was never the case, even at the height of the anti-inventive climate in mid-seventeenth century England, that all poems had to be grounded in verifiable occasion. It was, however, the case that poems not so grounded (paraphrases of scripture, translations of Classical texts, non-occasioned moral verse) rarely aroused in their readers the intense emotional reaction (pathetic response) which could be generated by occasional poetry. And of all such grounded poems, those concerned with belief in the narrative of poetry trusted in an individual's passage from life to death as an unambiguous event which could easily be verified. Edward King was known to have died; thus the poems collected in a memorial volume like *Justa Edovardo King* were grounded in fact. Literal belief leads to real tears.

Along with intensity of pathetic response, the funeral-volume genre benefited from its dramatization of a competition. The memorial volume exemplified by *JEK* has the latent structure of a tournament. All the poets face the same challenge. The number of variables being tested by this tournament is reduced to the one essential: the skill with which each poet handles the given subject. The volume becomes a funeral game, at which a dozen or more poets compete to create the definitive poem commemorating the deceased most memorably – the laureateship of a particular occasion.

Another attractive feature of the genre was the fact that contributions were generally signed. This was not always the case for most poems of the first half of the seventeenth century; poets – especially those with pretensions to gentility – were loath to let their names appear too openly on published poetry, or, in some cases, to publish at all. Ambition is thus usually a disingenuous process of *samizdat* dissemination among one's friends. But a memorial volume's epideictic function provided an excellent cover, since this genre had so much social sanction that the odour of ambition was less pronounced; and poets were clearly not shy about appending their names to their contributions. All but two of the contributors to *Justa Edovardo King II* provide either full names or clues to their identities which would have been sufficient for any member of the literary elite (*JEK II*, xii–xiii).

The volume might also have a built-in constituency. In the case of King's memorial volume, the contributors were competing not only against each other but, as a poetry-writing 'team', with Oxford. Cambridge's great rival was producing a memorial volume, *Jonsonus Virbius*, on the death of Ben Jonson, who had died in the summer of 1637:

The desire to commemorate the death of Edward King led to the publication at Cambridge early in 1638 of a Memorial Volume. Under Oxford auspices, a similar offering of poetical effusions was being brought out in honor of Ben Jonson, who also had died during the summer of 1637; and, no doubt, there existed an element of rivalry between the two university groups. (*Justa Edovardo King*, vi–vii)[16]

Thus the increasing popularization of the memorial volume – the genre to which *Justa Edovardo King* belongs – as a chance for young poets to enjoy a rhetorical saturnalia in a literary culture usually hostile to poetic displays, an adult version of the schoolroom versifiying competitions. And, as in the school exercises, topic is set – not by a master this time but by the event, the whole constellation of circumstances involved in a death.

3. 'A YOUNG MAN'S DEATH AT SEA, TO BE TURNED INTO ENGLISH VERSE': ELEGIAC ETHICS IN THE 'OTHER' POEMS OF *JUSTA EDOVARDO KING II*

As they considered the many ways in which King's death could be turned to poetry, the poets invited to contribute to his memorial volume would have begun thinking over King's character as poetic material, using their training in rhetoric to make the best case for the deceased, and for themselves as his commemorators. To clear the way for this effort, they first had to convince readers of the legitimacy of the commemorations.

The rhetoric of arrangement, an essential component of the rhetorical curriculum (Sloane 9–11; 180–202), is one way in which the composers of the volume dealt with the ethical legitimacy of elegiac verse. Thus the poems will be discussed in their order of appearance. First the deceased's family must be consulted and shown to take part in the commemorative enterprise. This is why the volume begins with a long poem by Henry King, brother of the deceased. It is not particularly distinguished poetry, but its placement at the beginning of the volume suggests that it need not be; it is there in part as a release, sent by the family of the deceased allowing the other commemorations to begin. Henry King's poem stresses the notion of permission in his elegy for his brother. After an aporia confessing his inability to go on forming verses about the family tragedy, he addresses the poets who will follow him in the volume:

> You then whose pious unconfounded wit
> Truly can apprehend this grief, and yet
> Not be struck silent; here, take up this theme,
> And sing the world his Epicedium.
> Pattern a grief, may serve us all to mourn
> For future losses, like the actours urn;
> That all that read your well-spunne lines with tears,
> May envy you, and wish your grief were theirs.
>
> (Mossner, ed. *JEK II*, 2)

Here the brother of the dead man presents a familiar antithesis between true grief – his own, the grief of a kinsman – which he depicts as inarticulate and dumb ('struck silent'), and the 'unconfounded wit' of the professional poets who will take up the song. This dilemma – that true grief could not rhyme well – and its corollary, that good rhymes make one suspect the sincerity of the writer's grief – is what Samuel Johnson was to argue in doubting the sincerity of grief in 'Lycidas'. Here is the same argument, spoken by Henry King in 1637 – which suggests that Milton's generation had similar reservations about the legitimacy of rhymed mourning. King calls the poets whom he is introducing 'pious' yet 'unconfounded'; that is, the poets can grasp, but do not feel the paralysing effect of, the family's grief. King himself, as a victim of what Johnson terms, 'Passion', is struck mute; to alter Johnson's famous comment, where there is this sort of grief there is no capacity for fiction.

Continuing the antithesis between real grief and that of the poets, King compares the aspiring poets to actors miming true emotion, and declares that they have the ability to make their sham passions so appealing that readers 'may envy you, and wish your grief were theirs'. This brief mention of envy in the elegiac context is typical of the uncanny complexity of tone which one finds again and again in seventeenth-century elegiac hyperbole. On a first reading, King is simply flattering the poets. But poets did in fact *desire* to be the singers of the grief. The funereal occasion was the occasion also of envious jostling. Thus the deceased's brother here obliquely depicts the 'wish' of the reader to be in on that competition. As is often the case in the hyperboles of *JEK*, elegiac hyperbole ends up not far from truth.

Having raised this troubling conjunction of desire and the corpse, King proceeds to discuss the way the reputation of the deceased affects the living:

> ... in him [Edward King]
> I lost my best life, which I did esteem
> Farre beyond Nature's, reputation
> And credit, which the mere reflection
> of his worth, like a twilight, cast on me....
> (Mossner, *JEK II*, 3)

The body of the deceased constitutes the life of reputation. This comparison is extended, throughout almost 40 lines of verse, into the perspective of the entire King family, which mourns its lost member on the ground that they will lose all their 'fame' through his death. Even here, in the ostensibly sincere grief of a brother, the themes of mourning and of literary fame are found bound up together, so that apparently empty, conventional hyperboles resonate with tension. For the King family, the death of Edward is an unambiguous loss. This means that they are mute; for them this is not an opportunity. For the other poets, whom Henry King has given licence to write, the death is a more complex event, with opportunity as well as grief. Thus, as King points out, they can speak while the family must be mute.

Joseph Beaumont's poem, which is first to follow Henry King's prefatory verse, epitomizes the anxiety about death and fame. Beaumont uses a central trope involving a protracted argument between the elegiac poet and 'Fame' herself, attributing to that goddess envy of the deceased, and consequently an eagerness to whisper his death:

> I check't that fame, and told her how
> I knew her trade, and her; nay, though
> Her honest tongue had given before
> A faithfull echo, yet his store
> Of grand deserts, which did prepare
> For envies tooth such dainty fare,
> Would tempt her now to fain his fate
> And then her lie for truth relate.
> (Mossner, *JEK II*, 5)

Beaumont's conceit of a personified 'Fame' who feels literary envy of the deceased, like Milton's evocation of fame in the context of a niece's death (Jenkins, 18), is a seventeenth-century commonplace; but the range of topics to which he was led – the idea of 'Fame's' contributing to King's death out of envy – displaces his own uneasy participation in this funereal exercise onto an invented enemy with whom the poet struggles on behalf of the deceased. The jealous feminized 'Fame' is made to carry the envy, ambition and craft of the poet. This is the first of many praeteritic attacks on invented targets whom the poets will burden with their own mixed motives.

John Cleveland's two contributions to the volume (*Justa Edovardo King II*, poems 3 and 4), which follow Beaumont's in the volume, are the most direct of all the contributions in their discussion of the moral problem of using a colleague's death as a springboard to literary fame. Cleveland's sensibility, for all its surface cynicism, strikes me as the most delicate of all the contributors and the most self-conscious of the rhetorical purpose of ostensibly-grieving poetry. Cleveland's background may account for this self-consciousness: he had been appointed Reader in Rhetoric at Cambridge in 1634. Cleveland's two contributions depict the writing of funereal poetry as a competition. There is a sense of jostling against rivals in both poems. This awareness of rival poets is a common theme in Cleveland's other works; the opening to 'The Hecatomb to His Mistresse', for example, vividly displays Cleveland's awareness of his rivals in verse:

> Be dumb ye beggers of the rhiming trade,
> Geld your loose wits, & let your Muse be splaid.
> Charge not the parish with your bastard phrase....

Here, having accused his rivals of impoverishing the poetic parish by breeding bastards in rhyme, Cleveland sharpens the implication that his fellow poets are making it harder for *him* to write; comparing rival poets to spiders, who travel wound in the products of their own entrails, Cleveland says:

> So it is with my Poetry and you.
> From your essence must I first untwine,
> Then twist again each Panegyric line.
>   (Cleveland, 50)

Here Cleveland portrays the problem faced by most poets trying
to operate within the shrinking range of invention available. So
many school-bred poets have learned the formulae for writing
genre poems (in this case, the praise poem to one's mistress) that
their accretions must be chipped away before the aspiring poet can
hope to begin. Jostling between poets replaces the encounter of
poet and object (in this case the beautiful mistress), dimming the
view of the object to be praised.

This is the same situation depicted by Cleveland in his two offer-
ings in *JEK II*. Cleveland's first contribution begins conventionally
enough, with a display of skill in the juggling of the astronomical
metaphor in a funereal context (a common elegiac move, also
notable in Henry King's contribution):

> Whiles Phoebus shines within our hemisphere,
> There are no starres, or at least none appear;
> Did not the sunne go hence, we should not know
> Whether there were a night and starres, or no.
> (Mossner, JEK II, 8)

But Cleveland sets up this apparently conventional opening,
with its hyperbolic cosmic grief, only to begin playing with the term
'stars'. First, Cleveland makes explicit the sense that these 'stars' are
King's competing elegists: 'Till thou ly'dst down upon thy Western
bed, / Not one *poetic* star durst shew his head.' [emphasis added] It
was awe of King's talent, in other words, that caused fellow-poets
to lie low until his death. There is no evidence that King had any
such talent; 'King's life ... had ... been all promise – no fulfilment.'
(Parker, 156) But in the uncanny way which is typical of funereal
hyperbole, this exaggerated claim turns out to be no more than the
truth; in a poetics limited to the exploitation of a few suitable occa-
sions, poets did lie dormant, waiting for the death of someone they
could commemorate – not out of fear of his (King's) talent, but
because of the rules of occasionality. For these 'stars' to shine, it
really was essential that their fellow 'star', the sun-like Edward
King, should set forever '... down upon his western bed'. Sunset, in
an ancient metaphor, is death; and so it is here: while the surface
meaning of these lines is simply that King's talent hid the stars as
does the Sun the lines also mean: You, Edward King, had to die for
us to write these poems. King sank into the Irish Sea, west of
England, completing the parallel which implies that the poets must

have been half-grateful for this timely sunset. Cleveland says so in line nine, in a brutal apostrophe to the deceased: 'Thy death makes poets....'

Having confessed the corpse's function in serving surviving poets' ambitions, Cleveland goes on to discuss the situation with the corpse he is exploiting, explaining to the dead Edward King exactly how his former friends are going to use his demise as poetic grist:

> ... we who had the happinesse to know
> Thee what thou wast ...
> Enjoy thee still and use thy precious name
> As a perfume to sweeten our own fame.
>
> (Mossner, *JEK II*, 8)

That is: King's contemporaries are going to use his corpse ('we ... enjoy thee still ...') for their own 'perfume'. This theme – the use of King's reputation to 'sweeten' one's own – is found in many other poems in the volume, but Cleveland is the poet who stresses the fact that the deceased is of more use to fellow poets dead than alive. But the question of intention arises in my reading of these verses; were the contributors aware of the moral problems of elegy?

Cleveland the teacher of rhetoric probably was thinking about this problem as he wrote. Indeed, as if he wanted to emphasize his own moral problem with this sort of elegiac poetry, Cleveland adds a second poem (*JEK II (4)*) which I find remarkable (though it has received little critical attention), in which he explicitly discusses the question of lyrical sincerity. Cleveland's second poem begins with a direct statement of the elegiac dilemma: 'I like not tears in tune....' This phrase prefigures the line of attack pursued over a century later by Samuel Johnson in his dismissal of 'Lycidas'; that the patterned, premeditated language of verse bears little resemblance to the effusion of real passion. Cleveland continues to argue about the value and sincerity of versified grief throughout his second contribution to *JEK II*:

> I like not tears in tune; nor will I prize
> His artificial grief, that scannes his eyes:
> Mine weep down pious beads; but why should I
> Confine them to the Muses rosarie?
> I am no Poet here; my penne's the spout

> Where the rain-water of my eyes run out
> In pitie of that name, whose fate we see
> Thus copied out in griefs Hydrographie.
> The Muses are not Mayr-Maids; though upon
> His death the Ocean might turn Helicon.
> The Sea's too rough for verse; who rhymes upon't,
> With Xerxes strives to fetter th' Hellespont.
> My tears will keep no channel, know no laws
> To guide their Streams; but like the waves, their cause,
> Run with disturbance, till they swallow me
> As a description of his miserie.
>   (Mossner, *JEK II*, 9)

The basic trope here is a praeteritic antithesis which distinguishes the poet's 'real' grief from the suspect, exploitative grief of other (rival) poets. Cleveland exploits the possibilities of praeteritic form to the utmost; the entire poem employs elegiac hyperbole while continually protesting its disdain for such rhetoric ('I will not do X … nor Y … nor Z'). This markedly 'poetic' (trope-laden, rhythmic) poem dissociates itself from other elegiac poetry, which, in the grand structure of the praeteritic antithesis, represents 'artificial grief'.

With the paradox between stylized literary product and real grief, Cleveland begins to call into question the legitimacy of elegy. He is not the only contributor to the volume to do so; antithesis between tears, as emblems of real grief, and metered language ('tune', 'scans'), as product of mere craft, is quite common in *JEK II*, as for example in this almost boastful conclusion to John Hayward's poem 'To the deceased's vertuous sister':

> My verse and tears would gladly sympathise,
> And be both without number; but my eyes
> Are the best Poet, for they shed great store
> Of elegies, when I have not one verse more.
>   (Mossner, *JEK II*, 17)

But Cleveland does more tonally complex work with the basic trope, calling into question the entire elegiac process in the catachresis 'Scans his eyes' where the notion of poetic scansion is contrasted to that of a true, intense self-examination represented by the poem itself. Verse, Cleveland implies (anticipating Johnson), is the product of premeditated ambition, not grief. Funereal poetry, he implies, is thus fundamentally corrupt. And his attacks on this corrupt poetic intention lead, finally, to a disavowal of the entire profession: 'I am no poet here'.

Both of Cleveland's contributions display the ambivalence of the elegiac contestant in this structure. Both poems begin with critiques of elegiac ethics conveyed via praeteritic antithesis. But both poems, as if shrugging at the hopelessness of the task, then turn gleefully to the attempt to win the competition, regardless of its moral base. For when he condemns ornate, insincere elegiac poetry, Cleveland gives himself the chance to show his skill in it – all in the name of showing the reader what is to be condemned. Both Cleveland's contributions begin with condemnation of the genre and move on to displays of elegiac skill. The first poem, for example, ends with an outrageous pun on King's name ('… to the highest heav'ns: where being crown'd / A King …') and a pedantic joke about which ancestry to claim for the deceased: Edward the Confessor or Saint Edward. The progression here is the same as that of the three poems Carew wrote on the death of a toddler: beginning with pious rejection of poetic display, then embracing it anyway.

Cleveland's second poem executes the same tonal turn halfway through. The fact that King died by drowning now becomes for Cleveland, as for every one of his rival co-contributors to the volume, the irresistible basis of poetic display. This is the sure sign of school-training; the topic is given ('A young scholar's death at sea, to be turned into verse') and the elements are instantly recognizable to the rival elegists: *youth, virtue, water, ships, sea, tears.*… Even for Cleveland, who was clearly aware of the doubtful moral basis of the competition, the temptation to indulge in a display of virtuosity at the expense of his initial moral critique of the genre is triumphant. Showing his skill in using the marine metaphor, he gives way to witty, grief-free flattery of the deceased:

> Some have affirm'd, that what on earth we find,
> The sea can parallel for shape and kind:
> Books, arts and tongues were wanting; but in thee
> Neptune hath got an Universitie.
> (Mossner, JEK II, 10)

School training comes through again: *young scholar … death at sea … Neptune …* one can hear the machinery creaking. Having decried the temptation to funereal eloquence, then praeteritically refused it, Cleveland returns at last to the funereal/pastoral repertoire of classical allusion. The conclusion of his second poem emphasizes the temptation to use the death as the foundation of poetic creation:

> When we have fill'd the rundlets of our eyes,
> We'll issue't forth, and vent such elegies,
> As that our tears shall seem the Irish seas,
> We floating islands, living Hebrides.
>
> (Mossner, *JEK II*, 10)

In the latter part of both of Cleveland's elegies, the corpse has disappeared; it is the living heirs, the elegists empowered by his death, who are the sole subject of this almost eager promise. They will 'issue forth' to create, by their tears, the sea in which King drowned. And, having created this sea which drowns the object of the elegies, the elegists become 'floating islands' – become that which is raised above the sea by the same action which sank King below it. Here again is the odd refraction of apparently hyperbolic elegiac rhetoric; on one level, this is nothing more than a fantastical conceit – exactly the sort of excess Cleveland at first rejects. But at another level, the conceit metaphorically reveals the way the mourners rise as (because) the mourned sinks.

The manipulation of marine metaphor is, naturally enough, a feature common to most of the contributions. Elegies often (though not always) focus on the manner of death, and death by drowning seems to be a particularly dramatic, frightening sort of death. But the common topic ('death by water') only intensifies the school-type competition. It is a specification of the 'assignment,' and the poets will try to outdo each other in making it new, doing something metaphorically impressive with it.

Marine metaphors are essential to W. Hall's contribution, which follows Cleveland's. Hall, like Cleveland, first makes a disclaimer about exploiting the deceased, then reveals through metaphorical manipulation exactly why the manner of King's death was so providential for the aspiring elegist. Hall's opening lines are particularly clear in their attempt to placate the deceased:

> Pardon, blest soul, the slow pac'd Elegies
> Of sad survivors; they have pregnant eyes

> For vulgar griefs. Our sorrows find a tongue,
> Where verse may not the losse or merit wrong:
> But an amazed silence might become
> Thy obsequies, as fate deni'd a tombe.
>
> (Mossner, *JEK II*, 12)

Hall's first words are apostrophe to the corpse, begging its pardon for what is to come – the elegy itself. The terms of Hall's plea are the familiar terms of the antithesis between real grief – which is silent – and stylized grief (elegy). The implication of these first lines is that there is indeed something to forgive or excuse in composing elegies, but that King's soul must overlook this 'vulgar' exercise on the basis of the quality of the mourners.

Even after reassuring himself about this, Hall repeats that the particulars of King's end might have made aposiopesis more appropriate than the usual aporia ('But an amazed silence might become / thy obsequies, as fate deni'd a tombe.') Since King's body cannot be recovered, a traditional funeral is impossible – and traditional elegy is in question as well. A drowned corpse, lost in the depths – who has the rights to such a corpse? In this way, the manner of King's death oddly anticipates the way in which the *habeas corpus* requirement will be manipulated and finally transcended by poets of the mid-eighteenth-century. In King's case, there is a death but not a corpse – King's body is lost at sea. This source of anxiety (from failure to satisfy the *habeas corpus* requirement of the genre) is revealed in Hall's poem to be equally a source of opportunity for the elegist; though the *habeas corpus* requirement is not met, the absence of a corpse makes King's body, which would otherwise be claimed and interred by his family, *public domain:*

> Heav'n would (it seems) no common grave intrust,
> Nor bury such a jewel in the dust.
> The fatall barks dark cabbin must inshrine
> That precious dust, which fate would not confine
> To vulgar coffins....
>
> (Mossner, *JEK II*, 12)

Conscious hyperbole as unconscious truth; conscious insincerity disguising simple truth. This is the pattern of hyperbolic rhetoric throughout *JEK II*. Here Hall, like Cleveland seems merely to be piling up conceits in order to impress the judges of the elegy–tournament. But there is something almost like glee here, at the notion that King's body is unavailable for inspection and thus open to the manipulations of the elegist. Later in the poem, Hall makes his glee explicit via yet another antithesis which drives home the theme of King's body as public domain:

> Should some enriched earthly tombe inherit
> The empty casket of that parted spirit,
> The easie world would idolize that shrine,
> Or hast to mix their dust with that of thine …
> To spare them, fate to interre thee forbears.…
> (Mossner, *JEK II*, 13)

The entry of Sampson Briggs, which follows Hall's in *JEK,* also emphasizes the public-domain status of King's death and the triumph of elegy: '… each wave / swell'd up, as coveting to be his grave …' is Briggs's conceit describing the storm which drowned King. Briggs's effort abounds in typical nature-based hyperboles which reflect a mental landscape dominated by the ideas of competition and overcrowding, as in his fanciful depiction of elegies falling thick as raindrops: '… the pitying skies / Melted and dropt in funerall elegies'.

In this, as in so many of the water-based hyperbolic metaphors of *JEK II,* can be heard the echo of Milton's school-poem on the miracle at Cana: 'The conscious water saw its God and blushed.' Indeed, the contribution of Isaac Oliver has a strikingly Miltonic tone, composed of a mosaic of classical and Christian allusion on a basis of hyperbolic 'hydrography':

> So seem'd [King's] soul the struggling surge to greet,
> As when two mighty seas encountring meet;
> For what a sea of arts in him was spent,
> Mightier than that above the firmament?
> As Achelous with his silver fleet
> Runnes through salt Doris purely, so to meet
> His Arethusa; the Sicianian maid
> Admires his sweetnesse by no wave decai'd:
> So should he, to have cut the Irish strand,
> And like a lustie bridegroom leapt to land;
> Or else (like Peter) trode the waves; but he
> Then stood most upright, when he bent his knee.
> (Mossner, *JEK II*, 15–16)

In Oliver's text, the disappearance of the corpse is complete; the occasion becomes a mere convenient trellis on which to train the familiar school-bred elaborations. Greco-Roman references yield, in the well-known Miltonic pastiche, to the more earnest Christian ones – such as the reference to Saint Peter, Fisher of Men, who, by the same school-trained association of sea and piety, occurred to Milton as a useful invention. This raises the question: how does 'Lycidas' compare, in its treatment of the deceased, with the lesser-known poems in *JEK II*?

4. 'LYCIDAS' AS MEMORIAL-VOLUME VERSE

Milton often thought that occasions had been given to him, that he had been called to give witness on these occasions, and that such expressions as he makes of this kind are rhetorical devices but also more than rhetorical devices. (Cedric C. Brown, *John Milton…*, xvi)

Over the centuries, 'Lycidas' has produced a huge volume of criticism, much of it touching nervously – often without any awareness that it is doing so – on the question of elegiac ethics. The issue is complex because, even by comparison with its fellow contributions to *JEK II*, 'Lycidas' is a subtle poem, carefully tailored to its context:

['Lycidas' is] … a text intricately woven into its occasion, perhaps overambitiously writing it into its text. It demands a reading mindful of the conventional expectations of its funerary functions as well as its institutional and political situations,… and the challenges it has presented to its readers over the centuries … have spelled out a wonderful story of difficulty. (Brown, 'Mending and Bending the Occasional Text: collegiate elegies and the case of "Lycidas"' in *Texts and Cultural Change in Early Modern England*, eds Cedric C. Brown and Arthur Marotti)

In his youth, Milton was hesitant about attempting major poetic projects and slow to take advantage of most conventional occasions (Brown, 'Mending and Bending …', 3), so his decision to commemorate King's death is an important one. It seems to have signalled the end of several years' indecision, after Milton completed his

studies at Cambridge, about how he should pursue his mixed liter-
ary/clerical/scholarly vocation (Parker, 153), and seems to have
been the subject of his excited confession of fame-seeking in the
letter to Diodati cited above (Brown, *John Milton…*, 38). Milton
certainly failed, as far as we know, to commemorate occasions
which belonged to him by right, like the death of his former head-
master Mr Gill in 1635 (Parker, 151) – a particularly notable 'refusal
to mourn' because headmasters, for obvious reasons, tended to
attract many elegies.

'Lycidas' thus dramatizes Milton's '… *re-entry* into this sort of
writing' (Brown, 'Mending and Bending …'), and makes the act of
commemoration the subject, and the unwilling elegist the protago-
nist, of the poem: 'It is … the character of the speaker – Milton, the
self-created public poet – whose dramatized actions provide the
shape and are themselves the intention of the work.' (Sloane, 54)
The first issue to be dramatized is Milton's decision to take up the
duty of elegizing King. Thus the first part of 'Lycidas' raises the
issue of the poet's role in relation to the legitimacy of the poetic
occasion:

> Yet once more, O ye laurels, and once more
> Ye myrtles brown, with ivy never-sere,
> I come to pluck your berries harsh and crude,
> And with forc'd fingers rude
> Shatter your leaves before the mellowing yeare.
> Bitter constraint, and sad occasion deare
> Compells me to disturb your season due;
> For Lycidas is dead, dead ere his prime,
> (Young Lycidas!) and hath not left his peere.
> Who would not sing for Lycidas? he knew
> Himself to sing, and build the lofty rhyme.
> He must not flote upon his watry biere
> Unwept, and welter to the parching wind
> Without the meed of some melodious tear.
>   (Mossner, *JEK II*, 20)

Milton's first line, 'Yet once more, O ye Laurels, and once more'
strikes the note of constraint and belatedness (in part the belated-
ness of a man five years out of university speaking on a Cambridge
occasion). The 'forc'd fingers' of line four again emphasize the
numbing formality of the occasion. Milton uses this 'constraint', this

aporiac impression of the poet beginning his elegiac task grudg-ingly and awkwardly, to apologize for the invention of the poem and to dramatize his unwilling (almost Christ-like) acceptance of the task, reattributing it in a quite conventional anti-inventive way to events outside the poet's control. The emphasis on compulsion may also have hinted to the more acute readers '... that John Milton, at Cambridge and now after Cambridge, was in demand as occasional rhetor'. (Brown, 'Mending and Bending ...') All this self-dramatising rhetoric implies that it is the *occasion* ('sad occasion deare') and not ambition which forces ('Compells') the poet to write. If Guillory's notion of impure inspiration applies to the occa-sional poem, then that same impurity – the fact that the poem originates in a public demand rather than a pentecostal inspiration – can become the basis for a strategy of reattribution of the inven-tion. It is an exercise – like a much more demanding, grown-up version of the competitive exercises at St Paul's.

But this is only the first of the justifications for the poem's exis-tence to be tried in 'Lycidas'. The second (lines 11–14) is the conventional notion of elegy as one of the needs of the deceased: 'He must not lie upon his wat'ry beir / Unwept....' The third and most important justification of the text is the notion of identifica-tion, actual interchangeability between the deceased and his elegist, which begins the second stanza:

> Begin then, Sisters of the sacred well ...
> Begin, and somewhat loudly sweep the string;
> Hence with deniall vain, and coy excuse.
> So may some gentle Muse
> With lucky words favour my destin'd urn,
> And as he passes, turn
> And bid fair peace be to my sable shroud.
> (Mossner, *JEK II*, 20)

The poet drops all discussion of occasional legitimacy by, in effect, offering licence to exploit his own death in exchange for the right to 'sweep the string' on this present decease. If Milton is willing to suffer becoming poetic fodder, so should King be. The pastoral lines which follow emphasize the interchangeability of Milton and King:

> For we were nurst upon the self-same hill,
> Fed the same flock ...
> Together both, ere the high lawns appear'd
> Under the glimmering eye-lids of the morn,
> We drove a-field....
>
> (Mossner, *JEK II*, 21)

Johnson's famous attack on the sincerity of the poet focused on the pastoral allegory in these lines: 'We know that they never drove a field, and that they had no flocks to batten' (Chalmers, 7: 302). More recent critics have also been troubled by the autobiographical claim implied in this pastoral part of the poem. What does the pastoral actually claim? The simplest claim is one which plays on the double sense of 'shepherd' as scholar and as minister (pastor). These are the claims which Milton can make in linking himself to the deceased. Both were Cambridge men bred for learning and the Church; and this connection with the Church will be used later in 'Lycidas' not just to link Milton to the deceased but to link both men to the party of 'good shepherds' who oppose the Bishops. As a well-trained rhetorician, Milton uses the pastoral allegory for more than one purpose: he first deploys it to build his own ethos – establishing his own legitimacy as elegist and his character as good shepherd – then later uses it to attack clerical enemies later on.

With his ethos as good shepherd established, Milton can return to the theme of his longing for fame by discussing King's own fame as did so many other contributors to the volume. The theme is cleansed because the distinction between corpse and elegist has collapsed. Milton then blurs the intensity of the desire for fame by giving it a spiritual gloss:

> Fame is the spurre that the clear spirit doth raise,
> (That last infirmitie of noble mind)
> To scorn delights, and live laborious dayes;
> But the fair guerdon where we hope to find,
> And think to burst out into sudden blaze,
> Comes the blind Furie with th'abhorred shears,
> And slits the thin-spun life; But not the praise,
> Phebus repli'd, and touch'd my trembling eares:
> Fame is no plant that grows on mortall soil....
>
> (Mossner, *JEK II*, 22)

This section of the poem amounts to a direct question about the utility of the hard, scholarly life Milton dramatized via the pastoral. If fame, the only thing which makes such shepherdly labours worthwhile, may be denied by sudden death, why go on? As this argument implies, Milton's identification with, or rather replacement of King is now complete. Going on is not an issue in King's case. That career is already punctuated by death; it is the literary/clerical career (Parker, 153) of John Milton which is in question, the subsumption of King into Milton emphasized by the inclusive pronoun ('... *we* hope to find / and think to burst out into sudden blaze'). King has no opportunity to raise the question; it is Milton who faces it, and thus it is Milton whose present life is dramatized.

Critics have been made nervous by the appearance of ambition and the related disappearance of King, the ostensible focus of grief, from the poem. Most have attempted to rationalize this change in the same way they rationalize Milton's longing for fame: by Phœbus' distinction between 'good' and 'bad' fame. But Phœbus does not define 'good' fame in terms of art-for-art's-sake or Christian duty; he merely reassures the poet that fame is in fact still a valid goal, since it may be redefined as immortality (the definition Milton employs in the letter to Diodati cited above); that is, as a literary reputation which survives the poet's death. Even if we accept Milton's fame-assigning 'Jove' as the Christian God, it is not at all orthodox Christian doctrine to envisage Heaven as the attainment of one's deserved literary renown. Far more typical of the orthodox Evangelical position are the anti-literary pamphlets which were so common in Reformation England, which dismissed all literary effort as, at best, a waste of precious time and at worst a deeply sinful vanity.

What the introduction of this mixed Christian/Pagan pantheon does do in terms of developing the theme of fame is to allow Milton to make his famous digression on the Simoniacs in the Church. Though this passage has as its primary context the debates about the place of the clerical hierarchy in the English church, it is interesting that Milton here develops a theme similar to that made by Cleveland and other less well-remembered contributors to *JEK II*: an attack on one's rivals for their unscrupulous scheming for fame:

How well could I have spar'd for thee, young swain,
Enough of such as for their bellies sake

Creep and intrude and climbe into the fold?
Of other care they little reckoning make,
Then how to scramble at the shearers feast,
And shove away the worthy bidden guest.
(Mossner, *JEK II,* 23)

The parallel between fame-seeking elegiac poet and simoniac preacher is made explicitly by Milton in the lines which follow:

And when they list their lean and flashie songs
Grate on their scrannel pipes of wretched straw,
The hungry sheep look up, and are not fed....
(Mossner, *JEK II,* 23)

Here Milton changes the referent of the pastoral allegory from shepherding in general terms to shepherding as song. By defining shepherds as makers of 'songs', he conflates the shepherd's poetic and clerical functions. In this context it seems to me that, though Johnson's attack on the pastoral allegory in 'Lycidas' may be unfair in some ways Johnson, as so often, had the right instinct in pointing to it as the most disingenuous part of the poem. By blurring shepherd-as-minister with shepherd-as-poet, Milton sets himself apart from his poetic rivals while ostensibly attacking only his doctrinal enemies. The good and bad shepherds certainly refer to good or bad pastors; but they also refer to good or bad singers, and in shifting blame to the bad singers, Milton follows a tactic common to all the poems in *JEK*: the redirection of the reader's anticipated mistrust of elegiac poetry to other, 'bad' poets and away from himself.

'Lycidas' emerges from its memorial-volume context as in many ways a typical, though superior, effort of a school-bred anti-inventive competitor. Its arrangement follows a standard elegiac form; like the other contributions to *JEK II,* 'Lycidas'

- begins with an attempt to resolve occasional ethics;
- moves to a discussion of fame;
- digresses to castigate incompetent rivals; and
- closes ('fields and pastures new') asserting the elegist's right to write.

Justa Edovardo King II was a typical memorial volume, and thus a good example of the context and conditions in which most seventeenth-century funereal-occasioned verse was created. Such volumes were designed to do several things, all of which are involved in the appearance of *JEK*. As a Cambridge production, it was intended to compete with *Jonsonus Virbius*, Oxford's memorial volume to Ben Jonson, due to appear as *JEK II* was being compiled. As an anthology of pieces produced for the occasion, it was a chance for ambitious young poets to showcase their talents in open tournament with more renowned rivals. And for some of the contributors, like John Cleveland, it offered an occasion within the funereal occasion, a chance to talk about the conventions of the elegiac, and in the process to raise doubts about 'sincerity' of the form, long before the pre-Romantics made sincerity an explicit part of the poet's qualifications. This strange and largely forgotten spectacle helped to mould the modern lyric: dozens of young men, trained at school and at Cambridge to try to outshine each other in assigned poetic invention, carry on the struggle for fame in the more meagre world of the adult occasional poet, wrestling over the prize: the corpse.

3

Carrion Crows: Occasion in the Beginning and End of Dryden's Literary Life

Events are not delivered to one's home, events are not a public utility ...

Paul Nizan, *Aden, Arabie*

But now, since the rewards of honor are taken away, that virtuous emulation is turned to direct malice ...

Dryden, 'Essay of Dramatick Poesie'

W. H. Auden called Dryden '... the greatest Occasional poet in English.'[1] Dryden is the premier occasional poet of this language not necessarily because that is where his talents lay, but because he was the best poet writing at a time when invention was becoming more and more constricted, and poets were forced to try to hide behind the claim of occasionality. This chapter focuses on the beginning and the ending of the life of Dryden (to the exclusion of the distinguished, successful, mid-career period) to illustrate the way that mid-seventeenth-century English poets lived and died by the poetic occasion. As noted in the analyses of the contributors to *Justa Edovardo King II,* it is in the beginning of poems (and, by extension, the beginnings of poetic careers) that the poet's claim to the right to write is established. As Richard Helgerson puts it in describing his focus on the career-trajectories of his *Self-Crowned Laureates,*

I give more attention to how the poet gets to his laureate destination than to what he does when he gets there.... For in those crossings of the threshold, when the author first appears before his audience, the pressure on self-presentation is greatest. To some extent, each beginning – beginnings of individual works as

56

well as beginnings of careers – brings a renewal of self-presentational pressure. (Helgerson, 13)

Just as the first lines of the truth-grounded epideictic text establish its legitimacy with respect to the occasion, the beginning of the poet's career establishes the name, the legitimate presence. Once that name is established, authority is less of a problem; the established poet in the mid-century period is usually embroiled, in a wonderfully fecund manner, in poetic sparring which spreads ever outward, in the form of a stylized literary feud, from some original, occasioning text, often forgotten. Thus one sees in Dryden's mid-career period a tendency which becomes even more prominent in Pope; the famous poet is himself an occasioning presence; he attracts the ostensibly hostile attention of hungrier, unknown poets who hope to attach their claims to authority to his via attacks on his already-accepted texts. Thus *de facto* laureateship is both a cruel and a nurturing institution; cruel because the opportunities to move from obscurity to fame in an invention-starved literary culture are few, but nurturing because the figure of the successful poet provides a sheltering reef, under which many lesser poets can find shelter.

But when the laureate, the top of the literary food chain, falls, there is the rather appalling spectacle of these smaller creatures swarming over the great body. The occasional poet becomes the occasion; the bland permission, abstractly granted by the young and healthy Milton in 'Lycidas', that some day other occasional poets may use his corpse, as he is using King's, for his own nourishment, becomes reality. Dryden's funeral occasioned one of the most extraordinary (and little-studied) frenzies of legend-making ever recorded. Even Johnson records, in his *Life of Dryden*, a legend about Dryden's funeral which he suspects to be untrue yet still found resonant enough to be worth retelling. This grisly legend, which is treated in this chapter and included in full in an appendix, embodies the culture's revenge on and digestion of the premier occasional poet, putting his corpse through a series of humiliating funereal mishaps. 'In my beginning is my end', might be said of Dryden; and his ending, his funeral – not the real funeral, which seems to have been uneventful, but the riotous nightmare of legend – represents the nadir of invention in English poetry. The arc of Dryden's career, then, rises from the grim mortuary waiting-room of occasionality and falls back into that same darkness; and as

Lawrence Lipking has demonstrated in his *Life of the Poet: Beginning and Ending Literary Careers,* it is the beginning and ending of the literary career which are its most complex and most important moments. The brilliant flare in between cannot be underestimated; but it is the moments of first rise and last fall in which the weight of the occasion are best observed.

1. BEGINNING: WEEPING PUSTULES AND THE NOISE OF THE GUNS

Dryden, one of the products of the new schooling and model of literary celebrity, attempted a literary career just as the constriction of invention was worsening. If Milton's career represents the deployment of aporia as a trope for this constriction, Dryden's early career is best figured as aposiopesis – absolute silence, the silence of an ambitious poet not merely talking about waiting, as Milton did, but *actually waiting* for the occasion which would get his career going.

The grim implications of occasional poetry on the literary career are detailed by Johnson in his Life of Dryden:

> We know that Dryden's several productions were so many successive expedients for his support … his poems were almost all occasional.
>
> In an occasional performance no height of excellence can be expected from any mind, however fertile in itself, and however stored with acquisitions.… The occasional poet is circumscribed by the narrowness of his subject. Whatever can happen to man has happened so often, that little remains for fancy or invention. We have been all born; we have most of us been married; and so many have died before us, that our deaths can supply but few materials for a poet. In the fate of princes the public has an interest; and what happens to them of good or evil, the poets have always considered as business for the Muse. But after so many inauguratory gratulations, nuptial hymns, and funeral dirges, he must be highly favored by Nature, or by fortune, who says anything not said before. Even war and conquest, however splendid, suggest no new images; the triumphal chariot of a victorious monarch can be decked only with those ornaments that have graced his predecessors.

Not only matter but time is wanting. The poem must not be delayed until the occasion is forgotten. The lucky moments of animated imagination cannot be attended; elegances and illustrations cannot be multiplied by gradual accumulation; the composition must be despatched, while conversation is yet busy, and admiration fresh; and haste is to be made, lest some other event should lay hold upon mankind. (Chalmers, 8: 461)

Johnson's look back at the occasional poem reflects the taste of his own old age and that of his time, the mid-eighteenth century, which had begun to find ways out of the dilemma of poetic truth and the consequent reliance on occasionally-grounded texts. Nonetheless, Johnson's depiction of the implications of occasional poetics on Dryden's early work is typically acute. Johnson's central metaphor in the cited passage is that of the occasional poet as a merchant. He makes a quick equation of occasional poetry and writing to survive: 'expedients for his support' means, for Johnson, that '[Dryden's] poems were almost all occasional.' This disdain for the occasional basis of Dryden's work still endures; a twentieth-century editor says, 'We must not infer, because [Dryden's] work was occasional, that his inspiration was not genuine' (Bredvold, L. in *The Best of Dryden*, xxvi). The implication is that occasional poetry is poetry with the 'inspiration' – that is, invention – excluded. The motive force of the occasional poem, Johnson suggests, is the marketplace. The occasional poem is a kind of souvenir ware; 'business for the Muse' is Johnson's periphrasis for occasional legitimacy, and he portrays the occasional poet as a sort of concessionaire, trying to sell his wares while they are still hot.

Dryden also used this and other, crueller metaphors to describe his own 'trade rivals' to a career in obtaining commemorative rights to the great occasions of 1665. He was as unhappy about the implications of occasionality as were his later critics. But unlike them, he had no choice. A generation younger than Milton (Milton b. 1608; Dryden b. 1631), Dryden faced a situation which had markedly worsened. The mid-seventeenth-century audience had been seared by civil war and endless doctrinal quarrels; the tenor of the literary culture harshened, and readers grew increasingly preoccupied with truthfulness in narrative. Another cultural trend contributed a new sort of difficulty: the reintegration of England into mainstream European culture, the very trend which created poets like Milton and Dryden, also intensified the pressure of literary rules, imposed by the teachings of Continental critics. As the number of school-produced English literary minds increased, the Unities joined their strain of pedantic suspicion with the more profound religiously-grounded objections to invented narrative. This trend reached its height in learned late-century readers like Rymer, who were insistent that, if mere invented tales were to be produced, they must at least conform to the rules of Ancient Greece as retailed by European judges.

At the same time, the number of aspiring poets continued to grow, and the competition over the limited number of occasions necessarily intensified. This climate is described by one of Dryden's biographers as: '[A] world of sharp competition and rapidly evolving trends and fashions' (Hopkins, 37). But Dryden carved himself a place in the diminished literary sphere. His beginning is a story of tough, ruthless literary warfare.

As might be expected, his first attempt to gain the world's attention was an elegy in a memorial volume for a dead schoolmate. The deceased was Lord Hastings, who died of smallpox on June 24, 1649. The volume produced in his honour was *Lachrymae Musarum: The Tears of the Muses; Exprest in Elegies; Written by divers persons of nobility and worth* .... This forgotten volume had an impressive list of contributors, including Denham, Marvell and Waller. Dryden, typically, had a problem with deadline of the sort mentioned by Johnson: 'Not only matter but time is wanting.... The poem must not be delayed until the occasion is forgotten'. Dryden's contribution was included only in the second edition dated 1650.

Dryden's effort tries to make up in hyperbole what has been lost in timeliness. The young Dryden has no time to play with aporia as Milton did; he has to take maximum advantage of this opportunity by submitting to the memorial volume an entry which would command attention. Milton, with solid social standing and the support of a father who had 'destined [him] from a child to the pursuits of literature', could afford the long labour of study; a poet like Dryden, of uncertain social position and less certain income, literally could not afford to do so. He had to rise quickly, find a patron, or find a more mundane employment; and he had to do so in a situation growing more and more difficult for the inventor of poetry.

The difficulty of his situation comes through clearly in 'Upon the Death of the Lord Hastings': gross flattery of the deceased interlarded with remarkable displays of Cowley-derived hyperbole. The clear rhetorical purpose of this first work is the straightforward effort to claim the corpse in as dramatic a manner as possible. Dryden was admitted to the company of Herrick and Marvell only because, by his status as alumnus of Westminster, the deceased's alma mater, he could claim some rights to commemorate Hastings' corpse (in order to stress this link to the deceased, his poem was signed 'Johannes Dryden, Scholae Westm. alumnus'). And, in an epideictic context like this one, a mere schoolboy can speak with authority: '… the teenage poet is given licence to command and teach the mourners hieratically'. (Brown, 'Mending and Bending …') In many ways, then, it was a marvellous opportunity for an aspiring poet.

Yet the schoolboy-poet's task is formidable, as comparison with Milton shows. Milton was not only financially independent but a grown man, five years out of Cambridge, when he contributed 'Lycidas' to *JEK II*. Dryden is much younger (eighteen), much poorer, and facing fully-grown, eminent rivals. Worse still, the given theme is a difficult one; Hastings was only nineteen when he died, and had died without having done much which could be converted to elegy by the usual formulae listed by Johnson: he had no military triumphs, no offspring, no service to the state, no literary successes – not even the dramatic manner of death seized upon by the elegists of Edward King. In fact, the manner of his death (smallpox) was horrible – a difficulty which Dryden will turn to advantage.

But youth and obscurity also help Dryden, when one compares his situation in celebrating Hastings' death to Milton's in 'Lycidas'. There is in Dryden's poem little of the anxiety and self-justification found in the contributions to *Justa Edovardo King II*. Dryden is too desperate to worry about elegiac ethics. It is elegiac *tactics* which concern him. This is a cultural, not just a biographical difference; this desperation becomes a constant feature of English elegy as the seventeenth century passes midpoint. The demand for authenticity paradoxically but not perhaps surprisingly gives rise to more and more cynical exploitations of the few available occasions. Thus Dryden's elegy hardly so much as bows in the direction of elegiac decorum, let alone 'sincere grief' – the topics which obsessed the contributors to *JEK II*. The most notable feature of 'Upon the Death of the Lord Hastings' is its immediate employment of witty tropes which have little to do with even the pretence of guilt, as its abrupt beginning shows:

> Must noble *Hastings* Immaturely die,
> (The Honour of his ancient Family?)
> Beauty and Learning thus together meet,
> To bring a *Winding* for a *Wedding-sheet?*
>
> (Dryden, 1: 3)

In line four, after the briefest imaginable bow towards elegiac decorum, the author introduces an alliterative tmesis ('a *Winding* for a *Wedding-sheet'*) clearly comic in its effect and designed to show the elegist's skill in wordplay – with the alliterated adjectives italicized to alert slow readers to the joke. Dryden, continuing to exploit the deceased with 'any available means of persuasion' to impress potential patrons, slyly reveals to the reader the paucity of material he has to work with in the late Hastings, as if he wants his readers to be aware of his difficulty in finding topics to amplify. He shows the reader just how much he can do with the deceased's rather modest accomplishments, such as Hastings' schoolboy skill in language-acquisition (as the product of a pedagogy devoted so heavily to languages, Hastings' skill would not have been remarkable), devoting ten lines to a *gradatio* of praise on Hastings' mastery of Greek, French and Latin:

> Rare Linguist! whose Worth speaks it self, whose Praise,
> Though not his Own, all Tongues Besides do raise!
> Then Whom, Great *Alexander* may seem Less;
> Who conquer'd Men, but not their Languages.
> In his mouth Nations speak; his Tongue might be
> Interpreter to *Greece, France, Italy.*
> His native Soyl was the Four parts o' th' Earth;
> All *Europe* was too narrow for his Birth.
> A young Apostle; and (with rev'rence may
> I speak it) inspir'd with gift of Tongues, as They.
>
> (Dryden, 1: 3)

The poet even asserts the deceased's superiority to Alexander in lines 17–18. This sort of rhetoric raises the question of the real purpose of elegiac hyperbole: is the reader supposed to be convinced that this schoolboy's linguistic skill is worth more than Alexander's conquests? It seems unlikely. Nor is this reader likely to believe that Dryden, consumed with grief, thought so – since Dryden devotes no effort at all to a simulation of personal grief.

Rather, poet and reader enter a cynical compact over the corpse, in which the poet, following Johnson's dictum about the tedium of elegies, tries to come up with something bigger, wilder, newer than has been done before. The corpse is only the grounding, the permission of the text; the rhetorical purpose is display of epideictic skill; and the paucity of material is an enjoyable challenge for reader and poet.

A clear indication that Dryden actually *wants* the reader to feel the hyperbole of his praise of the deceased comes in lines 24–5, where, in an intentionally awkward parenthetic apostrophe, he actually makes a display of embarrassment for asserting that Hastings' linguistic gifts entitle him to be called an apostle: 'A young Apostle and (with rev'rence may / I speak it) inspired with gift of Tongues, as They.' It is rare for Dryden to break a line in mid-phrase, as here with 'may'; the enjambed parenthesis calls attention to itself thus by prosody as well as punctuation and tone.

When he comes at last to the manner of Hastings' death, Dryden again is concerned to show his difficulties as elegist. Hastings died of smallpox, a particularly horrible disease. Dryden could simply have passed over this aspect of the occasion; instead, he turns it into another hurdle over which to show himself leaping, displaying his poetic agility to good effect – and dropping all pretence of grief in the process. He begins his discussion of the manner of Hastings' death by making a display of horror at the cause of death: Why '… such a Foul Disease?' – as if grumbling at the difficulty it poses for the elegist – and then proceeds to show how much can be done even with such loathsome material:

> Was there no milder way but the Small Pox,
> The very Filth'ness of *Pandora's* box?
> So many spots, like *naeves,* our *Venus* soil?
> One jewel set off with so many a Foil?
> Blisters with pride swell'd; which th'row's flesh did sprout,
> Like Rose-buds, stuck i' th' Lily-skin about.
>
> (Dryden, 1: 4)

He reiterates the grossness of the disease: 'the very Filth'ness of *Pandora's* box …' but, overcoming this difficulty and turning it into a rare opportunity for invention, he immediately begins metaphorical alterations of the crude epidemiological facts: 'So many spots, like *naeves* … / One Jewel set off with so many a Foil' (lines 56–7). The alterations continue, each one turning a brutal fact of the disease into a beautiful trope; the pustules are first portrayed as evil and ugly ('Blisters with pride swelled') and then transformed into beautiful flowers ('Like Rose-buds, stuck i' th' Lily skin about'). Lines 59–66 bring the portrayal of the pustules to a boil, as it were, by offering an auxesis of metaphorical explanations for the symptom:

> Each little Pimple had a Tear in it,
> To wail the fault its rising did commit:
> Who, Rebel-like, with their own Lord at strife,
> Thus made an Insurrection 'gainst his Life.
> Or were these Gems sent to adorn his Skin,
> The Cab'net of a richer Soul within?
> No Comet need foretel his Change drew on,
> Whose Corps might seem a *Constellation.*
>
> (Dryden, 1: 4)

Here, in two perfectly matched sets of four lines each, Dryden offers the reader two brilliantly realized readings of the fatal blisters; the metaphor in lines 59–62, obviously referring to the Civil War and fall of Charles, is that of blisters as insurrectionists; they weep (line 59) even as they slay their lord.

The second quatrain follows what we have seen to be typical elegiac hyperbolic pattern in that it takes off on a less moralistic, wilder, more purely verbally-inventive tack, grounding itself in the pious banality of its predecessors (compare the progression from simple commemoration to wild metaphorical improvisation in Carew's three elegies on Mary Villiers). The blisters are now (line 63) offered to the reader as gems, forced through the skin by the sheer pressure of Hastings's inner goodness. But this more decorative reading turns to one of the more grotesque extremes imaginable, even by the standards of 'Metaphysical' poetics; the pustules, forming a pattern of dots on Hastings's disease-ridden corpse, are compared to an astronomical augury of greatness (lines 65–6).

Most criticism, faced with such bizarre excess, has explained the poem's excesses, somewhat tautologically, as typically 'Metaphysical' or dismissed them, and the entire poem which contains them, as youthful ineptitude. Dryden deserves more credit than this. If the strangeness of these tropes is taken as the work of an intelligent, ambitious young poet, what purpose can they have

Occasion in the Beginning and End of Dryden's Life 65

been meant to serve? They can hardly have been composed as comfort to Hastings's family – imagine his relatives hearing the pustule-dotted skin of their deceased scion compared with macabre playfulness to 'a *Constellation*'. Nor do they seem to offer much fulfilment of Eric Smith's so very earnest 'human needs' (speculation about the poet's own mortality in another's guise, etc.)

In fact, these lines are born of the school exercise. Like Milton's youthful version of the miracle at Cana, they can best be understood via their conditions of production: schoolboys competing to find a new metaphorical texture for a given, fixed invention. Dryden's comparison of Hastings's corpse to a constellation is a product of the same poetics. The subject is fixed; the materials are few, due to the youth and mediocrity of the deceased. The assignment is roughly like that given the contributors to *Justa Edovardo King II*, but while their assigned topic was 'The death of a promising young man by drowning', Dryden's assigned topic was: 'The death of a youth, versed in languages and of good family; from the smallpox'. The manner of Hastings's death is clearly the most promising element in the assignment; naturally, the aspiring elegist tries to make it even more dramatic, bizarre, extreme.

Dryden has already demonstrated his ability to amplify Hastings's few accomplishments to the maximum; he has milked Hastings's one modest accomplishment, his linguistic prowess, in lines 14–20. The only useful material which remains of Hastings's *ethos* is the manner of his death. And so Dryden makes the most of it; invention takes precedence over decorum as Dryden allows a succession of apparently inconsistent metaphors about the pustules, which are first jewels, then proud blisters, then rosebuds, then teary faces, then rebels, then jewels yet again (Dryden, 1:4) and then the crowning image, the stars of a constellation.

This inconsistency is entirely consistent with the *rhetorical* intention, and indeed offers a good instance of the utility of rhetorical rather than purely intellectual readings of seventeenth-century elegy. Dryden *wants* to demonstrate his ability to come up with an impressive number of metaphors. The ability to bewail the corpse in print is one of the few opportunities a poet of his generation would get to display his powers in a pathetically-charged environment; why should he not take maximum advantage of the rare opportunity? If this is a display piece intended to gain the author admission to the Writers' Guild, then inconsistency and mixed metaphors are a demonstration of potential power. And it is an impressive one; these lines on the pox have made generations of readers uncomfortable – a reaction Dryden might not have minded at all. For the occasional poet, the Hollywood adage that there is no such thing as bad publicity is simple fact.

In fact, 'Upon the Death of the Lord Hastings' is (among other functions) a self-advertisement by Dryden; and the size of the advertisement – that is, the length of the poem – is itself part of the appeal. (Quantitative terms are used as praise unabashedly in seventeenth-century English literature, a product of school training in *copia,* the ancient rhetorical skill of amplification.) Dryden, repeatedly hinting at the thinness of the biographical material he has to work with, demonstrates his ability to produce 110 lines of glittering, clever elegiac product. In the process, he not only switches tone and trope repeatedly but does so intentionally, to show prospective patrons his ability to work in a variety of styles and tone. This time the corpse is not merely the object of struggle, as in the poems surrounding King's body; this time, Hastings's corpse is a prop for the elegist's display of wit. The poet's real purpose is clear in the lines in which he imagines the corpse as the subject of combat, like that of Patroclus or Hector:

> O had he di'd of old, how great a strife
> Had been, who from his Death should draw their Life?
> Who should, by one rich draught, become what ere
> *Seneca, Cato, Numa, Caesar,* were:
> Learn'd, Vertuous, Pious, Great; and have by this
> An universal *Metempsuchosis.*
>
> (Dryden, 1:4–5)

If John Dryden, pupil, had anything to say about it, it was quite clear 'who … from [Hastings's] Death should draw [his] Life': *Johannes Dryden, Scholae Westm. alumnus.* Dryden's early career illustrates the scarcity of literary opportunities for a poet committed, as he was at this stage, to exercising poetic invention only when the occasion permitted. His next major composition was the 'Heroic Stanzas' on Cromwell's death in 1658 – almost a decade after the verses on Hastings' death. Dryden's late development as a poet has often been noted:

Although [Dryden] had probably long been nursing literary ambitions, it is remarkable that at the age of twenty-seven he had published only three brief poems, all occasional in nature. (Bredvold, L. xv)

There is a clear connection between the fact that all of Dryden's early works are 'occasional in nature' and the fact that there were so few of them. The legitimate occasions which came his way were few; Dryden exploited them as he could. Dryden had to wait for someone to die about whom he was qualified by social position to write. Westminster School had provided him with a sort of attenuated kinship to Hastings, allowing him to enrol in the memorial volume; the death of Cromwell, the next opportunity of which it is known that Dryden availed himself, was nine years later.

Cromwell was a legitimate object of elegy for any poet; as head of the nation, he was related, as it were, to everyone in the country, so Dryden could claim the attenuated kinship of elegiac decorum. But the grim geometry of occasional poetics meant that, just as Cromwell could be considered a relative of everyone in England, so every aspiring elegist in the country was certain to turn out an elegiac offering on his death.

Dryden clearly felt the odds worth taking; he produced the 'Heroique Stanzas' on the Protector's death. This poem has been the subject of a great deal of politically-oriented criticism, most of it aimed at convicting or exonerating Dryden of the charge of political opportunism. This is an odd sort of argument, explicable only in terms of the degree to which modern criticism has accepted Romantic poetics. The death of a Lord Protector is an absolutely legitimate occasion for displays of elegiac skill; but the *right* to write elegy must not be confused – as it often is – with the *rhetorical purpose* of the elegy so written. Dryden's right to commemorate Cromwell is undoubted; this is in no way to suggest that the purpose of the resultant poem is the expression of grief. The rhetorical purpose here, as always in Dryden's early work, is simply the furthering of the poet's career. The major difference between this sort of elegy and the more private schoolmates' volumes is that Dryden is aiming higher, seeking the patronage, as it were, not of a single family but of the nation (which patronage, in the form of the laureateship, he did in fact later obtain). Johnson casually treats the lust for fame as the obvious purpose of the 'Heroique Stanzas':

It was not till the death of Cromwell, in 1658, that [Dryden] became a public candidate for fame, by publishing [in 1659]

Heroic Stanzas … which, compared to the verses of Sprat and Waller on the same occasion, were sufficient to raise great expectations of the rising poet. (Chalmers, 8: 424)

The difference between the sort of occasion presented by the death of a schoolmate and the death of 'His Late Highnesse Oliver, Lord Protector …' is a difference in the kind of obstacle the poet had to overcome. The elegist of a death like Cromwell's does not face the problems presented by a subject like Hastings; the events of Cromwell's life were such that amplification would hardly be a problem. But these apparently positive aspects of the occasion were precisely the problem: an occasion so widely felt, and so obviously worthy of celebration, would inevitably produce thousands of elegiac entries. The poet's problem, then, is to stand out from his rivals.

Dryden, composing these verses, is in the position of a merchant facing the competition of thousands of other entrepreneurs; it is not surprising, therefore, that this poem marks the appearance of a theme which Dryden, frustrated by the perennial famine of occasions, was to develop fully in the next decade: the poet's fear and hatred of those he regarded as purveyors of hastily produced, shoddy occasional wares: that is, of trade rivals.

Cromwell died on September 3, 1658. His funeral was held on November 23. Johnson, in the passage from the *Life of Dryden* cited above, cited the extreme perishability of the occasional poet's ware, which, essentially, is a corpse – what could be more perishable than a corpse? Dryden faced the problem of perishability in commemorating Cromwell and again in commemorating the events of 1665 in 'Annus Mirabilis'; both times, his occasional product was late in reaching the market. He was not, evidently, the sort of quick, journalistic composer the occasional market required. Dryden, in a resourceful and audacious manner typical of him, turns this defect into a boast. Since he cannot be first to sing over the corpse, he turns haste into ghoulish vice; his slowness is now decorum, defined as waiting for the funeral – a rule which had never been a part of occasional ethics until Dryden invented it as such. Dryden emphasizes the propriety of his timing in the first stanza of the 'Heroique Stanzas':

> And now 'tis time; for their Officious haste,
>   Who would before have born him to the sky,

> Like *eager Romans* ere all rites were past
> Did let too soon the *sacred Eagle* fly.
>
> (Dryden, 1: 11)

'And now 'tis time'; – Dryden means to imply that *his* effort displays a respectful diffidence, as opposed to the 'officious haste' of those who published elegies without waiting for the funeral. Anxiety about the efforts of rival elegists reappears in the fourth of the 'Heroique Stanzas', when Dryden sketches the other, related strategy he will develop in the coming decade: the notion that he writes only to forestall the less worthy, less legitimate efforts of those poets who would otherwise fill the elegiac void:

> Yet 'tis our duty and our interest too,
> Such monuments as we can build to raise;
> Lest all the World prevent what we could do
> And claim a *Title* in him by their praise.
>
> (Dryden, 1: 11)

Here appears again that remarkable feature of elegiac rhetoric which was so marked in the contributions to *JEK II:* what seems to be mere hyperbole when read according to the conventional literary-intellectual context suddenly appears as simple fact when read in the context of poetic ambition. The surface intellectual content of these lines is that England must celebrate Cromwell before other nations come and claim his heroic qualities; but if this is the elegist speaking, then the stanza simply says, 'I, the aspiring occasional poet, must commemorate the deceased before someone else comes along and does so' – which, of course, is precisely the focus of Dryden's anxiety as he performs above the fast-decaying corpse. Cromwell's corpse, of course, was, figuratively at least, *decaying* quickly as a valuable source of political or poetic capital; the smart money was not betting on the survival of Richard Cromwell's rule, and elegies to Cromwell therefore might have a particularly short time of sale.

The surface meaning – the nation's claim to the corpse – serves the poet's ambitious purpose. By assuming the role of England's poetic champion (laureate), Dryden generalizes and legitimizes his own fear of being eclipsed by the many other poets who will undoubtedly crowd around this public, valuable corpse. Dryden's professional argument, which he will articulate more fully a few years later in the 'Essay of Dramatick Poesie' and 'Annus Mirabilis', is that he *must* compose an elegy ("'tis our duty, and our interest too') in order to fence out foreign interests who would take over English trade otherwise: 'Lest all the world prevent what we should do / And claim a title in him by their praise.' Thus, like Milton in 'Lycidas', and indeed like more and more English poets as the seventeenth century progressed, Dryden tries to avoid the imputation of voluntary invention; tries, that is, to reattribute the creation of the poem to something outside the ego of the poet.

Dryden continued to try to play by the severe rules of occasional poetry, waiting to pounce on the appropriate event. He was a talented aspirant; in Johnson's judgement, cited above, he 'won' the funeral tournament over Cromwell's corpse. Dryden produced two major poems occasioned by the restoration, 'Astrea Redux' in 1660 and 'To His Sacred Majesty, A Panegyrick on His Coronation', in 1661. But he was not the winner of this major poetic competition; the poem most popular with contemporary audiences was Robert Wild's 'Iter Boreale', while the one which best captured the sense of relief and pride immediately following the success of the Restoration effort was Waller's 'On St. James's Park, as Lately Improved by His Majesty'. Having failed to make poetic capital from this once-in-a-lifetime occasion, Dryden must have been especially anxious to win the next major occasional tournament.

When such an opportunity finally came, it arose from the crises of the mid-1660s. Dryden found himself in the exciting position of having not one but two great public occasions to celebrate: the naval war with the Dutch and the Fire of London. For the occasional poet, this was of course a great opportunity; but it was a moment of danger and panic, too. Such public events would inevitably be preempted by hordes of humbler, quicker occasional poets of proto-Grub-street mould. Dryden's response, one of the most remarkable in the history of literature, is a multi-genre counter-offensive which includes the ostensibly theoretical, drama-centred 'Essay of Dramatick Poesie' as a sort of silent partner and protector of the more popular occasional poem 'Annus Mirabilis'.

The 'Essay of Dramatick Poesie', because of its apparent character as theoretical discussion, has been analysed largely for its content as a piece of Restoration criticism, and considered, as such, only as it applies to 'Dramatick Poesie' (Verse Drama). But the beginning of the 'Essay' can also be considered as bearing on *occasional* poetry, and as it links up, via the overarching metaphor of trade rivalry, to Dryden's simultaneous practice of occasional poetry in 'Annus Mirabilis.'

Critics, struck by the apparent slovenliness of the 'Essay' have taken its casual, colloquial style to be another sign of what they deem Dryden's 'inconsistency' – his all-too-pliant, facile mind. Indeed, the first written response to the 'Essay' focuses on an accusation of inconsistency; while, three hundred years later, Donald Davie continues the tradition, dismissing the 'Essay' as no more than an unfocused 'Conversation-Piece'. Such are the perils of viewing literary texts purely as vessels of intellectual content; for these works possess an iron unity, not merely within themselves but among each other. This unity has gone unmarked because it is a unity of rhetorical purpose, not intellectual content. When examined for rhetorical purpose, the 'Essay' becomes clearly understandable as a defence of Dryden's own work in theatre and of his own 'Annus Mirabilis'. In fact, the 'Essay' is more of a weapon than it is a 'conversation-piece'; seen in its original context, it glows with malice, and is at once a low blow directed by Dryden at rival occasional poets and a furious expression of the tremendous frustration felt by a hungry, ambitious and talented poet trying vainly to operate within the rules of occasionality and their cousins, the 'Unities', which tied the hands of dramatists as occasionality tied those of lyric poets.

The 'Essay of Dramatick Poesie' is of course constructed as a dialogue between four characters who are floating down the Thames while the battle of Lowestoft was taking place off the mouth of the Thames. The 'Essay' begins in a quiet, almost incidental way with a discussion of occasional poetics. But, quiet as it is, Dryden has packed this opening narrative with hidden, career-driven literary propaganda. A striking case in point is the narrator's mention of 'the noise of the guns'. The scene is set: the four principals have decided to float downstream toward the naval battle taking place off the coast. As they move downriver, they are hoping to be able to hear some sound of the distant battle. It is the noise of cannon which connects the battle to the four principals and, finally, to 'Annus Mirabilis':

> . . . the noise of the Cannon from both Navies reach'd our ears about the city: so that all men being alarm'd with it, and in a dreadful suspence of the event, which they knew was then deciding, every one went following the sound as his fancy led him; and leaving the Town almost empty, some took towards the Park, some cross the river, others down it; all seeking the noise in the depths of silence. (Dryden, XVII: 8)

'Seeking the noise in the depths of silence' – in this phrase
Dryden hints at the true rhetorical purpose of the narrative
prologue to the dialogue, and its secret link to his effort to fend off
trade rivals of 'Annus Mirabilis'. By placing a thinly-disguised
version of himself in a boat floating towards the battle, flanked by
three equally thinly-disguised distinguished witnesses, Dryden
hopes to emphasize his qualifications to be the poet of this desir-
able occasion, first as a poet of noble acquaintance (unlike his
quicker Grub-Street rivals), and, even more importantly, as a man
who was *there,* at ground zero of the occasion, or at least as close as
a civilian could get; and whose effort to be on the scene can be
confirmed by the impressive three companions (the narrator slyly
mentions *'three [of the four]'* as 'persons whom their witt and
Quality have made known to all the Town …'. (Dryden, XVII: 8)

The three companions thus amount to a sort of disguised testi-
monial to the occasional legitimacy of the poet, the fourth member
and the narrator of their voyage. The more this fourth passenger
basks in his friends of 'quality', and the further he moves down-
river toward the guns, the more he becomes likely to be named,
among the numerous contenders, as *the* poet laureate of the Battle
of Lowestoft.

Dryden thus had urgent reason, grounded in the notion of occa-
sional poetry as testimony, to 'seek the noise of the Cannon'. That
those guns could have been heard at all from London is doubtful;
Dryden in fact makes many references to the strain he and his
companions faced in trying to hear the noise of battle. First, the four
principals of the dialogue, using a boat provided by 'Lisideius',
'made haste to shoot the bridge, and leave behind them that great
fall of waters which hindered them from hearing that which they
desired'. Next they have to force their way through a crowd of
moored vessels who obstruct their pilgrimage to 'the noise'. Like
trade rivals, these 'hulks' are described as dull, annoying obstruc-
tions in the way of the occasion and the poet laying claim to it. At
last, in a passage central to Dryden's strategy, the four men find
'that which they desired'; having made their way through the
distractions of the urban Thames,

they order'd the Watermen to let fall their Oares more gently;
and then every one favouring his own curiosity with a strict
silence, it was not long ere they perceiv'd the Air to break around
them like the noise of distant Thunder, or of Swallows in a

Chimney: those little undulations of sound, though almost vanishing before they reach'd them, yet still seeming to retain somewhat of their first horrour, which they had betwixt the Fleets: after they had attentively listned til such time as the sound by little and little went from them; *Eugenius* lifting up his head, and taking notice of it, was the first who congratulated to the rest that happy Omen of our Nations Victory; adding, that we had but this to desire in confirmation of it, that we might hear no more of that noise which was now leaving the *English* coast. (Dryden, XVII: 8–9)

This is the moment when Dryden claims the occasion; this, he hopes, entitles him to get the preference he desires for 'Annus Mirabilis'. Dryden writes the scene (quite beautifully) so as to create an almost reverent tone – each of the four maintains a devout silence, '*strict* silence' as he puts it, while awaiting the noise of cannon. Their prayers are ambiguously answered; when the sound does come, it is described in similes emphasizing its distance and quiet; the sound is compared to distant thunder, or swallows in a chimney. Dryden actually stresses the doubtfulness of the sound, emphasizing that 'those little undulations of sound almost vanish[ed] before they reach'd them'.

From little to less; the tiny sound of the distant battle is then described as vanishing completely: '… the sound by little and little went from them'. Why does Dryden, trying to claim first-hand experience of the occasion he hopes to commemorate, go to such lengths to stress the doubtful, distant quality of that which [he] desired? Part of the answer lies in the goal which defines all of the prologue of the 'Essay': the desire to pre-empt trade rivals. Dryden, in his description cited above, completely shuts down the noise, denying it to any rivals; Eugenius, who first declares the sound inaudible, turns this silence, which might have been a declaration of failure to reach the occasion, into the occasion of patriotic joy; he states that the fact that the four *had* been able to hear the guns, and now cannot, means that the battle is 'now leaving the *English* coast', implying an English victory.

'*Did Dryden Hear the Guns?*' asks a mid-twentieth-century academic article, implicitly accepting Dryden's stress on the importance of actually hearing the guns, without questioning why it is so important to decide whether Dryden heard them or not. The article begins with the premise that the (alleged) four men in the (alleged) boat heard *something,* but – working directly on Dryden's own literary description of the difficulty of hearing that noise – offers an alternative explanation of those 'little undulations of sound'.[2] The article suggests that those sounds, described by Dryden as resembling 'distant thunder', *were* in fact distant thunder, and goes on to prove this thesis by examining meteorological records for the London area on the day of the battle of Lowestoft. This thunder becomes a providential grounding – a sound which any well-meaning listener might easily have taken for cannon, and which thus absolves Dryden of the charge of *lying*.

'Annus Mirabilis' commemorated three events: the naval war, the plague, and the fire of London. If Dryden were to invent a narrative which would allow him to lay claim to unique intimacy with even one of the three occasions, he would necessarily have chosen the war; the fire and plague were too widely experienced by all Londoners. He cannot put himself and his distinguished friends in a boat and get them nearer the centre of those occasions; London was itself the centre of both the fire and the plague. Moreover, the battle was perhaps a more savoury occasion than the plague to hug to himself (though we have already seen, in 'Upon the Death of the Lord Hastings', that Dryden was not shy about amplifying the symptoms of a fearful disease when it served his purpose). So his flagship-occasion becomes the battle, and only by moving out of London in an expensive hired boat can Dryden hope to use his aristocratic connections to batter his quicker, more numerous proto-Grub-Street foes, who would not have had the resources to follow downriver.

But by far the most convincing evidence that the frame-tale of the boat-trip exists to serve career purposes is the way in which Dryden carefully blends the opening, narrative frame of the 'Essay' into the dialogue proper. The opening narrative of the four companions' search for the noise of battle allows Dryden to lead into a discussion of occasionality in poetry, which is in many ways the true subject of the 'Essay'. The way in which this discussion begins is telling: Eugenius, having made of the diminishing sound of battle a good omen, makes silence a desired goal – and this silence soon becomes explicitly that silence which Dryden desires to impose on his occasional rivals. As the [alleged] sound leaves the coast, the first extended speech begins. It is spoken by Crites, usually identified as Sir Robert Howard, Dryden's friend and patron. Crites' speech is an attack on the very basis of occasional poetry, as practiced by Dryden's rivals. It proceeds, with Dryden's usual deceptive ease, from Eugenius' interpretation of silence as good news; building on the 'silence is golden' theme, Crites says

> if the concernment of this battel had not been so exceeding great, he [Crites] could scarce have wish'd the Victory at the price he knew he must pay for it, in being subject to the reading and hearing of so many ill verses as he was sure would be made on that Subject; adding, that no Argument could scape some of those eternal Rhimers, who watch a Battel with more diligence than the Ravens and birds of Prey; and the worst of them surest to be first in upon the quarry, while the better able, either out of modesty writ not at all, or set that due value upon their poems, as to let them be often desired and long expected! (Dryden, XVII: 9)

In this passage, we find our 'premier occasional poet' comparing occasional poets to carrion-eaters, and suggesting that those with any decency would prefer not to write at all, rather than write such a despicable sort of poetry. The self-loathing which the poetics of occasionality, advancing in the decay of invention, created is made explicit here: a poet is someone who waits for a great disaster, then gleefully attempts to write up a verse on it as quickly as possible – before the corpses are cold, if possible.

But Dryden has no intention of abandoning his chosen profession. He intends to continue writing occasional poetry; this attack is directed at his rivals, not himself. The viciousness of the attack must not be ignored – Dryden makes Crites say that occasional poetry *per se* is a loathsome profession – and may well express his sincere doubts about the genre. But the emotional matrix of a text is not identical to its rhetorical purpose, and here, the rhetorical strategy is part of an aggressive attempt to claim the occasion, not – as it might be seem to a modern critic – an introspective confession.

The loophole by which Dryden hopes to exculpate himself from the general condemnation of occasional poets comes with a division in the category: '… and *the worst of them* surest to be first in upon the quarry [my italics]'. This suggests that speed of production is one way the consumer can tell the bad occasional poets – the *paparazzi*-like carrion crows – from the better sort. The good ones work slowly. Dryden clearly intended to let his own work, 'Annus Mirabilis', fall into the category of those occasional verses which are 'often desired and long expected' – i.e. which take a great deal more time to appear than do the broadsheet ballads.

This strategy of turning a professional liability – slow rate of production – into a sign of virtue is a favourite one of Dryden's. Dryden made his silence a sign of talent, much as Milton had made the aporia on 'writer's block' a part of his self-created legend. The tardy appearance of his poem is proof of its integrity, just as the difficulty of hearing the noise of battle becomes proof of the auditors' patriotism.

Crites' speech exposing the ghoulish basis of occasional poetry leads, in Dryden's strategy, directly to the suggestion of restricting trade rivals. Lisideius, seconding Crites' attack, depicts the occasional poets as low men, mere tradesmen, who hawk their stock of commonplaces cynically, adjusting it according to any outcome of the battle then in progress:

> There are some of those impertinent people of whom you speak, answer'd *Lisideius,* who to my knowledg, are already so provided, either way, that they can produce not onely a Panegireck upon the Victory, but, if need be, a funeral elegy on the Duke: wherein after they have crown'd his valor with many Lawrels, they will at last deplore the odds under which he fell; concluding that his courage deserv'd a better destiny. (Dryden, XVII: 9–10)

This is an extraordinarily violent strategy, amounting to the revelation of some trade secrets in the hope that their revelation will damage one's rivals more than oneself. But Dryden's strategy of revealing sordid secrets of the elegiac trade may have been especially prominent in his mind at the time of writing because he planned to make use of these tricks himself in 'Annus Mirabilis'. For example, the topic of greater numbers (the Dutch fleet) versus greater valour (the English), mocked by Crites in the passage cited above, is one of the most frequently used in 'Annus Mirabilis' (see especially lines 210–300); and the depiction of the valour with which the English dead fell, also named by Lisideius as an elegiac cliché, is interwoven with it in an earlier section of the poem (see the death of Lawson, lines 81–5).

In impugning the integrity of his chosen genre, Dryden seems to invoke the notion of restraint of trade by force – which happens to be the central argument of 'Annus Mirabilis' and of the 'Essay' as well. Certainly the direction taken by the dialogue after Crites and Lisideius make their attack on the genre suggests that the author wants something done about his many occasional rivals; the next speech, by Crites, amounts to a demand for government action against unlicensed poets. Crites, excited by Lisideius' endorsement of his attack on occasional poetics, lashes out at several of Dryden's real-life rivals piecemeal, then broadens the attack to the suggestion of preventing these rivals from breaking into print at all:

> *Crites,* more eager then before, began to make particular exceptions against some Writers, and said the publick Magistrate ought to send betimes to forbid them; and that it concern'd the peace and quiet of all honest people, that ill Poets should be as well silenc'd as seditious Preachers. (Dryden, XVII: 10)

This is not idle hyperbole. The silencing of seditious preachers was, after all, an activity regarded as central to the survival of the state in the early years of the Restoration. Crites' suggestion is deeply serious and arises out of the easily-summarized formulae used by occasional poets, as noted in his earlier speech against them. Occasional poets write at times which are easily guessed – like crows, they appear after a great carnage. The magistrates could plausibly 'send betimes to forbid them' from exercising their craft.

Convincing the magistrates of the seditious nature of poetry Dryden happened to find professionally inconvenient would not, of course, have been so easy; so, falling back on the class-based strategy he used earlier, Dryden has Eugenius respond that official action is not necessary; scorn will dispose of these 'poets of the people', though he adds, in a speech through which Dryden's envious irritation shows through plainly, that though 'a few … about the town' may have the grace to see through these lowly poets' pretensions, there are many willing buyers in the City (that is, of the mercantile class) who know no better, and even interrupt their pursuit of gain to read them 'in the midst of "Change time"' [i.e. during business hours].

Here, transfigured, is Dryden's own rhetorical/commercial situation: facing the rivalry of a host of poets who had produced faster, cheaper, more accessible poems on the three great occasions which Dryden had entrusted to one huge, erudite umbrella-occasional-work, 'Annus Mirabilis'. How to market such a thing, when its rivals were already being successfully hawked to the ignorant

customers of the City? Clearly, Dryden had to try to capture a
different audience: the Town (the aristocratic reader); and with the
town, the patronage of the crown itself, made visible in the award-
ing of the laureateship. Dryden may not have hoped to secure the
literal prohibition of his lowly, seditious rivals, but rather the iden-
tification of himself with elegance, restraint, 'The Town'; and his
rivals with commerce, low tastes, and 'The City'.

As Dryden (and a great many other English people) saw it, the
restraint of rival trade was the whole motive for the Dutch war, the
occasion which occupies most of 'Annus Mirabilis'. That work
begins by arousing hatred of the Dutch for their trade supremacy:

> In thriving Arts long time had *Holland* grown,
> Crouching at home, and cruel when abroad;
> Scarce leaving us the means to claim our own.
> Our King they courted, & our Merchants aw'd.
>
> Trade, which like bloud should circularly flow,
> Stop'd in their Channels, found its freedom lost;
> Thither the wealth of all the world did go,
> And seem'd but shipwrack'd on so base a Coast.
> (Dryden, 1: 59–60)

The Dutch are caricatured in 'Annus Mirabilis' in the same way
that Dryden's rivals are caricatured by Eugenius in the opening of
the 'Essay'. Like those rival poets, the Dutch are 'base' tradesmen
who have somehow gained the advantage over their more warlike
but less grasping English trade rivals. In the complex interlocking
strategy of the occasional poem and prose 'Essay', Dryden is to his
rivals, (those crude 'poets of the people') as England is to Holland
– the nobler, slower but finally more powerful entrant usurped
temporarily by a base, enterprising rival.

> Dryden=England=The Town;
> Dryden's occasional rivals=Holland=The City.

The plot of that part of the poem dealing with the war is simple;
the Dutch supremacy in trade is restrained by the English
supremacy in courage and power. There is no hint that the English
ought to compete more efficiently as traders; they are exhorted
simply to hound the Dutch into a less aggressive trade posture and

regain the mercantile 'laureateship' of Northern Europe. This is the import of the last stanzas (303–4) of the poem:

> The wealthy *Tagus,* and the wealthier *Rhine,*
> The glory of their Towns no more shall boast;
> And *Sein,* that would with *Belgian* Rivers joyn,
> Shall find her luster stain'd, and Traffick lost.
> (Dryden, 1: 104)

Once the Navy has removed the Dutch fleet, more peaceful persuasions will make London the preferred commercial destination:

> Our pow'rful Navy shall no longer meet,
> The wealth of *France* or *Holland* to invade:
> The beauty of this Town, without a Fleet,
> From all the world shall vindicate her Trade....
>
> Thus to the Eastern wealth through storms we go;
> But now, the Cape once doubled, fear no more:
> A constant Trade-wind will securely blow,
> And gently lay us on the Spicy shore.
> (Dryden, 1: 104–5)

This is the vision with which Dryden leaves the reader – a pure monopoly, in which all trade rivals have been beaten, or intimidated out of competing. Johnson finds this an odd ending: 'The poem concludes with a simile which might have better been omitted' (Chalmers, 8: 465). But within Dryden's actual rhetorical conception of the interlocking essay-and-poem strategy for his own trade war, it makes perfect sense to end the poem with a vision of riches, rather than martial glory. For the aspiring laureate, the prospect of a poetic monopoly was a vision of paradise, too; a spicy heaven in which magistrates might suppress the horde of rivals who, aroused by the all-too-public, all-too-rare occasions of poetry, sprang up to sell their cheaper and more quickly produced goods to the City before the higher sort of poet, aiming at the Town, could even get his offering on the market. Dryden, faced with such a situation, wistfully lets his characters in the dialogue of the 'Essay of Dramatick Poesie' toy with the idea of trade restrictions; but he lets his stronger hopes rest on a strategy of scorn, in which the poem and the 'Essay' combine to present a multi-generic offensive emphasizing the superior nature of Dryden's product. Such a strategy, though it may seem cynical, was in fact absolutely necessary to an ambitious poet trying to play by the rules of occasionality in a climate where a profusion of suitable occasions like that which burst over England in the mid-1660's comes rarely; the opportunity must be taken as aggressively as possible. Another *Year of Wonders* might not have arisen until Dryden was too old to make his way.

2. ENDING: HIJACKING THE LAUREATE'S CORPSE

> Polemicization of the dead ... is ... a central feature of the mid-
> and late-seventeenth-century epitaph.
>
> Scodel, 139

An eloquent picture of the state of invention and occasional poetics is provided by Johnson in his *Life of Dryden.* To end the *Life,* Johnson chooses a story about the final events in the life of the greatest occasional poet in English, John Dryden, making his own corpse the object of occasional strife by the sort of 'carrion crows' he vilified in the 'Essay of Dramatick Poesie'. (For the full text of this account of Dryden's funeral, see the Appendix.)

The story is not biographically true; as early as Scott's *Life of John Dryden* the funeral of Dryden is described as decorous (398–401).[3] Johnson seems to have taken the scurrilous story of a disturbance at Dryden's rites from a 12-page biographical sketch written by Thomas Birch, general editor of the English edition of Bayle's *General Dictionary* (Osborn, 12; 60; 138).[4] An authoritative account of the actual proceedings can be found in James Anderson Winn's recent biography:

> [Dryden's] body was quickly buried on 2 May in St. Anne's, Soho; Charles Montagu ... helped defray the expenses of this first burial. But a few days later, probably at the intervention of Dorset, the corpse was exhumed and embalmed, lay in state at the College of Physicians, and was finally buried in Chaucer's grave in Westminster Abbey on 13 May. The undertaker's bill, with its charges for velvet hearse coverings and plumes for the six white horses, gives some sense of the pomp involved. Dr. Garth made a funeral oration in Latin, and two collections of

generally dreadful poems on the death of the poet were published the next fall. (Winn, 512–13)[5]

The only elements of the actual funeral which are absorbed into the legend are the idea of two funerals (a modest, and then a grand one); the continual transfer and decoration of the body; and the involvement of Garth and the physicians. Beyond that, the cultural forces at work invent the wild story of riot and decay. But it is precisely the fact that someone invented this story, which readers evidently believed as something which could or should have happened at Dryden's funeral, that makes it so significant. It stands as an allegorical confession of the culture's own horror at the ghoulish struggles over a corpse produced by occasionality – in this case, with bitter irony, the corpse of the occasional poet himself – which had come to characterize English poetry. Thus, whatever its origin, the fact that this remarkable tale existed at all suggests that English poetics in 1700, the year in which Dryden died, had reached a nadir which the culture itself attributed to reliance on funereal occasion.

One could not possibly invent a story which reveals more poignantly the perils of occasionality. Dryden, the outstanding occasional poet of the day, reduced to becoming himself 'the corpse' and as such the object of self-serving pretence of grief; 'the corpse' literally hijacked by one (Lord Jeffries) who hopes to grab the occasion and its pathos for himself; 'the corpse' then abandoned by the self-serving hijacker and rotting, ignored; the second funeral, which becomes an excuse for low comedy (the beer-barrel) and the riot of the mob vs the arrogance of the sword-wielding 'gentlemen' as they surge forward to try to get at 'the corpse'; and finally Dryden, the premier practitioner of the poetics of occasion and 'truth' laid *on top of* the remains of Chaucer, perhaps the greatest of the fictional, inventive poets in the English tradition – the occasional poet's corpse clumsily ('with as much confusion and as little ceremony as was possible') overlaying the corpse of the inventive power of English poetry.

Dryden's death spawned many Grub-Street responses, all of which emphasize to varying degrees the image of the occasional poet becoming itself the helpless occasioning object, jostled and tossed about, as in Johnson's account, and hijacked for the purpose of maudlin display by whatever faction of the literary scene the writer happens to find most objectionable. In the Johnson account, it is the drunken aristocrat who asserts power over the corpse; the middle-class literary/professional sector, as represented by Garth, is treated with more respect. In Tom Brown's 'A Description of Mr. Dryden's Funeral', it is Dryden's fellow literati who are the hijackers of the corpse. Brown begins by stressing the power of the laureateship (using the term in its broad, unofficial sense) which Dryden had commanded:

> A bard there was, who whilome did command,
> And held the laurel in his potent hand;
> He o'er Parnassus bore imperial sway,
> Him all the little tribes of bards obey;
>
> (Pinkus, 123)

The death of such a figure represents the fall of the top of the literary hierarchy, and as such an opportunity for all 'the little tribes of bards'. Brown, of course, is one such, a Grub-Street entrepreneur of the new type, living by the sort of occasional pamphlet-and-poem writing described by Johnson; thus his poem on Dryden's death is both a description and an instance of the work of decomposition of the 'imperial' corpse. Brown is well aware of this dimension of his work; in fact, after narrating the death of Dryden in the passage cited above, he describes the commemoration of that death in the familiar metaphor of carrion-eating birds gathering around a corpse:

> The day is come, and all the wits must meet
> From Covent Garden down to Watling Street;
> They all repair to the Physicians dome,
> There lies the corpse and there the eagles come ...
>
> (Pinkus, 123)

These 'eagles' are named by their professional relation to the literary trade; first 'A troop of stationers' including Tonson, then the less-respectable remainder of the literary world:

> ... poets, fiddlers, cut-purses, and whores,
> Drabs of the play-house, and of common shores;
> Pimps, panders, bullies and eternal beaux,
> Famed for short wits, long wigs and gaudy clothes;
> ... All these the funeral obsequies do aid,
> As younger brothers of the rhyming trade.
>
> (Pinkus, 124)

Inevitably, the gathering of the carrion-eating birds here listed turns into a struggle over the corpse: 'About the corpse in state they wildly press...' (Pinkus, 124). Brown reserves his most savage attack for the funeral procession itself (which is in fact the focus of almost all the legends involving the funeral). In his account, which differs in most points from Johnson's, there is this point of agreement: the notion that the corpse is degraded by the slapstick, self-serving attempts to commandeer it during the funeral procession:

> Now, now the time is come, the Parson says,
> And for their exeunt to the grave he prays:
> The way is long, and folk the streets are clogging,
> Therefore my friends away, come let's be jogging ...
>
> One pocky spark, one sound as any roach,
> One poet and two fiddlers in a coach;
> The play-house drab, that beats the beggars bush,
> And bawdy talks, would make an old whore blush ...
> Was e'er immortal poet thus buffooned?
> In a long line of coaches thus lampooned?
>
> (Pinkus, 125)

As Brown comments at the end of his poem, after such a cere-mony even the life-weary Dryden 'would rather live than thus be buried'. The degradation of the corpse by the 'long line of coaches' is so painful to the sight because it is a gross, visual representation of the piling-up of 'tributes' to the deceased – the physical repre-sentation of a memorial volume. The villain changes; in Johnson's account it is the social élite which wants to hijack the corpse, in Brown's it is rival poets; but in both accounts there is a striking feeling of the helpless body being subjected to ludicrous and essen-tially self-serving commemoration.

A third account, by Ned Ward in the *London Spy*, combines elements of the Johnson and Brown accounts, in spite of Ward's evident attempt to maintain funereal decorum. This time, Jeffries is the hero of the story:

> '[T]is credibly reported the ingratitude of the age is such that they had like to have let [Dryden] pass in private to his grave. But a true British worthy, meeting with the venerable remains of the neglected bard passing silently in a coach, unregarded to his last

home, ordered the corpse (by the consent of his few friends that attended him) to be respited from so obscure an interment; and most generously undertook, at his own expense, to [pay for a better funeral]. Lord Jeffries [was] concerned chiefly in the pious undertaking. (Pinkus, 213–14)

Ward's characterization of Jeffries is the direct opposite of that in the Johnson account, and reflects a desire to preserve the tone of the funereal occasion; Ward, like Brown, reserves blame for the lower-ranking denizens of Grub Street, who disrupt the funeral. In Ward's account, decorum gives way to comedy slowly. Ward tries to begin in an uncharacteristically solemn, decorous tone:

A deeper concern has scarce been known to affect in general the minds of grateful and ingenious men, than the melancholy surprise of Mr. Dryden's death has occasioned through the whole town. (Pinkus, 213)

But this unaccustomed severity (note also the typical usage of the verb 'occasioned') gives way to farce at the crucial moment of the funeral procession. In a manner typical of the professionalized literary man of the turn of the century, Ward interprets the problem in commercial terms; the 'hackney whore-drivers' (carriages hired as mobile bedrooms for short-duration sex) are annoyed by the congestion created in the streets by the press of carriages in the procession of Dryden's funeral (once again, the notions of corpse and congestion, jostling, and overcrowding come together). Trouble breaks out between the rival groups of cab-drivers:

The great number of qualities' coaches that attended the hearse so put the hackney whore-drivers out of their bias that against the King's Head Tavern there happened a great stop, occasioned by a train of mourning coaches which had blocked up the narrow end of the lane, obstructed by an entangled number of movable bawdy-houses who waited to turn up the same narrow gulf the others wanted to go out of. Some ran their poles into the windows of another coach, wherein fat bawd and whore, or mother and daughter, squeaked out, for the Lord's sake, that some merciful good man would come in to their assistance. (Pinkus, 216)

This farcical encounter quickly becomes the focus of the narrative for Ward; once again, the corpse is lost in a jostle over it. The corpse emerges nonetheless in these accounts as a character of sorts – note that Ward uses the pronoun 'his' to describe it, as if it still possessed personhood. It becomes an object of competition but also a dramatic figure in itself, tossed from one to another, hijacked from the procession and then used as a threat from the undertaker (i.e. that he will leave it on the Dryden family's doorstep if not paid) and then made to lie there, centre stage, while 'poets, fiddlers, cut-purses and whores' shove each other (in Brown's account) or while the gentry and the populace ('The City' and 'The Town' as Dryden put it in the 'Essay of Dramatick Poesy') fight with sticks and swords (weapons which are themselves class markers) over the right to get close to the death (much as the young and ambitious Dryden had fought, by other and more imaginative means, to get close to the deaths arising from the battle of Lowestoft, or to the corpse of Lord Hastings, or Cromwell). Through it all, the glib, aggressive seizer of occasions is reduced, in a remarkable sort of ceremonial vengeance by his culture, to lie there, dead and still, as these jostles crash around him. When the orator falls off the barrel, smashing it, it is a thinly-disguised joke about the coffin being broken into. In all these ways, the corpse is violated; and in its nature, it is, as both Johnson's and Ward's account describe it, 'gross'. Both these accounts stress the idea of decay; Johnson adds to the drama of the homeless, graveless corpse by remarking on the stench arising from its advanced state of decay. Season cannot go far in explaining this particular rottenness ascribed to the corpse; Dryden died in the springtime. There is clearly something of the corpse, the *corpus*, in Dryden even before his death – this is the key to the comic treatment of that corpse. Ward even goes out of his way to imply that Dryden had begun to become a corpse even before his official death:

> The occasion of his sickness was a lameness in one of his feet ... and, being a man of gross body, a flux of humours falling into the part made it very troublesome, so that he was forced to put himself into the hands of an able surgeon, who, foreseeing the danger of mortification advised him to part with the toe affected, as the best means to prevent the ill-consequence likely to ensue. This he refused ... till at last his whole leg gangrened; This was followed by a mortification, so that nothing remained to

prevent death but an amputation of the member thus putrefied. He refused…. (Pinkus, 215–16)

The repetition of terms implying death ('Putrefaction', 'mortification' 'gangrened') and the basis of the narrative – that Dryden died by inches until his entire body was a mass of rotting flesh – suggests the way that he is becoming an *occasion* even before the moment of death. Dryden, who is used to taking the corpses of others, refuses to consent to the loss of any of his own *corpus*. This results in the loss of the whole and the giving over of that whole body to the saturnalian comedy featured in all three accounts. Regardless of the identification of the parties responsible, all three accounts aim at the same sort of comedy (and it *is* comedy, and rather low, slapstick comedy at that, which all three of the accounts invoke, as the proper sort of vengeance (or 'poetic justice') on the enforced seriousness of the occasional poet, the function represented by Dryden's corpse.) The comedy involves the helpless corpse of a major poet becoming the occasion of the most degrading, low sort of quarrels – it is in this sense that the accounts of Dryden's funerals may well be placed in the line of psuedo-Homeric mock-heroic poetry which flourished at the time of his death.

This is serious comedy. The jostling around the corpse is fit vengeance for its profit from a lifetime of occasional poetry, and enacts a ritual, saturnalian revenge on the literary élite which survives by means of that poetics. The legends of Dryden's funeral thus suggest a deep unhappiness and impatience with the poetics of occasionality. As Dryden wrote in commemorating the end of the century in which he had plied his trade,

> All, all of a piece throughout …
> 'Tis well an old age is out,
> And time to begin a new.

But in fact the famine in poetic invention was intensifying at the time of Dryden's death, and the poets who made up his funeral procession had to live on, scheming ways to cope with the increasingly overcrowded and ambitious world he had at last left behind.

4

Nadir: the Generation of Namur and the Famine of Occasions

All were abused, as was his intention,
And underwent the lash of his invention.
'An Elegy' [1699, Attributed to Tom Brown]

1. THE DISSEMINATION OF THE POETICS OF ENVY

The latter years of the seventeenth and the first years of the eighteenth century represent the nadir of poetic invention in modern England, a nadir lived through by the Generation of Namur – the generation which is defined by its desperate participation in great occasional tournaments to commemorate a few great occasions: the death of Queen Mary (1694) and the decisive battles of Namur (1695) and Blenheim (1704). My decision to call this the 'Namur Generation' reflects the belief that prevailing terms, notably 'Augustan', convey a sanitized impression of the literary culture of the period, turning what was a nadir of poetic invention and, consequently, a period of vicious occasional competition into an altogether more noble enterprise. Close examination of the literary warfare of the period can only emphasize that the early-eighteenth-century world was a rough place which underwent a sort of posthumous rehabilitation into the modern scholar's Arcadia of stability and reason. (This is emphasized in many of the essays of Nussbaum and Brown[1] and Rawson.)[2]

It is easy enough to demonstrate that this period represents a low point in the history of English poetry in the minds of twentieth-century readers. The *Norton Anthology of Poetry* (3rd edn), a standard anthology in use at most American universities, contains over 1300

pages of verse, arranged in chronological order. To the poets
between Dryden (b. 1631) and Pope (b. 1688), the *Norton Anthology*
allots no more than 25 of those pages. One might, of course, argue
that the bias indicated by allotment of space in contemporary
anthologies does not prove the real failure of the poetry of the
Namur era. It could certainly be said that the judgements of the late-
twentieth century on the verse of the late-seventeenth mean little.
But there is considerable textual evidence that the period at the end
of the seventeenth and beginning of the eighteenth century was
experienced at the time as one of failure in English poetry; that the
poets and readers of the time, constrained by occasional truth, had
to force an ever-increasing volume of literary ambition into an ever-
shrinking, increasingly overcrowded and violent literary world.

This is certainly the view developed by critics closer in time to the
period in question – for example, Samuel Johnson, looking back
from the 1770s at the age of Namur. In signing a contract to write,
as he put it, 'little lives' of English poets, Johnson had essentially
agreed to take a contemplative, evaluative look back at English
poetry from Milton's time to his own. Often his judgements are
skewed by factional or religious enmity (as in his comments on
Milton); but more often, bias in his judgements reflects the bias of
the moment of writing – the time, past the crucial mid-eighteenth-
century period, when the crisis had passed, and English poetry had
at last begun to escape from what Edward Young himself called
the 'famine of invention'. (Young, Conjectures on Original
Composition, 54) Thus it is worthy of note that in the 'Lives' the
poets of the Namur generation are consistently treated by Johnson
with a violent contempt unlike anything he expresses toward the
poets of any other time, even those (like Milton) whom he clearly
dislikes; and that this particularly virulent contempt is directed at
the Namur poets precisely for their practise of occasional poetics.

What is most remarkable is that Johnson consistently (as in the
following passage from his 'Life of Prior') distinguishes the practice
of occasional poetics as an outmoded habit characteristic of this
particular generation of poets:

> Every thing has its day. Through the reigns of William and Anne
> no prosperous event passed undignified by poetry. In the last
> war, [i.e. the Seven Years War] when France was disgraced and
> overpowered in every corner of the globe, when Spain, coming
> to her assistance, only shared her calamities, and the name of an

Englishman was reverenced through Europe, no poet was heard against the general acclamation; the fame of our counsellors and heroes was intrusted to the Gazetteer. (Chalmers, 10: 108)[3]

Here Johnson, as is his wont, pursues several ends at once; he is simultaneously slighting the occasion-chasing poets of the turn of the century, while, somewhat inconsistently, castigating the poets of his time for 'intrust[ing]' the successes of English arms 'to the Gazetteer'. But, his political grumbling aside, Johnson clearly posits a change in the practice of occasional poetry which has taken place at some point in the first half of the eighteenth century. It was not actually the case that no poets celebrated English victories in the Seven Years War; nonetheless, Johnson was right to imply that the mid-century reader had come to look for patriotic pathos from the 'Gazetteer', not the poet. While the occasional poems of the Namur generation represent their best work, mid-century occasional martial poems are usually found in journals like the *Gentleman's Magazine,* and are usually the work of poets not of the first rank. The best, most technically advanced mid-century poets – Gray, Young, and Collins – had found a way out of the gazette-like practice of journalistic poetry; Prior and his contemporaries in the generation of Namur had not. Johnson, after looking over the mass of obviously hastily-produced odes and elegies on battle, marriage and birth, rightly saw a difference in the practice of poetry in the two eras.

Johnson, in dealing with occasionality in the 'Life of Prior' – whom, in fact, he respects more than almost any poet of the Namur generation – still allows himself a breezy contempt about the most deeply occasionally-grounded texts of the time:

[Prior's] occasional poems necessarily lost part of their value, as their occasions, being less remembered, raised less emotion. Some of them … are preserved by their inherent excellence … [but] the poems to King [William] are now perused only by young students, who read merely that they may learn to write; and of the Carmen Seculare, I cannot but suspect that I might praise or censure it by caprice, without danger of detection; for who can be supposed to have laboured through it? Yet the time has been when this neglected work was … popular. (Chalmers, 10: 114)

Implying that occasional verse is ephemeral verse designed to elicit pathos ('their occasions ... less remembered ... raised less emotion'), Johnson ends by saying that this once-popular sort of work now need not even be read. At no other point in the series 'Lives of the English Poets' does Johnson reveal anything like this sort of violent alienation from the texts he is discussing. It is clear that a sharp break has occurred, in his view, between the generation of Namur and his own, and that the decline of occasional poetics seems to him the point of the break.

Part of the scorn with which Johnson looks back at the turn-of-the-century practice derives from his argument that occasional poetry was devoted, not simply to pathos, but to that fatal triad, 'poetry', 'patronage' and 'preferment' which he slyly hints characterized the generation of Namur. Referring to Prior and his collaborators in 'The City Mouse and the Country Mouse', the Protestant reply to Dryden's 'The Hind and the Panther', Johnson observes, '[The poem] procured its authors more solid advantages than the pleasure of fretting Dryden; for they were both speedily preferred'. (Chalmers, 10: 106)

In the Namur environment – which added the lure of state preferment to literary ambition, oxymoronically combined with disdain for original invention – it is not surprising that the desire to write might be connected to the desire for ambitions other than literary. In fact, as literary creation became dissociated from invention, it acquired the sense of an accomplishment, a sort of preliminary examination for preferment – thus reinforcing the association of mainstream English poetry with the classroom and the school. Successful completion of the sort of academic poetry-writing exercises exemplified by Prior's works were of tremendous value in making one's career. In Boswell's *London Journal 1762–1763* the pedagogue Thomas Sheridan recalls the turn of the century in a tone very different from Johnson's scorn. For Sheridan (whose pension came later than Johnson's) Prior's time represented a lost Golden Age of preferment:

> Mr. Sheridan said that this age was ... a trifling age. 'In the reign of Queen Anne,' said he, 'merit was encouraged. Then a Mr. Prior was Ambassador, and a Mr. Addison Secretary of State. Then genius was cherished by the beams of courtly favour. But in the reigns of George the First and George the Second it was a disadvantage to be clever ... I knew several people when at school whose Juvenalia were equal to those of the great men of letters in

Queen Anne's time; but as true great genius is always accompanied with good sense, they soon saw that being men of literary merit was not the way to rise. (*Boswell's London Journal*, 91)[4]

In Queen Anne's time, then, according to Sheridan, 'being men of literary merit' *was* the way to rise, not only in literature but in gaining any lucrative state office. William and Mary had reason to disburse as much support as possible to potential laureates in its effort to consolidate their legitimacy. Johnson sums up the situation thus:

King William had no regard to elegance or literature; his study was only war; yet by a choice of ministers, whose disposition was very different from his own, he procured, without intention, a very liberal patronage to poetry. ('Life of Addison', Chalmers, 9: 488)

As Johnson hints, the poets of this age were defined not only by a particularly desperate reliance on occasion but on a particular kind of occasion – one in which reasons of state and the requirements of poetic pathos were combined. Such an event would be the death of one of the ruling couple; thus, Johnson notes:

The death of Queen Mary (in 1695) produced a subject for all the writers; perhaps no funeral was ever so poetically attended. Dryden, indeed, as a man discountenanced and deprived, was silent; but scarcely any other maker of verses omitted to bring his tribute of tuneful sorrow. An emulation of elegy was universal. Maria's praise was not confined to the English language, but fills a great part of the *Musae Anglicanae*. (Chalmers, 10: 106)

'Tuneful sorrow' is of course meant as a sarcastic oxymoron by Johnson. It is the same sort of derision directed at all forms of stylized grief, but notably elegiac poetry, which underlies Johnson's famous comment, cited above, about 'Lycidas'. Thus it is inevitable that, as he discusses the Namur poets, who relied on elegiac and martial occasions almost exclusively – far more than did poets of Milton's generation – his scorn increases.

Indeed, one gets a sense, while reading his 'Lives of the English Poets' with care, that Johnson has made an association between Whiggish surface piety and latent ambition which finds its nexus in the elegy, as practised by a poetic line running from Milton or Prior

– a genealogy termed 'Whig Panegyric Verse' and traced by Cecil Moore in *Backgrounds of English Literature, 1700–1760* (Minneapolis: University of Minnesota Press 1953). For Johnson, writing at a time in which expanded opportunity has made the luxury of 'sincerity' possible, crass struggles like that of the Namur poets over the body of Queen Mary seem contemptible.

Another familiar factor combines with reliance on occasionality and the ignoble struggle for preferment by a quasi-legitimate regime to produce the surplus of ambition and dearth of invention which characterize the Namur generation: the proliferation of new-modelled schooling of the sort which produced Milton.

Pope stands alone in his refusal to engage in occasional poetics/politics – a striking anomaly in the poetics of the Namur era. As a Catholic born in the year of the 'Glorious Revolution', with its revival of anti-Catholic bigotry, he could not go to the elite schools which bred the Namur poets. In fact, Pope, so elusive and subtle on many issues, is very straightforward and consistent in his hatred for formal education ('Essay on Criticism' lines 25–7; Dunciad II). A comparison of Pope's early poems to those of his contemporaries (and his elders of the Namur generation) shows that Pope was remarkably uninterested in strictly occasional verse – perhaps because the verse surrounding the struggle for laureate-ship required full citizenship in the English polity (since it involved celebrating state occasions) – which Pope, as a Catholic, could not hope to obtain. Nor could he hope for 'preferment' in the Civil Service as reward for literary distinction. Joshua Scodel cites Pope's early decision to look to his own mythologized persona, rather than public occasions, for poetic material:

> In a letter of 1710 the young Pope wonders whether "'tis a kind of sacrilege … to steal epitaphs?' Instead of stealing others' epitaphs, he continually rewrites them in order to affirm … what is, finally, his own. (Scodel, 276)

In his 'First Epistle of the Second Book of Horace Imitated', Pope attacks '… the authors as well as the subjects …' of occasional poetry (James D. Garrison, *Dryden and the Conventions of Panegyric* Berkeley/Los Angeles: University of California Press 1975, 255), '… step[ping] forth from behind his ironic mask to belittle those poets who had written in praise of kings':

And when I flatter, let my dirty leaves
(Like Journals, Odes, and such forgotten things
As Eusden, Philips, Settle, writ of Kings)
Cloath spice, line trunks, or, flutt'ring in a row,
Befringe the rails of Bedlam and Sohoe.
(cited in Garrison, 226)

Instead of resorting to strictly occasional poetry to establish himself as a poet, Pope developed a two-stage strategy for grounding his poetry: first defining himself as 'translator' (rather than composer) of his true love, epic poetry; and then, once his fame was secure, using his own literary combats and adventures to write a new, autobiographical epic – not mock-epic but urban, urbane epic.

It is clear that the epic poem was Pope's first and deepest love ('There was probably no major poet after Dryden who devoted himself so intensively and indefatigably to the idea and practice of the epic as Pope' [Ulrich Broich, *The Eighteenth-Century Mock-Epic Poem,* Cambridge, 1990, 110]; see also Mack, 44–50, 94n, 837n). Eighteenth-century neo-epic genealogy stretches from Blackmore to Chatterton, with Pope as its greatest critic, prophet, and 'translator'. I have traced the moment of its failure (Dolan, 'Poetry', 'Fiction', and 'Found Texts of the 1760's' *Genre* XXVIII – Spring/Summer 1995, 35–50). In *Peri Bathous,* a sophisticated prediction and critique of the road a romanesque poetics might take, Pope makes it clear that he resents Blackmore for daring to write epic in a belated, minor era in which only poetry of 'judgement', not true 'invention', can be composed. Clearly worried that Blackmore's very stupidity had a somewhat Homeric flavour to it, Pope raged against this fool who rushed in where the yearning but intimidated Pope feared to tread. In the second half of the century, MacPherson and Chatterton were to use almost exactly the set of 'sinking' devices which, Pope predicted, could be used to make epic poetics appealing to degraded modern tastes – the enterprise in which he saw Blackmore as being engaged. Rather than try, as Blackmore did, to rewrite (or, as Pope would put it, 'sink') ancient epic, Pope settled for translating and editing Homer. Summarizing his career, Pope said, '[I have] become, by due gradation of dulness, from a poet a translator, and from a translator a mere editor' (Bloom, ed. *Alexander Pope,* 3) – the diminished role appropriate to a belated writer or epic ('Preface to the *Iliad*' in *Poetry and Prose of Alexander Pope,* New York, 1969, 440).

Though it began as a sort of consolation prize after his acceptance of the impossibility of writing original epic, Pope's enthusiastic acceptance of the secondary roles of translator and commentator provided him with the opportunity to write a new kind of auto-biographical epic by using his own difficulties as the basis for an apparently autobiographical narrative of war – an epic with himself as improbable Achilles, as in the 'Epistle to Doctor Arbuthnot'. As Helgerson says of an earlier analogue to this autobiographical-heroic poem, 'For a poem like [this] to work, the poet's name must already mean something…. At such moments, the poet draws on an account to which he has been making deposits for many years.' (Helgerson, 12–13)

This technique also characterized the latter stages of Dryden's career, when he defined the laureateship as single combat against a series of challengers (and even adumbrated the lone-catholic-against-the-host-of-whigs stance Pope was to perfect). But it is a technique available only to a poet already famous. Pope could not begin to use his own career as occasioning material for poems until he had already attained considerable fame – at the least, enough to inspire many anti-poems directed at himself and his work. In this strategic impasse, translation served for him, as it had for many Namur-era poets, as a way of putting his skill as poet before the public without incurring the accusation of actual invention. As critics attacked his translations, Pope became the protagonist of his own epic, and could write from within a public narrative which was not, as far as suspicious, invention-hating readers were concerned, of his own making.

But while Pope, a shining anomaly, turned his disabilities into the stuff of epic, an increasing number of over-educated, under-funded young people continued to attempt to make a living by literature, pursuing the occasion-centred poetics taught in the schools from which Pope had been excluded. These are the pool from which the bulk of the Namur poets and Grub Street hacks are drawn. As Philip Pinkus states: 'In the 1690s, it seemed possible, for the first time, for [English] hack writers to live by their writing' (Pinkus, 15).

If the notion of citizenship will not suffice as a metaphor for this 'Grub Street' literary world of the 1690s, perhaps free enterprise or entrepreneurship will; for the sociology of literary enterprise is a vital factor in the way that the literary world is changing at this time. The class of young writers who flock to London to make their living with their pen, caricatured as 'Grub Street' hacks, in fact shades easily into higher literature, as cases like that of the remarkable Tom Brown demonstrate. Brown's literary career was much like Edmund Smith's in that he combined, in his early life, a good training at a good school with a willingness to engage in the grosser sort of 'Grub Street' writing – writing burlesques and occasional verse for quick sale. But in fact, the 'Grub Street' model does not suddenly lose its applicability to the Namur Generation at a certain socio-literary level; there is more of 'Grub Street' about even the best poets of the time (e.g. Prior and Addison) than it is comfortable to admit; these well-remembered poets began, as Johnson stresses, by competing in servile occasional tourneys for the ruling couple, and lived in a literary/political environment in which 'preferment' was, if more genteelly, at least as intensely sought as a Grub-Street pamphleteer with lower aims might seek a fee or a dinner.

A larger reading public, with the increase in periodical literature to satisfy its demand for material, enticed these aspirants to London. As the reading public grew, capital invested in publishing grew to attract sales; this enticed more and more aspirants to Grub Street. As the number of literary aspirants increased, the pressure on each suitable occasion naturally grew; thus struggles over the right to commemorate eminent corpses, characterized by Dryden as resembling the scrabbling of 'carrion crows', grew far more intense toward the end of the seventeenth century in the London literary world. The obsession with controlling the occasion, as Pinkus demonstrates, was no longer limited to poets; as the reading audience grew, a new faction, the booksellers, became more and more of a factor in the struggle over the corpse. These booksellers had the capital to define and control the issuing of memorial volumes on a popular deceased; but they had to be agile and ruthless to exploit an important death, as the career of the notorious literary pirate Edmund Curll, described by Pinkus indicates:

A few verses might appear by an anonymous writer. Some weeks later [Curll would issue] a 'biography' of the supposed writer. Then the two pamphlets would be issued together as 'Poems on Several Occasions, with some account, etc.' Then a preface would be added, creating another edition. And if some brief comment on the book was then discovered, it also would be added to the text, which became 'The Poetical Works of....' And when the poet died his Last Will and Testament was incorporated and the book became 'The Whole Works of …' or 'The Life and Times'. In this way the poet received Curll's undivided professional attention, and perhaps little else, almost from the cradle to the grave. (Pinkus, 55–56)

Profiteering over the corpse thus was becoming, for entre-peneurs like Curll, a more organized, corporate venture; individual aspirants could be hired, lending their skills to the bookseller's cause rather than their own. Curll now had a huge pool of hungry writers from which to draw; not only those who worked for him, but those who entered the literary tournaments, often employing the device of anonymity became, as Pinkus notes, fair game for a reinvented *ethos* to be nurtured for the bookseller's profit.

The formulaic, mediocre quality of Namur-era verse might be explained by the oversupply of writers which created such enter-prises. But while this oversupply does account, perhaps, for the peculiar viciousness of the poetic trade in England circa 1700, it cannot explain the formulaic nature of the verse, since even in successful writers of the Namur era, one retains a powerful impres-sion of belatedness and second-order invention, on which poets grounded their works. Poets of the time had so internalized the poetics of occasion that they wrote anti-inventively by preference. The preference is a matter of internalized training – the institution-alization of reactive poetry. The biographies of the Namur poets have a striking sameness to them, quite unlike the varied, not to say roguish, careers which characterized the Jacobean poets. A strik-ingly high percentage of the poets of the 'Age of Preferment' were the products of Westminster School, where they were tutored (and flogged) by the famous Busby; after Westminster they went on to Oxford or Cambridge, and often tried to get a fellowship and remain at college as long as they could. If no fellowship was forth-coming, they tried to obtain some governmental sinecure, often, as in the case of Addison and the commemoration of Blenheim, by producing occasional verse which served the regime's purposes.

This is the life-trajectory of a Namur poet; and its impact on the potential for invention was malign. As Mack asserts, 'the curricu-lum of studies in a late-seventeenth-century school was not well calculated for the meridian of a lively imagination' (Mack, 51).[5] The deadening progression of such a life is exemplified by careers like that of Edmund Smith – whose libertinage actually made his biog-raphy rather more exciting than those of most of his peers, but who otherwise follows the dull, pedantic course of a Namur poet. This is his career, as acidly summarized by Johnson:

> Edmund Neale, known by the name of Smith ... was educated at Westminster. It is known to have been the practice of Dr. Busby to detain those youth long at school, of whom he had formed the highest expectations. Smith took his master's degree on the 8th of July, 1696; he therefore was probably admitted to the university in 1689, when we may suppose him twenty years old.
>
> His reputation for literature in his college was [great]; but [so was] the indecency and licentiousness of his behavior.... [He received] while he was yet only bachelor a public admonition.... At Oxford, as we all know, much will be forgiven to literary merit; and of that he had exhibited sufficient evidence by his excellent ode on the death of the great orientalist, Dr. Pocock, who died in 1691, and whose praise must have been written by Smith when he had been but two years in the university....
>
> He proceeded to take his degree of master of arts, July 8, 1696.... As his years advanced, he advanced in reputation ... though he did not amend his irregularities; by which he gave so much offence, that, April 24 1700, the dean and chapter declared 'the place of Mr. Smith void....'
>
> But he was still a genius and a scholar, and Oxford was unwilling to lose him; he was endured, with all his pranks and his vices, two years longer; but [in] ... 1705, at the instance of all the canons, [he was expelled from Oxford].
>
> ... He was now driven to London, where he associated himself with the Whigs. (Chalmers, 9: 171–2)

This is the life of someone comfortable only in the permanent adolescence of student life; Smith leaves the university, against his will, when almost forty years of age. He was obviously continually getting himself into trouble with schoolboy pranks well into middle-age, and continually getting himself out of them by, in effect, adding to the university's lustre by offering occasional poetry. In the instance mentioned in detail by Johnson he proved his usefulness by producing the winning entry, 'Pocockius', on the death of Dr Pococke, a well-known Orientalist whose death was an important test of the literary prowess of his university. The presence of a good occasional poet like Smith at such a moment was important enough for the University to forgive his transgressions when he came through with an adequate verse on the deceased.

Smith's poetry is straightforwardly occasional, without exception. For Smith, a non-occasional poem would have been a pointless, unprofitable business. The list of titles is like a summary of the major legitimate poetic occasions of his time: 'On the Birth of the Prince of Wales', 'On the Inauguration of King William and Queen Mary', 'On the Return of King William from Ireland' and so on. The poems are formulaic and, as Johnson implies in the passage cited above, all but unreadable to audiences removed from the pathos-context of the original occasion. They are standardized and businesslike in their exploitation of the available topoi; Smith clearly wrote them according to order and produced according to demand. Thus his occasional works lack either the guilt-haunted, macabre irony of the contributions to *Justa Edovardo King II* or the wild amplifications of topos found in Dryden's work. By Smith's time, as the summary of his career above suggests, the occasional genre is institutionalized, and its training ground, the Westminster-model school, has drilled into its pupils the precise formulae necessary for poetic preferment. As the century closes, this result of school-training becomes the norm: instead of defending their right to the occasion, most poets become defensive about their right to write anything which extends, however slightly, outside strict occasionality.

The cynicism which naturally arises from these conditions of production distinguishes the occasional productions of Smith and the other products of the Namur generation. It reaches its height in Smith's elegy for John Philips. Philips had been one of Smith's close friends; and so, motivated, ostensibly, by grief, Smith wrote an elegy for the occasion. But the real purpose of the production of this text is clear from Smith's employment of the occasional text as mercantile product. Johnson describes Smith's sales strategy: 'This elegy it was the mode among [Smith's] friends to purchase for a guinea; and, as his acquaintance was numerous, it was a very profitable poem'. (Chalmers, 9: 174)

This highly trained, standardized practice of occasional poetics combines with his narrowly academic experience to produce in Smith's work a pedantry characteristic of post-Miltonic school-bred poets. Johnson emphasizes the school-bred aspect of Smith's poetry; of Smith's play, *Phaedra and Hippolitus,* he says, 'It is a scholar's play' (Chalmers, 9: 173) and of Smith's manner, he says, 'scholastic cloudiness still hung about him' (Chalmers, 9: 175).

Smith may not have been by nature more of a pedant than the poets who preceded him; rather he is representative of a generation which had been trained by the schools to treat poetry as a path to academic success, and which could manage to eke out its entire adult life moving from the narrow environment of school- and university-life to the service of the State, populated with former classmates now in powerful office.

The creative life epitomized by Smith – writing to order, waiting for occasional licence, and relying on school-taught literary formulae – is not likely to produce a great deal of worthy invention, especially when it is remembered that the entire focus of education at a school like Westminster was the development of formulaic literary competence. This levelling of literary production is one of the most notable effects of school-training of poets (and may still be observed in contemporary literary workshops). Literary instruction tends to produce a regression to the mean, as the worst and the best efforts of the students are tugged by powerful social pressures towards that formulaic mean.

This regression to the mean led in turn to a frightening inability to distinguish good from merely ordinary verse. It is illustrated by an anecdote from Johnson's *Life of Addison*; Johnson is discussing the simile of the Angel, one of the most often-praised features of Addison's most famous occasional work, 'The Campaign', devoted to the glories of Marlborough:

> Marlborough 'teaches the battle to rage'; the angel 'directs the storm'; Marlborough is 'unmoved in peaceful thought'; the angel is 'calm and serene'; Marlborough stands 'unmoved amid the shock of hosts'; the angel rides 'calm in the whirlwind'. The lines on Marlborough are just and noble; but the simile gives almost the same images a second time.
>
> But perhaps this thought, though hardly a simile, was remote from vulgar conceptions, and required great labour or research, or dexterity of application. Of this Dr. Madden ... gave me his opinion. 'If I had set', said he, 'Ten school-boys to write on the Battle of Blenheim, and eight had brought me the angel, I should not have been surprised'. (Chalmers, 9: 508)

When eight out of ten schoolboys – let us say, allowing for malice or hyperbole in Madden's or Johnson's account, when even one in ten, one in a hundred, or even one in a thousand – when *any* significant percentage of the brightest schoolboys can replicate the poetic strategies of Addison, considered the best poet of the Namur generation – then there is clearly a crisis in the poetic hierarchy. In the early eighteenth century, more and more readers confess their inability to tell good from ordinary verse. This is the consequence of an educational system devoted to the mass production of formulaic efforts on topics imposed from outside; but its immediate consequence is the diversion of poetic effort into the search for preference, since quality of verse alone is not enough to win through. When the artistic product cannot be judged as better or worse than others of its genre by consumers, it is the self-promotional skills, rather than the inventive talent of the artist, which comes to the fore; career strategies replace quality of invention as the criterion of success. This is the meaning of Sheridan's nostalgic assertion that, in the Namur generation, 'men of sense' pursued poetry.

Of course, not all critics have shared Johnson's (or the *Norton Anthology's*) dim view of the poetry of the Namur generation; there have been several attempts, which deserve serious consideration, to rehabilitate the poetry of this period. Eric Rothstein, in his *Restoration and Eighteenth Century Poetry 1660–1780*[6] attempts to explain the apparent willingness of English readers, circa 1700, to be entertained by poetry which seems to consist of nothing but 'staid metaphors,… stilted diction,… largely standardized speakers who intone generalities, invoke personification, call birds "plumy people" … and dignify the unworthy' (Rothstein, 49). How, Rothstein asks, could readers capable of appreciating Shakespeare find pleasure in such texts? His explanation is that readers of this era were particularly concerned with 'contexts and placement', and that many of the devices later readers have found numbingly dull must be seen as attempts to satisfy that longing for contextual ordering (though 'placement', in the Namur-era jargon, often means something more down-to-earth). Rothstein's reading illuminates much of what is valuable in this poetry, yet fails to take into account one telling aspect of the poetic culture of the period: its own sense of failure, of inferiority in poetic accomplishment. The generation of Namur, the generation between Dryden and Pope, represented a nadir of poetic production in England, and knew it.

This is not to slight the poets of that era; talent is no doubt evenly distributed over time, but opportunity is not. As Edward Young, speaking of the dearth of poetic invention, put it, 'I think that human souls, through all periods, are equal ...' but 'Reasons there are why talents may not *appear*, none why they may not *exist*, as much in one period as another.' (Young, *Conjectures* ..., 47) Young places the blame on the weight of example (55):

> But why are originals so few? Not because the writer's harvest is over ...; nor because the human mind's teeming time is past, or because it is incapable of putting forth unprecedented births; but because illustrious examples engross, prejudice, and intimidate ... Nature's impossibilities, and those of diffidence, lie wide asunder.

Those difficulties 'of diffidence' were formidable enough, however. Poets born to spend their career in a bad moment for poetic invention must spend all their time jostling for the right to write. In so doing, the Namur poets laid the groundwork for the mid-eighteenth-century renewal of invention; out of their nadir grew the great technical innovations of the early and mid-eighteenth century. Therefore it is not in order to attack these poets that their inventive failure must be recognized; rather, in order to appreciate the innovations which came after them, we must understand the bleakness of the poetic landscape circa 1700 – for it is that bleak environment which provided the force for the innovations which led to a brighter poetic landscape. The beginning of an appreciation of the Namur poets begins with the acknowledgment that, no matter how much they may appeal to twentieth-century scholars of their period, the poets of that generation felt themselves to be and have consistently been judged since to be lacking in poetic invention.

Rothstein's defence of the poetry does not correspond to the view expressed of their craft by the poets themselves. 'Context', Rothstein's term for the central preoccupation of the poetry of the period, is, in a sense, truly crucial; context actually represents the desperate efforts of this generation of poets to satisfy tightening demands for 'truth' or occasional grounding in their work. But Rothstein and other twentieth-century defenders of the Namur generation seriously underestimate the extent to which this was actually a violent, envious, desperate world. Rothstein's conception of the importance of context in poems of the period emphasizes a harmonious inclusiveness:

The [early-eighteenth-century] poem as constructed object should be related to other poems, the speaker to other members of his society, the perceiver to the perceived objects, and the perceived objects to each other and to larger defining categories.

Of these, the relationship most apparent to modern readers is that between a given late-seventeenth- or eighteenth-century poem and other poems, since so many major works of the period assiduously define themselves through genre or allusiveness to earlier poems and poetic traditions. One repeatedly finds versions of the heroic, the pastoral, the traditional ode, sometimes used straight, sometimes ironically, sometimes with the intention of great change in the old meaning of the form involved. Such works announce their poetic citizenship not out of caution or awe for the past but out of a desire for location within the shared, understood esthetic space that poetry, as a social heritage, occupies. (Rothstein, 50)

Rothstein has undoubtedly isolated a central feature of this poetry: its reliance on a prior claim to legitimacy, increasingly resting on descent from another poem. But his interpretation of the motives and tone in which this struggle for legitimacy was carried out arises from the desire to legitimize the poetry of this era (a common feature of criticism of early-eighteenth-century poetry). 'Such works announce their poetic citizenship not out of caution or awe for the past' – perhaps not precisely out of those concerns, but out of the need to *ground the reactive text* – since the reactive, rather than inventive, text is taken for granted as one of the generic markers of a poem by the turn of the eighteenth century. The urgent drive to place one's poem within a context is thus not a humane, civic obligation but a Darwinian need to hook the suspect, invented text into an earlier, more legitimate invention; the poet of the generation of Namur realizes that, in the anti-inventive climate, the poem must place itself somehow; otherwise it has no right to exist.

It is for this reason that English poetry of this time is characterized by increasingly elaborate titles and subtitles (which even now evoke a 'turn-of-the-eighteenth-century' feeling.) Those titles and subtitles, cumbersome as they seem, were essential; they became, to the Namur generation, as important or even more important to the reading experience than the poem itself. Here, for example, are the titles of Chalmers' selection of the poems of Halifax, poet and patron of the Namur generation:

'On the Death of his most sacred Majesty King Charles II'
'Ode on the Marriage of the Princess Anne and Prince George of Denmark'
'Latin Ode on the Same Occasion'
'The Man of Honour, occasioned by a Postscript of Penn's Letter'
'An Epistle to Charles Earl of Dorset, occasioned by His Majesty's Victory in Ireland, 1690'
'Written at Althrop in a Blank Leaf of Waller's Poems, *upon seeing Vandyke's Picture of the old lady Sunderland*'
'Verses written for the toasting-glasses of the Kit-Kat Club, 1703'
'On the Countess Dowager of _____'
'Verses by Lord Halifax from Dr. Z. Grey's mss.'
'On Orpheus and Signora Francisca Margarita'. (Chalmers, 9: vii)

The first impression here is of the absolute reliance on occasionality; the titles alone identify all but the last three poems as occasional – and on closer examination, two of those three turn out to be occasional also. The occasions on which Halifax relies are, as Johnson hints, much more those of state than the deaths of private individuals. The first poem combines state and funereal occasion on the death of Charles II; the next two serve the new order by celebrating Anne's marriage. These two are taken from the commemorative volume produced for their marriage, *Hymenaeus Cantabrigiensis* (1683); Halifax, in traditional manner, had taken full advantage of the occasion by contributing both a Latin and an English ode. The 'Epistle to Dorset,' occasioned by William's victory at the Boyne, is also occasional in the strict, traditional sense – the victory at the Boyne produced an outpouring of rejoicing in verse which was only a little less fulsome than that occasioned by Namur and Blenheim.

It is in the other poems by Halifax, though – those which, at first glance, seem not to be so rooted in occasionality – that the pervasive requirements of occasional grounding are revealed most strongly. These are poems which are not direct products of a public event; 'The Man of Honour', for example, is a type-poem like 'l'Allegro', in which the delineation of the 'Man of Honour' is the topic. But Halifax, a typical school-bred poet, cannot simply begin detailing his portrait; no one has given him an assignment. If the work had begun as response to a school assignment, Halifax would have taken care to say so; since it did not, the inventive part of the poem has to be tied, however artificially, to some event occurring verifiably in the public world – that is, to some artificial occasion. Here, in a manner which anticipates much of Romantic poetics, the occasion is precisely the associative mental event which sparked invention: reading a postscript in one of Penn's letters. But whereas a Jacobean poet would have suppressed the actual source of the moment of invention in favour of developing that invention in its own terms, Halifax, attempting to ground an invented text, stresses the source of his idea; the moment at which he allegedly read this postscript becomes an occasion of its own, connecting the mental world to the world of verifiable truth. Another of Halifax's poems makes the same sort of strategic move in its extended title: 'Written at Althrop, in a blank sheet of Waller's poems, *upon seeing Vandyke's picture of the old lady Sunderland.'* [italics in original] Note that this title does not even bother to indicate the subject of the poem; its entire effort is to construct an artificial occasional scaffolding for the poem. The title acquires something of the detail and precision of a legal deposition – because that is its function. The title amounts to a deposition by the author that the text arose not out of any vain ambition to invent on his part but as a result of the sequence of occasioning events detailed in the title. First the location is given, fixing the place of the occasion; then the actual material on which the occasioned writing was transcribed; then the occasioning stimulus (the sight of Van Dyke's picture).

A moment of irony in literary history: the poor Halifax, a mediocre poet courted in his life and scorned in his death, becomes, for a moment, a precursor of the sort of Romantic topos employed, for example, in Wordsworth's poem, 'Elegiac Stanzas: Suggested by a Picture of Peele Castle, in a Storm, Painted by Sir George Beaumont'. The relationship of title to invention is the same; the title throws the responsibility of invention onto an object perceived by the poet. This strategic opening makes, of a landscape poem, an occasional, and thus pathetically charged, work which asserts that the stimulus (the painting) provokes a mental event, occasioning the text. (Significantly, both titles are long – seventeen words for Wordsworth and nineteen for Halifax.) This depositional assertion of mental event is the basis of the Wordsworthian – and thus the prototypical Modern English – first-person narrative poem. But Halifax's poem cannot keep up with his titles. (Titles, in fact, evolve faster toward Modern poetics than the texts they attempt to legitimize; Halifax's title here is a hundred years in advance of the poem that it introduces.)

The difference in the texts which follow Halifax's and Wordsworth's poems indicate the primitive status of Halifax's work; the first line of his poem (after the title) is 'Vandyke had colours, softness, fire and art' while the first line of Wordsworth's 'Elegiac Stanzas' is 'I was thy neighbour once, thou rugged pile!'. What Wordsworth exploits in his opening is the first-person pronoun in immediate response to the stimulus of the extended title. Halifax, in a manner typical of these early efforts at artificial occasion, keeps up the effort only for the duration of the title. He occasionalizes the title only in order to ground an otherwise purely descriptive poem; his effort in this sense could be called defensive. Wordsworth, with a century of such efforts behind him, was able to realize the offensive potential of this sort of artificial occasion, and thus to maintain the 'I' as occasioned and occasioning in the text of the poem as well as the title.

The basic urge driving such odd evolutionary developments as the elaborate occasioning title might be termed 'reattribution'. That is, the poet of the Namur generation strives to place the responsibility for the poem elsewhere – other than in his own imagination – at all costs. The artificial occasion is the most advanced, and would be over the next centuries the most successful of these devices; but it was not by any means the only such means available. Many other reattributive strategies are visible in the poems of the era. The problem with most of them is that of pathos. That is, they could legitimize the poem quite successfully; what they could not do was to provide it with an emotional charge strong enough to make an impression on the reader. An example of this sort of re-attributive strategy is the proliferation of poems which are either translations of Greek or Roman poems. Rewritings like this are certainly, as Rothstein points out, an attempt to contextualize invention, but while acceptable to the reader, they are not usually very powerful texts. An audience which demanded truth in poetry was not willing to become excited over mere translations.

But rewritings are only the most obvious of the many reattributive/reactive strategies which suffuse the Namur poets; another, far more successful in terms of creating pathetic charge, was the sort of reattribution by which one's poem came into being solely as a response to an earlier work which thus bore the entire responsibility for the existence of both texts. Earlier texts join the other occasioning pretexts – the sight of a painting (as in Halifax's poem cited above), the arrival of guests, a household accident, or a change in the weather – as the basis of reattribution. Every being from God to the housemaid – everyone, that is, other than the poet – is made responsible for the act of writing the poem.

These are clearly strategies which evolve in a hostile environment; and the resultant poetry is formulaic, mediocre, and, because one poem is difficult to distinguish from another, all the more violently competitive and full of envy and resentment by each poet for all others. While it is true that 'such works [lean on earlier texts] not out of caution or awe for the past'; it does not seem to me an accurate summary of the conditions of writing at the turn of the eighteenth century to say that they do so 'out of a desire for location within the shared, understood esthetic space that poetry, as a social heritage, occupies'. One might get that impression reading the contributions of rural amateurs who sent poems in to the *Gentleman's Magazine* somewhat later in the century; but for the truly ambitious professionals, circa 1700, the conditions of writing verse were more like Churchill's later image of the Scottish cave 'where half-starved spiders prey'd on half-starved flies' than the dignified transmission of a cultural heritage. A passage from an anonymous response to Tom Brown's 'Satyr upon the French King', a savage dissent from the laudatory occasional poems on the Treaty of Ryswick, ends with a curse upon the entire poetic profession:

> And has this Bitch, my muse, trepanned me;
> Then I'm as much undone as can be;
> I knew the jilt would never leave me
> 'Til to a prison she'd deceive me;
> Cursed be the wretch, and sure he's cursed
> That taught the trade of rhyming first …
>   (Pinkus, 41)

Poets leaned, more and more, on earlier texts because they had to; because the poetics of truthfulness, translated into a poetics of occasionality, left them no choice. Even as poets struggled to find opportunities for invention, the prevailing anti-invention climate infected them; the host of hostile parodies which any original work instantly raised up testified not only to poets' hope of trellising their own on an earlier text, but their infection with the hatred of literary creation of the first order.

The works of John Sheffield, Duke of Buckinghamshire, provide extensive testimony to the climate of envy and competition in which Namur-era poets worked. In Buckinghamshire one encounters a literary ego atypical of its era only by way of being far less desperate than most of those competing without the social position and wealth he could command; yet even so, Buckinghamshire's work is suffused with ambition, envy and something like loathing for the literary world in which he operates. A typical Buckinghamshire poem (entitled, aptly enough, 'On Mr. Hobbes') begins with a depiction of this violent milieu:

> Such is the mode of these censorious days,
> The art is lost of knowing how to praise;
> Poets are envious now, and fools alone
> Admire at wit, because themselves have none....

> As strings, alike wound up, so equal prove,
> That one resounding makes the other move;
> From such a cause our satires please so much,
> We sympathize with each ill-natured touch;
> And as the sharp infection spreads about,
> The reader's malice helps the writer out.
>
> (Chalmers, 10: 96–7)

Buckinghamshire points out in the final couplet of this passage the crucial compact between reader and writer which evolved at this time and which allowed the huge, always-increasing numbers of mediocre, envious writers to help pull down any work which seemed capable of climbing out of mediocrity. This was indeed a striking new feature of the literary scene in the age of Namur: the increase in predatory poems, poems whose entire existence was not only grounded in but ostensibly devoted to 'answering' earlier poems.

2. 'SACRED SILENCE': STRATEGIES OF ANTI-INVENTION IN PRIOR

The early works of Matthew Prior, one of the most successful of the Namur poets, exemplify the fecundity with which a talented poet could exploit the anti-inventive preference. From first to last, Prior's works' titles are like a catalogue of ways in which a poet may ground the poetic text on anything but invention. Prior's first work is a straightforward occasional Latin poem, 'On the Marriage of

George Prince of Denmark, and the Lady Anne', which, like the two poems by Halifax cited above, was produced as a contribution to the *Hymenaeus Cantabrigiensis*. Prior's next effort is listed as yet another school exercise, a version of Exodus III.14, 'I Am that I Am, an Ode written 1688, as an exercise at St. John's College, Cambridge.' Here, typically, the text finds a ground in Scripture and a second grounding in the master's assignment; next we find another college exercise; an amplification of 'Part of the LXXXVIIIth Psalm, a college exercise, 1689', then 'To the Rev. Dr. F. Turner, Bishop of Ely, Who Had Advised a Translation of Prudentius', followed by, 'A Pastoral to the Bishop of Ely, on His Departure from Cambridge'. Next a more privatized occasional lyric; 'To the Countess of Exeter, Playing on the Lute'. (Chalmers, 10: vii)

These titles imply a pattern which continues for most of Prior's work: the poet attempts to find, as Rothstein rightly claims, a way to place his work in a prior (as it were) context; but the manner in which Prior does this seems not so much civic as apologetic (re-attributive). In each of the titles cited above, Prior's title and subtitles – which, again typically for the period, become more and more elaborate – attempt to *excuse* the creation of the text.

The fourth poem is perhaps the most interesting of all in terms of an approach to invention as crisis: 'To the Rev. Dr. F. Turner, Bishop of Ely, who had advised a Translation of Prudentius.' The levels of apology are complex here; first of all, the poet in no way provoked the creation of the poem, but rather was requested to make it by this 'Dr. F. Turner' (note that, in true depositional style, the entire name is given); second, the literary task that Turner requested was, like the Biblical exercises which were Prior's previous material, merely a translation, and thus not a true invention; and finally, the request is one which, as the poem is meant to demonstrate, gave the poor tempted poet a great deal of worry before he forced himself to favour the demands of friendship over the risks of invention:

> To the Rev. Dr. F. Turner, Bishop of Ely
> Who Had Advised A Translation of Prudentius
>
> If poets, ere they cloth'd their infant thought,
> And the rude work to just perfection brought,
> Did still some god, or godlike man invoke,
> Whose mighty name their sacred silence broke;

Your goodness, sir, will easily excuse
The bold requests of an aspiring Muse;
Who, with your blessing, would your aid implore,
And in her weakness justify your power. –
From your fair pattern she would strive to write,
And with unequal strength pursue your flight;
Yet hopes she ne'er can err that follows you,
Led by your blest commands, and great example too.
Then smiling and aspiring influence give,
And make the Muse and her endeavors live;
Claim all her future labours as your due,
Let every song begin and end with you;
So to the blest retreat she'll gladly go,
Where the saints' palm and Muses' laurel grow;
Where kindly both in glad embrace shall join,
And round your brow their mingled honours twine;
Both to the virtue due, which could excel,
As much in writing, as in living well –
So shall she proudly press the tuneful string,
And mighty things in mighty numbers sing;
Nor doubt to strike Prudentius' daring lyre,
And humbly bring the verse which you inspire.

(Chalmers, 10: 130–1)

This is, of course, the sort of work which is usually identified, and dismissed, as a 'patronage poem'; Prior enacts a ritualized flattery of his patron. But 'patronage' here is a matter of responsibility for invention of the text, not money, and it interacts oddly with the aversion to invention: the patron, for the poets of the Namur generation, is not a necessary evil but a godsend, a scapegoat who is willing to bear the blame for the creation of yet another poem. Prior's title, as usual, lays out the accusation; it was Turner who caused this poem to exist by suggesting a translation of Prudentius. The poem goes on to flatter the Rev. Dr. Turner at some length, finally promising the requested verses. The poem, in this way, is all title, all promise and excuse, all prologue; there is no subject. The poem is at once an advertisement for the translation to come, a stroke for a valued patron, and an apology for its own existence. In this last aspect, the apparently cloying flattery has a serious purpose; by attributing the very existence of this work, and the translation to come, to Turner's influence, Prior grounds the work in someone else, more established than himself, and becomes the mere vehicle of Turner's designs, rather than a suspect inventor of verses. Patronage in this way could provide a kind of cover for invention; many of the more intricate dedications and attributions of verse to patrons amounted to a public declaration that one had protection, permission to invent.

Prior begins the poem by invoking the 'sacred silence' which precedes the creation of a poem, and which may be legitimately broken only by the intervention of a higher being – the patron. Nothing could reveal the almost Gnostic hatred of poetic invention which characterizes this poetics more than this worshipful invocation of poetic muteness.

The sort of courtship diction (using 'courtship' in the broad sense employed by Kenneth Burke) which follows the frightening notion of creating a poem is not mere flattery; like most of the poetic hyperbole of the seventeenth century, it means what it says, in a strange way, when read at the level of invention/anti-invention. Thus, when Prior, in lines 5–9, begs the aid of his patron in taking responsibility for the creation of the poem, he is speaking quite literally – in fact, in these lines, Prior actually asks Turner's pardon for using him as the trellis on which to build the poem. 'Your goodness, Sir, will easily excuse / The bold requests of an aspiring muse' – these lines are a direct response to the actual rhetorical situation faced by Prior. Turner, whose position makes him a useful grounding, will be exploited – so that a poem of a certain length, with Prior's name attached to it, can be grudgingly accepted into existence thereby. This is the 'point' of this poem and the tens of thousands like it: to exist, to occupy space on a page in the name of the poet who thus claims that bit of paper territory in the name of his own ambition. What is 'said' is secondary. In the case of this poem, what is 'said' is one long aporia, one lengthy aporaic frame for the existence of the lines themselves. Thus the difficulty of reading such poems for 'content', as Rothstein and many other commentators have attempted to do – content is beside the point; the point is to cause the poem to seduce its way into existence in a hostile environment, so that it may carry there the name of its maker and anyone the maker chooses to gratify.

Thus the odd structure which defines this poem: it is all preamble. This is a telltale characteristic of much of the poetry of the Namur generation: structure is lost and instead one finds poems which are all preamble, or rather all aporia. The poem apologizes for its existence for a certain number of lines (as in Prior's poem, cited above), then ceases, having only hinted aporaically about the possibility of an actual subject (in the case of this poem, the translation of Prudentius). This sort of poetry cannot be made to make logical sense; but it makes an excellent sort of sense in career/rhetorical terms: it defeats rival poems by preemptively occupying scarce and desired space on the page, and it does so by avoiding the appearance of anything like invention.

Thanks to invention-camouflaging tactics like the reattribution of his aporaic 'Translation of Prudentius' poem, Prior was capable of occupying such literary space without needing a standard, solid occasional base. But it is clear that he reacted with elation when such an occasion occurred. This excited eagerness to exploit a major, legitimate occasion suffuses his many productions related to the martial events of the turn of the century; these were the poetic focal point of the entire Namur generation, as Johnson, with his instinct for the point of tension in a poet's work, hints in the 'Life of Prior'.

The occasions involved actually became the focal point for a violent struggle between trade rivals in the panegyric which bears many resemblances to that catalogued in the last chapter; here, however, as the occasion is a battle between two nations which are culturally as well as militarily eminent, the fight is joined across national lines. Prior was one of the leading English participants in this 'Battle of the Poets' which fed on and mimicked that of the monarchs; he and Boileau made themselves into poetic caricatures of William and Louis and fought in rhyme what the kings had done in blood. Prior's response to Boileau on the loss and recapture of Namur (1692–1695) is particularly illuminating since, like Dryden in 'Essay of Dramatic Poesy', Prior is sufficiently agitated against foreigners and trade rivals to reveal the trade secrets of the occasional poet. Boileau's 'Ode sur la prise de Namur par les armes du roy, l'annee 1693' leaned heavily on stock classical turns, with all the familiar panegyric machinery: Thracian oaks, deified winds, and jingoistic muses; sharing the French joy. Now Boileau is attacked by Prior, gloating after the French loss of Namur, employing the same tone of self-disgust at the poetics of the heroic ode as that seen in Dryden's 'Essay':

An English Ballad, on the Taking of Namur by the King of Great Britain, 1695

Dulce est desipere in loco

Some folks are drunk, and do not know it;
So might not Bacchus give you law?
Was it a muse, O lofty poet,
Or virgin of St. Cyr, you saw?
Why all this fury? What's the matter,
That oaks must come from Thrace to dance?
Must stupid stocks be taught to flatter?
And is there no such wood in France?
Why must the winds all hold their tongue?
If they a little breath should raise,
Would that have spoil'd the poets song,
Or puffed away the monarch's praise?

Pindar, that eagle, mounts the skies,
While Virtue leads the noble way:
Too like a vulture Boileau flies,
Where sordid Interest shows the prey.
When once the poet's honour ceases,
From reason far his transports rove:
And Boileau, for eight hundred pieces,
Makes Louis take the wall of Jove.

(Chalmers, 10: 145)

This is a clever example of the sort of poem the Namur poets write best: the poem designed to annihilate a rival poem – the predator-poem. But in forcing its attack, it calls the entire genre into question in a manner reminiscent of Dryden. Perhaps the most striking similarity between Dryden's and Prior's attack on occasional poetics is their common employment, as a central trope, of the occasional poet as carrion-eating bird (this time a vulture rather than a crow). Boileau, here the type of the morally-bad occasional poet, is portrayed as exploiting the occasion in an openly venal manner ('Where sordid Interest shows the way' and 'eight hundred pieces' refer to the income Boileau derived as court poet). This exploitation is seen as an abandonment of poetic integrity ('Where once the poet's honour ceases'). The complexity of Prior's work in this case is that, having begun with this familiar attack on occasional poetics, he must still manage to exploit his own occasion, the English reversal of the triumph Boileau celebrated. In part, it is the determinedly low diction and scorn for classical metaphor which allows Prior to distinguish *his* celebration of a successful battle of Namur from Boileau's; thus the emphasis on 'An *English Ballad*' – that is, according to the self-congratulatory antithesis popular in English culture, an 'English ballad' is simple and straightforward, a 'French Ode' elaborate, insincere and fawning. Thus it is simply Boileau's allegiance to a rival nation which, Prior hopes, will keep readers from including him among the occasion-exploiting poets he terms 'vultures'. In their joy at seeing the French discomfited, and the pompous, grovelling poetics of their victory ode humiliatingly overthrown, the English reader and Prior can share for a moment revenge on a hated foreign king, and in a broader sense, can share revenge on the hateful poetics of occasionality under which the culture labours – safely projected onto the straw man, Boileau, laureate of a rival kingdom.

Boileau's exertions in attempting to whitewash Louis' turn-of-the-century difficulties proved an irresistible topic for Prior; a decade later, after the tremendous victory at Blenheim, he again tints his occasional contribution with an attack on his opposite number:

> A Letter to
> Monsieur Boileau Despreaux;
> Occasioned by the
> Victory at Blenheim, 1704
>
> … Since, hired for life, thy servile muse must sing
> Successive conquests, and a glorious king;
> Must of a man immortal vainly boast,
> And bring him laurels, whatsoe'er they cost,
> What turn wilt thou employ, what colours lay
> On the event of that superior day,
> In which one English subject's prosperous hand
> (So Jove did will, so Anna did command)
> Broke the proud column of thy Master's praise,
> Which sixty winters had conspir'd to raise?
>   (Chalmers, 10: 165)

The moment is one which a poet like Prior, toiling in the chronic difficulties of occasionality, had to savour: Boileau, designated bard of the French court, must now strain to find a way within the conventions of occasional form to write about this appalling defeat. Louis himself becomes, as in the commemoration of Namur, the point of difference between the English and French poet; Prior is praising 'one English subject [Marlborough]' while Boileau, servile court poet, must 'of a man immortal [Louis] vainly boast'.

But even in this moment of exultation, Prior's habit of attempting to conceal poetic invention is present here, underneath the sneer; as in his mild early works, Prior is here concerned to 'blame' the existence of his work on others – first on the occasion itself (the battle, whether Namur or Blenheim) – and second on the previous attempt to write about it by a rival poet (Boileau) – just as he hoped to attribute his translation of Prudentius to the urging of Turner, and his commemoration of the marriage of George and Anna on the assignment given him at Cambridge. Prior continues the 'Letter to … Boileau' as a chatty, cynical reminiscence about the difficulties which face the occasional poet – the poem begins almost to seem like a cheery conversation about the trade between two officers of opposing armies. Prior discusses the difficulty, one apparently shared by French and English poets, of fitting tongue-twisting Dutch and Flemish names into rhyme (Chalmers, 10: 165):

> What work we had with Wagenhinghen, Arnheim,
> Places that could not be reduc'd to rhyme!

demonstrating, in the process, his own ability to surmount the difficulty, and actually using 'rhyme' as a rhyme. In a further display of anti-poetic skill, Prior embeds this rhymed 'rhyme' in a military metaphor, by which the occasional duellist 'reduces' a besieged city by forcing it to rhyme, as a commander reduces it by breaching its defences. Then, twisting the knife, Prior ironically suggests to his rival that Anna kindly sent over English commanders in order to make the ode-maker's job easier (Chalmers, 10: 165):

> Her warriors Anna sends from Tweed and Thames,
> That France may fall by more harmonious names.
> Can'st thou not Hamilton or Lumley bear?
> Would Ingoldsby or Palmes offend thy ear?
> And is there not a sound in Marlborough's name,
> Which thou and all thy brethren ought to claim …?

The counter-ode developed here by Prior is clearly one of those genres mentioned by Rothstein which emphasize context; it is in fact *about* the literary context of the war. But Prior is not, obviously, acting like a 'citizen' here. He is clearly and simply attempting to punish a trade rival, Boileau; and, more fundamentally, to hijack the rival's text – to get the credit for the work while laying the blame for its invention on another. Prior uses Boileau as the true source of invention, with himself as mere respondent, correcting the initial poet's mistakes – as he takes care to mention in his depositional title, it was Boileau who started the war by writing the 'Ode sur la prise de Namur'; Prior is only striking back.

The notion of hijacking an earlier text may be extended beyond the simple rivalry of Boileau and Prior; it is in fact a feature of many genres, often appearing in rather subtle form. Consider the 'Instructions to the Painter' genre, which was popular in the late-seventeenth century; though painter and poets are not at odds in such poems, the poet is attempting to outdo the painter; the poet, by stepping into a painting in progress with hints and help, puts the painter in the position of original inventor and takes over the role of critic, correcting the landscape begun by the painter. Blackmore even managed to combine the 'Instructions to the Painter' genre with the commemoration of the great century-ending battles in poems such as 'Advice to Poets' and 'Instructions to Vander Bank'.

This sort of reattribution of invention is closely related to the proto-Wordsworthian stimulus/response form noted in Halifax's painter-poem on Vandyke. Prior, too, employs this sort of artificial occasion to ground his otherwise purely-invented texts. An entire toolbox of paraphernalia which may be employed to occasionalize an invented poem begins to develop around this time; the painting to be corrected is one such tool, but others – notably books, pets, and children – begin to coalesce into a vocabulary of 'light' occasions. Examples of this sort of light demi-occasion abound in Prior's early works, as these titles may suggest: 'To My Lord Buckhurst, very young, playing with a cat.' 'To the Countess of Dorset, written in her Milton.' The tone of flattery and lightness in these productions naturally lends itself to the production of verse on romance; but what is notable about the sexual verse of this sort in Prior's work is that he frequently uses long, depositional or actually narrative titles to ground and occasionalize the poem as autobiography. A remarkable example of this tendency is the well-known lyric,

TO A LADY:

SHE REFUSING TO CONTINUE A DISPUTE WITH ME, AND LEAVING ME IN
THE ARGUMENT

AN ODE.
(Chalmers, 10: 140)

The typography of the printed version of Prior's poem (whether
the product of Prior's, a copyist's, or a bookseller's sensibility)
reflects a significant generic tension within the grounding of the
poem. The beginning and end of the title are generic markers of a
love poem, and would suffice for a title in themselves. Why, then,
the long (14-word) autobiographical basis? Because thousands
upon thousands of poems have already appeared, entitled 'To A
Lady: An Ode.' The profusion of such formulaic odes makes
pathetic response unlikely. The mid-title in small type supplies the
documentation which alone could inspire an intense emotional
response from readers. Failing that, the reader was left with the
naked text – a vehicle of literary ambition; a hated invention.

3. THE SESSION OF THE POETS

The increasing popularity of the 'session of the poets' genre in the
early Eighteenth Century is clearly part of the poetics of trellised
envy. The proliferation of works of this genre is a clear symptom of
the increase in literary ambition, which must inevitably be frus-
trated by the decline in inventive scope. The 'Session of the Poets'
genre, first developed by Suckling and exploited in the Namur era
by Coppinger, Phillips and many other anonymous anti-poets,
literalizes the actual competition for attention among poets into a
tournament, game of chance, or judgment by God(s), dramatizing
the longing of the poets to rise above the scramble and be anointed
as *the* poet. Buckinghamshire's work includes an example of the
genre, entitled 'The Election of a Poet Laureate'. The poem is
typical in its rough, cynical treatment of poetic ambition; in a
common conceit, Buckinghamshire depicts all the poets of the day
(1719) gathering to compete for Apollo's favour on the occasion of
the granting of the laureateship to the obscure, place-seeking
Laurence Eusden. The ending of the poem is typical – no one is

found deserving of Apollo's favour (this is the outcome, in one
manner or another, of most early-eighteenth-century poems of this
form – usually the award is given backhandedly, if at all):

> Apollo, now driven to a cursed quandary,
> Was wishing for Swift, or the fam'd Lady Mary....
> But at last he grew wanton, and laugh'd at them all;
>
> And so spying one who came only to gaze,
> A hater of verse, and despiser of plays;
> To him in great form, without any delay,
> (Though a zealous fanatic) presented the bay.
>
> All the wits stood astonish'd at hearing the god
> So gravely pronounce an election so odd;
> And though Prior and Pope only laugh'd in his face,
> Most others were ready to sink in the place.
>
> Yet some thought the vacancy open was kept,
> Concluding the bigot would never accept;
> But the hypocrite told them, he well understood,
> Though the function was wicked, the stipend was good.
>
> At last in rush'd Eusden, and cry'd, 'Who shall have it,
> But I, the true laureat, to whom the king gave it?'
> Apollo begg'd pardon, and granted his claim,
>   But vow'd though, till then he ne'er heard of his name.
>   (Chalmers, 10: 99)

Clearly, the 'punch line' here is the obscurity of Eusden (who,
nonetheless, remained laureate until 1730). But the tone and
conception of the poem – a tournament of poets which no one is fit
to win – was clearly meant to satisfy 'the malice of the reader'
which Buckinghamshire mentions as a sort of silent partner in the
promulgation of bitter, envious works like this. These 'Laureate-
contest' poems are little represented in the major modern
anthologies of eighteenth-century verse, perhaps because they are
thought too ephemeral or topical in interest (or perhaps because
the naked malice of the form displeases post-Romantic editorial
tastes); but they are one of the most common genres of the period.
    The election of a new laureate always led to the production of
reams of viciously satirical verse on the 'Session of the Poets'
model, since the institutionalization of poetic formulae increased

the number of aspirants, and decreased the range of invention, with each generation. As the *Grub Street Journal* put it:

> Nothing has increased [the numbers of Grub-Street aspirants] so much as Poetry; We are taught it at School; if not, we believe we are born poets. Every corner abouds with its professors; the bellman nightly salutes his master and mistress; the Marshall, his Gentleman Soldiers every Christmas; Every street rings with Ballads, the Royal Palace resounds with Odes; and every Churchyard with its productions. (cited in *Gentleman's Magazine*, 1: 11)

The *Grub Street Journal* was, not surprisingly, delighted with this steady increase in potential subscribers. But what was good for the poetry industry as a whole was not seen so rosily by the individual aspirants, particularly those who were striving to write something which would stand above the facile mass of school-bred poems. The laureateship became, in the early decades of the century, a focus of envy and the drive to attach the responsibility for invention to something outside oneself. The Laureate was a poet not only entitled but required to produce verse which was certifiably occasioned. This inspired disappointed would-be laureates (in both the literal and the broader senses of 'laureate') to attack any productions by the laureate – not only because they resented his appropriation of valuable poetic occasions, but because his productions could serve as safely-grounded occasions in themselves. The succession of laureates from Nahum Tate to Nicholas Rowe (1715), and from Rowe to Laurence Eusden (1718) provoked endless parodies and mock-laureate congratulations, usually in the 'Session of the Poets' form; but it was the early years of the reign of Colley Cibber (appointed laureate 1730) which provoked the most severe attacks, as the bankrupt poetics of occasion reached a crisis.

This crisis, reflected in the pages of the *Gentleman's Magazine*, expressed itself in reams of bad, envious verse, all making use of the laureate-competition model. Although his accession to the laureateship was marked by many parodies (and a sharp rivalry with Stephen Duck, the ambitious thresher-poet, whose famous former occupation led to hundreds of bad puns in verse), Cibber's greatest contribution to the anti-poetry of the era was his 'ODE for His MAJESTY's Birth-Day, October 28, 1732'. The *Gentleman's Magazine* was typical in getting a great deal of verse from the badness of

Cibber's effort. In the October 1732 issue, a rival ode is printed '... as preferable to the Laureat's Ode on the same Occasion' (11: 1027). In the next issue (November 1732), the magazine does print Cibber's work, but only as a trellis to which it attaches a rival ode, 'The Laureat's ODE burlesqu'd', originally published in the *Grub Street Journal,* a sharper publication which tended to see poems from a professional literary man's angle. This burlesque, in which Pope himself may have had a share, is the first to associate Cibber with the throne of Dullness. In this it is actually only following a long line of anti-laureate poems, which at once attempt to unseat the present laureate while leaving on him the onus of poetic invention. But since the laureate is protected against the charge of true invention by his duty to produce poems 'upon certain occasions', the accusations tend to focus on the quality, rather than the invention proper, of his verse. And even this line of attack is not really very important: the real point of the anti-poems is to be published. The worse the Laureate's work, the greater room for reactive poems which 'answer' his official works. The verb 'to answer' actually assumes, at this late point in the famine of occasions, a particular importance. As usual, the *Grub Street Journal* is the first to report developments in the profession (August 1731):

> The Art of *Answering* a Book.
>
> ... Almost every thing being now controvers'd.... Here is a book, suppose, *unanswerable,* which makes a deep impression on a certain person. He mentions it to his friend, on which they fall to wrangling as in the following dialogue.
>
> DIAL. 1 A. That book's *answered,* those papers and pamphlets are *answered.* There are six or seven *answers* to them.
> B. Aye, but all those *answers* are as fully *answered.*
> A. By whom, pray?
>
> B. Why by Mr. W. by Dr. S. by J. T. esq. by my Ld W. and by three or four without names.
> > (*Gentleman's Magazine*, 11: 923 [italics in original])

The existence of the first book is necessary for its answerers; in the same way, the bad productions of the Laureate are essential to his answerers. The remarkable badness of Cibber's 'Birthday Ode' for 1732 (It began, 'Let there be light ...' and continued in as

fulsome a tone) made the parodies almost certain hits; the
November 1732 edition of the *Gentleman's Magazine* contains not
only the well-known 'Burlesqu'd' version of Cibber's Ode but
another, less polished parody, and even a sort of defence of him
against his attackers:

> An EPIGRAM on the GRUB
> Dear Grub! Don't so bejade your thought,
> Too much of one thing's good for naught;
> Eternal harping thus on Colly,
> Shows much of malice, more of folly:
> Striving his little errors to expose,
> You far much greater of your own disclose.
> > (*Gentleman's Magazine*, II: 1074)

This poem comes into existence as a 'defence' of Cibber; the
poems provoking it come into being as 'attacks'; but the 'striving' is
the same. Whether they strive to attack or defend – or attack the
attackers of the attackers, or defend those who defend the defend-
ers, and so on – these poems strive, above all, to find a way to attach
themselves to some original point which has been already 'contro-
vers'd' – that is, already designated a legitimate ground for verse.
No imputation of invention is thus attached to them. But the
formulae have, by this time, been in existence for a long time, and
there is a feeling of excess and sameness even among some of the
participants in the game. The mood in which Boswell's worldly
friend Eglington would say that poems were like whinstones in
Scotland – they could be found in any number in any field – was
already developing in Grub Street culture. The 'Grubs' went at
their ostensibly nihilistic task with the old enthusiasm – in January
1733 the *Gentleman's Magazine* reprints the Laureate's harmless
'Ode on New Year's Day, 1733' with a full page of pedantic attacks
from the *Grub Street Journal* – but the problem is essentially the one
facing all the school-bred poets: everyone knows how to produce a
poem which can see print; no one has any sense of a way to find a
poem which will escape the confines of an anti-inventive poetics.
   Here the anti-inventive ethos yields a paradoxical result: the
surface effect of these anti-poetic poems was to demolish an earlier
poem and thus reduce the number of envy-objects by one; but in
fact each such poem increases by one the number of poems extant,
and 'demolishes' nothing at all (the belief in parody as a powerful

weapon, capable of destroying the text parodied, is one of the cherished myths of the Namur era). In fact, such attack-poems multiplied endlessly, each parody being parodied and defended in turn. Thus their actual effect was a huge expansion in the volume of poetry produced – a volume which fills the burgeoning miscellanies and journals, all the while ostensibly devoting its verses to the annihilation of the form it embodies.

The clash of anti-poem and anti-anti-poem, in the ceremonial games on the accession of a new laureate, marks the most intense, desperate stage in English occasional poetics. From Dryden's death and the legendary battle over his corpse, to Eusden's death – the death of an insignificant poet whose place was far more important than his poems – the enviroment of the aspiring poet becomes more cynical, more formulaic, more dependent on a set topic or prior invention, and more crowded with fellow aspiring 'Grubs'. But the steady increase in aspirants not only made the environment of the aspiring poet more difficult; it also increased the odds that, after a certain number of years of stagnation, one of the burgeoning crowd of 'grubs' would find a way out of the poetics of the Namur generation. In fact, that way out came only a decade after the accession of Cibber to the laureateship. It came in 1742, the true *annus mirabilis* of English lyric poetry.

5

'To Darkness and to Me': Mental Event as Poetic Occasion

I have frequently seen a poet withdraw, having enjoyed the most valuable part of a farm, while the crusty farmer supposed that he had got a few wild apples only. Why, the owner does not know it for many years when a poet has put his farm in rhyme, the most admirable kind of invisible fence, has fairly impounded it, milked it, skimmed it, and got all the cream, and left the farmer only the skimmed milk.

Henry David Thoreau

Two blacks won't make a white. Neither will two Grays.

James Boswell

December 1762: James Boswell, just down from Scotland, circulates eagerly in London literary society, spending much of his time with a group of ambitious young literary men, most of them fellow Scots. Among these is James MacPherson, who provides the admiring Boswell, always in need of a literary model, with the pattern of quick literary success. In his entry for Wednesday, 29 December, Boswell mentions an interesting remark by MacPherson:

> Says [Eglington], 'I had a very good party with me last night, amongst whom was Fingal [i.e. MacPherson].... We were talking of Gray's fine *Elegy in a Churchyard* [*sic*]. 'Hoot!,' cried Fingal, "to write panegyrics upon a parcel of damned rascals that did nothing but plough the land and saw [*sic*] corn". He considered that fighters only should be celebrated.' (Boswell, *London Journal*, 110)

MacPherson resents Gray for tinkering with the rules of occasionality by commemorating persons too low in the social scale to be celebrated. Gray, by finding a way to commemorate the obscure, had opened up a vast new field (or cemetery) of poetic opportunity. Gray, with many contemporaries, notably Young, Shenstone, Robert Blair, and later associated poets like Cowper and Wordsworth, forms a distinct line of poetic innovation, in which poetry turned to a line of legitimization entirely unlike that of the modern novel. In this line, which may be called 'ethos-occasioned', the poet grounds the text in an *unverifiable occasion*. This is the basis of Gray's 'Sonnet on the Death of Mr Richard West', 'Distant Prospect' and unspecified 'Country Churchyard'; the basis of Young's unidentified 'Lorenzo', 'Philander' and 'Narcissa' in 'Night Thoughts'; the basis of Blair's massive metonymy in 'The Grave' and Shenstone's redefinition of the scope of the elegy. As the unverifiable occasion provides a satisfyingly opaque grounding for the mental event which it occasions, that mental event becomes the focus of the poem, until at last the mental event becomes itself the ground of the poem.

Few English poets of the first rank have been despised or ignored as intensely as Thomas Gray. Gray is the single most innovative technician in the history of English verse. Every time Gray wrote a poem, something technically interesting and *new* happened, as in his work on Welsh and Norse poetry, and his Odes. In his most important poems, especially the 'Elegy Written in a Country Churchyard' he virtually invented the basic occasioning device of the modern first-person narrative poem. Yet there is something about this dim, fussy figure which aroused hatred both in his contemporaries and even after his death. One still encounters, even in quite recent criticism of Gray, comments like this: '[i]t is hard to think of the author of the "Elegy Written in a Country Churchyard" as a member of the avant-garde' (Price, 43).[1] Regrettably, hostility to or dismissal of this important poet seems to unite different times and critical orientations; Dr Johnson clearly despised Gray, and Wordsworth, who owes much of his poetic technique to Gray's innovations, goes out of his way to malign him.

This hatred for Gray is so consistent in the English critical tradition that it offers a significant object of study in itself. Why is Gray so hated? MacPherson's grumbling, cited at the beginning of this chapter, exposes one reason for this hatred: Gray is like a financier who has cornered the market in a stock previously thought worthless. One reason he was hated by other poets is the fact that he found a way – admittedly a disingenuous, tortuous way – out of the restrictions and demands of occasional poetics, through the use of intentional obscurity.

Gray, whose greatest poem is the favourite of 'unsophisticated' readers, becomes the focus of dislike for the 'sophisticated' reader. In this, he is intriguingly like a poetic avatar of Pavel Ivanovich Chichikov, hero of Gogol's *Dead Souls (Myortvii Dushii)*.[2] Chichikov is a sly ex-bureaucrat, a fussy, ageing single man like Gray. He comes up with a scheme to buy up the 'dead souls' – that is, deceased serfs – of country landowners, so that he can claim them as his own and gain the status of a great landowner. Gray managed, in his 'Elegy Written in a Country Churchyard', to find a new technical means to do almost precisely the same thing: to buy up a graveyard full of dead peasants unknown to him in life.

This poem has a curious history of reader response: it has always received popular acceptance, but critical response has been grudging or even embarrassed. For instance, Martin Price, in the article cited above, uses the epithet 'author of the "Elegy"' to deprecate Gray, implying that this text is anything but 'avant-garde'. In another instance of hostility to this poem in particular, the editors of a major literary anthology call it 'the English poem best known and most loved by unsophisticated readers' (The *Norton Anthology*, 1: 1760), implying that a fondness for the 'Elegy' is a sure sign of the literary-critical outsider.

The professional critic's wariness toward the 'Elegy' is grounded on two closely related features of the poem: its origin in the Sentimental mode, and its complex treatment of attribution and occasionality. These features are related, as suggested above, in that the poet who satisfies epideictic/occasional tests is likely to obtain a less guarded pathetic response than one who is not forthcoming about the epideictic basis of the emotions stimulated by the text. Gray, as a poet experimenting within the sentimental tradition, accepts the premise that stimulating emotion is the basic purpose of the poem; therefore, the design problem which results in the 'Elegy' is the familiar one with which English poets had been tinkering for generations: how to beat the *habeas corpus* requirement by achieving epideictic intensity without sacrificing a friend or family member. A funeral oration without a corpse – this is the design goal of the 'Elegy' and of other innovative poems of the mid-century.

For Gray was of course only one of several poets experimenting with methods of obtaining occasional pathos without requiring an actual occasion. His greatest rival in the invention of new occasioning techniques was Edward Young, whom I will discuss in the next chapter. But Young was not the only other experimenter in this most innovative of poetic eras; in one important aspect of the technical revolution of the 1740s – the exploitation of the non-specific setting for ostensibly occasional poems – the better-known Gray and Young are more than matched by the single successful work of Robert Blair (1699–1747). Blair is now remembered for one poem: 'The Grave'. This fairly short work (approximately 800 lines) was produced in 1743, making it the contemporary of Gray's and Young's revolutionary works. 'The Grave' represents a third major strategy for expanding occasional pathos; while Gray encompasses a field of anonymous dead, and Young hints at an unstated occasion, Blair, with striking simplicity, simply employs a container-for-contained metonymy to avoid specifying the inhabitant of 'The Grave', focusing on the paraphernalia of the container (the grave) rather than the identity of the contained (the corpse). In fact, Blair cleverly devotes the first six-and-a-half lines of his work to maximal blurring of the identity of the corpse by emphasizing that 'The Grave' is the common denominator of all persons:

> While some affect the sun, and some the shade,
> Some flee the city, some the hermitage;
> Their aims as various as the roads they take
> In journeying thro' life; – the task be mine,
> To paint the gloomy horrours of the tomb,
> Th' appointed place of rendezvous, where all
> These travellers meet....
>   (Chalmers, 15: 63)

This venerable moralistic commonplace becomes something much more useful in Blair's work. Placed thus at the beginning of a poem devoted to arousing funereal pathos, it becomes a diffused occasioning claim and thus functions much like the placement of the 'I' in Gray's 'Elegy'. What is missing in Blair – what contributed to the brevity of its vogue, as compared to those of Gray's and Young's works – is its radical employment of the metonymic funereal landscape without the provision of an occasional narrative, and 'real' characters, to be placed in this landscape. As long as other mid-century writers were filling the poetic churchyards of England with sufficient characters and occasioning narratives, Blair's poem survived; but without particular people, more or less identical to the poet, to pity, Blair's landscape seemed empty and the metonymy suffered for the lack of a corpse.

'The Grave' is like an organism which cannot survive without the presence of many similar, but more powerfully-occasioned works to ground it. Blair's 'grave' is a purely generic, unparticularized one (that is, no named character, and thus no funereal occasion, is implied):

> The new-made widow, too, I've sometimes spy'd,
> Sad sight! slow moving o'er the prostrate dead:
> Listless, she crawls along in doleful black,
> While bursts of sorrow gush from either eye,
> Fast falling down her now untasted cheek.
> Prone on the lowly grave of the dear man
> She drops....
>
> (Chalmers, 15: 63)

Scenes like this are so common in 'graveyard poetry' as to become the stuff of parody; but they were also a source of intense pleasure to contemporary readers – they produced in such readers a drug-like 'high' which became, increasingly, the whole point of sentimental stories; thus the tendency, in the works of later sentimental novelists like MacKenzie (*The Man of Feeling*), to move with almost contemptuous speed through the actual narrative in order to reach the climactic picture of the weeping widow (or grateful orphan, or reunited relatives, etc.).

Gray, more than all his rivals, encompassed and profited from the nameless dead – and it was for this that he has been one of the most hated of all figures in the history of English poetry. Contemporaries hated Gray for several reasons (homophobia among them) – but most of all because he had invented a shortcut around the occasional problem which they could not copy. MacPherson hates Gray in the way that Chichikov, hero of Gogol's great *Dead Souls,* is hated by other serf-owners: because he has claimed many dead peasants to which he has no real right. Gray, an acute observer of the poetics of his time, seems to have known that the success of the 'Elegy' was a matter of design innovation rather than poetic texture; he is reported to have said that the 'Elegy' 'owed its popularity entirely to its subject, and that the public would have received it as well if it had been written in prose' (*The*

Correspondence of Thomas Gray, 896).[3] Gray cannot have meant 'subject' in the simple sense; the proliferation of elegies and funereal poetry at mid-century meant that literally thousands of poems with subjects similar to that of the 'Elegy' were read, dismissed and forgotten. His work survived because it had found a solution to the problem of grounding elegiac pathos. In this sense, his evaluation is correct; as the success of long, prosaic works like the 'Night Thoughts' showed, readers, once convinced that the author had properly grounded the text in a valid occasion, were more than forgiving of defects in prosody – even the virtual absence of any prosody, as Young's success demonstrated.

In order to develop his solution to the problem of grounding the text, Gray had to invent, virtually by himself, a vital component: obscurity. 'Obscurity' is the commonplace objection to Gray in his own time; everyone of note in the English literary establishment seems to have used this word about him at some point, even his ally, Horace Walpole (*Selected Letters* 178, Letter CXXX).[4] When the Cambridge students (who, not surprisingly, despised Gray) undertook to parody his work, they composed 'Two odes on Oblivion and Obscurity ...' (Johnson, 'Life of Gray' in Chalmers 14: 139). Johnson, in all his works, cannot say the name 'Gray' without adding the adjective 'obscure'. Goldsmith makes the same accusation in the following revealing dialogue with Boswell (as reported by Boswell): BOSWELL. "And what do you think of Gray's odes? Are not they noble?" GOLDSMITH. "Ah, the rumbling thunder! I remember a friend of mine was very fond of Gray. 'Yes,' said I, 'he is very fine indeed; as thus—

> Mark the white and mark the red,
> Mark the blue and mark the green;
> Mark the colours ere they fade,
> Darting thro' the welkin sheen.'

'O, yes', said he, 'great, great!' 'True, Sir', said I, 'but I have made the lines this moment'. BOSWELL. "Well, I admire Gray prodigiously. I have read his odes till I was almost mad." GOLDSMITH. "They are terribly obscure. We must be historians and learned men before we can understand them." (Boswell, *London Journal*, 105–6)

The exchange is a stylized (and stylistic) one; we need not take any part of it as historically true to see the way in which Boswell, with his usual uncanny insight, has constructed a scene which reveals the question at stake in the contemporary response to Gray, and particularly in the accusation of obscurity.

Goldsmith first refers to Gray's poetic tone as 'the rumbling thunder' – suggesting sound without meaning – and then offers the pseudo-Gray lines he claims were accepted by one of Gray's fans. The game Goldsmith claims to have played, in inventing fake lines of poetry, involves the rhetoric of attribution, with which Gray had learned to play in a sophisticated way. The incident Goldsmith describes may or may not have happened, but it is at least possible that it actually did; attribution was vital in determining contemporary readers' responses to eighteenth-century poetry. A reader who had once been satisfied by one of Gray's works might well decide in advance to like any others attributed to him, and might thus feel obliged, by virtue of an earlier decision accepting the validity of Gray's poetic ethos, to like everything else written by Gray.

Ethos is thus becoming more central to poetic response, with the embarrassing result that no one actually hears the lines anymore. This is exactly what MacKenzie means in his aphorism that 'one is ashamed to be pleased by the works of one knows not whom'; the most troubling corollary of this aphorism is that one is all too easily fooled by a faked attribution to someone one does know – that is, to a poet one has already decided to like and trust.

Mid-century literati were uneasily aware of the embarrassing tricks which attributive poetics allowed; Johnson performed, or claimed to have performed, the same sort of experiment described by Goldsmith. Johnson performed the experiment with a passage from Thomson (whom he generally admired), reading only every other line and getting the same excited response:

> Dr. Johnson said: 'Thomson had a true poetical genius, the power of viewing every thing in a poetical light. His fault is such a cloud of words sometimes, that the sense can hardly peep through. Shiels … was one day sitting with me. I took down Thomson, and read aloud a large portion of him, and then asked, – "Is not this fine?" Shiels having expressed the highest admiration, "Well, Sir," said I, "I have omitted every other line".' (Boswell, *Life of Johnson* 366)[5]

Johnson does not make up Thomson verses, but he does, by omitting alternate lines, destroy the integrity of the text. The committed fan of Thomson's work, like the fan of Gray in Goldsmith's anecdote, fails to detect anything wrong. The fact that Johnson even thought of performing the experiment shows that he was aware of the irrational loyalties ethos-based verse occasioned. This incident, like the one recounted by Goldsmith, may or may not have actually happened; but since it is reported appreciatively by Boswell and has provoked little comment since, it is at least safe to assume that it is something that Johnson's contemporaries could easily believe – that it was something which could plausibly have happened. Two such dramatic experiments in popular response to lyric, which seem to indicate that readers could not actually 'hear' the works they claimed to love, deserve more attention than they have received. This sort of deaf acceptance of faked text is certainly not part of the world of the eighteenth-century reader preferred by conservative critics – that world of sane and reasonable appreciation of good writing which one often finds nostalgically invoked, as antithesis to the alleged bedlam of the twentieth century, in the introductions to anthologies of the period (e.g. Paul Fussell's Introduction to *English Augustan Poetry*).[6]

These strange experiments deserve a closer look. Unfortunately, Boswell does not mention, in the *Life of Johnson,* which lines of Thomson, Johnson offered to Shiels, so it is difficult to analyse the Thomson-altering experiment. But thanks to Boswell's detailed report on his conversation with Goldsmith, Goldsmith's chimerical version of Gray can be examined for the markers which allowed the attribution-centred reader to accept it as authentic.

Goldsmith's version of Gray is not only a forgery but a parody of Gray's style. Parody is usually the most acute sort of criticism, and in the quatrain he invents, Goldsmith has made an acute, though hostile, sketch of Gray's method. The four lines Goldsmith invents are defined by obscurity. This is the trait the credulous reader accepts as genuine. The fake stanza begins with an imperative, related to vision: 'Mark ...'. The direct object of this imperative is not an object at all, but a list of colours without shape: 'Mark the white and mark the red, / Mark the blue and mark the green.' The effect – satiric for Goldsmith but not for the committed auditor on whom he imposes this forgery/parody – is of vagueness, a self-defeating command to 'Mark' that which is not defined .

This purposeful murkiness is then compounded by 'rapid fading'

as the imperative acquires new urgency by warning of the dis-
appearance of the shapeless colours: 'Mark the colours ere they
fade.…' The fading of the colours suggests the end of day, a moment
marked for the sentimental reader as pathos-charged, and associated
with Gray through the 'Elegy'; this is emphasized by the last (and
intentionally worst) line, 'Darting through the welkin sheen'. The
implied narrative ends here with the 'darting' flight of the obscure
and ephemeral subjects of the verse, with added pathos accruing to
the sentimental reader from the use of archaic or awkward diction
('welkin sheen') – another charge habitually made by the Johnson
circle against Gray. The sum of effects in the little verse is roughly that
of an actual verse by Gray: the reader follows the perception of a
speaker who seems to be alone in a dim landscape, trying to see an
object which is somehow obscured. The focus 'darts' from that
obscure object to the implied sensibility of the speaker himself. This is
the sort of obscurity which Gray made famous.

Obscurity of a different sort is the basis of the accusation
MacPherson makes about Gray's technique in the 'Elegy'; 'to write
panegyrics upon a parcel of damned rascals that did nothing but
plough the land and saw corn' is a form of cheating, MacPherson
implies, because the social obscurity of Gray's peasants makes them
ineligible for commemoration. But this single invention, the inven-
tion of the obscured, blurred occasion, is the biggest single
subsidiary innovation in Gray's overall design. Like Goldsmith,
MacPherson resents Gray for discovering a way through the poetic
snarl of the period – one which is more productive than his own.

The word 'obscurity' has, of course, many senses; and all of these
senses are exploited, in one poem or another, by Gray. Gray uses
literal obscurity (loss of light and outline) as well as social-class
obscurity (as in Goldsmith's parody and, of course, in the 'Elegy');
he uses obscurity of reference (in 'The Progress of Poesy', 'The
Bard' and many other poems from the Northern tradition) and of
allusion – Gray is the poet of footnotes.

Obscurity is the one theme all these techniques have in common.
The poetic landscape had been exposed to a shrivelling spotlight of
authentication by generations of truth-grounded poetry; Gray
wants to dim the light, 'and leave[…] the world to darkness and to
me'. Boswell, with that weird half-conscious brilliance of his, makes
a telling joke about Gray in a letter to Temple: 'Two blacks won't
make a white. Neither will two Grays' (*Boswell in Holland*, 83).[7] But
Gray was not aiming at 'white', at clarity; he was in fact aiming at

'gray', at a strategic blurring of the epideictic scene. This blurring effect appears in the early 'Ode on a Distant Prospect of Eton College' – in fact, it is the central theme of the poem, as the title suggests ('A Distant Prospect'). Eric Rothstein has argued, in a passage cited earlier, that the eighteenth-century poet's central concern is to place himself in a context. If this is so, it only underlines Gray's profoundly innovative technique; for Gray's central device here is placing the poet out of the context – excluded by distance (of time and space) from what is being celebrated in the poem.

The motto chosen by Gray for the beginning of this ode is revealing. It is a line from Menander: 'I am a man; that is reason enough to be unhappy'. This motto could serve as the slogan for Gray's career-long effort to expand the rights of the occasional poet; it would suit the 'Elegy' as well as the 'Eton' ode. The thrust of the motto is the right of a poet not directly involved in tragedy to commemorate the tragedy. Gray's speaker in the 'Eton' ode is not involved in the life of the school; Gray's persona in the 'Elegy' does not know the peasants he commemorates. But in both cases, the speaker is a man, and a man of feeling at that; and 'that is enough to make [him] unhappy'.

The decontextualization of the speaker in 'Eton' is evident from the beginning of the poem; he summons from memory a landscape he can only dimly see; at best, he gets a bit of the breeze blowing from the school (lines 15–16). Having placed the poet out of the landscape in this way, Gray has disturbed the focus of the poem in a way which will be especially useful to him at its conclusion. Like Milton in 'Lycidas' Gray is concerned with transferring the scene of the poem towards himself; the implication is that some of the perils of adult life which make up the poem praeteritically refer to the speaker's world, not that of the students. Some, not all – the list is exhaustive and some of its elements are incompatible (Poverty and Ambition). The reader thus senses that *somehow* the poem is about the speaker, not the students, but is not quite certain exactly what happened to this speaker. This blurring of the focus of pathos becomes explicit in the last stanza:

> To each his suff'rings; all are men,
> Condemn'd alike to groan;
> The tender for another's pain;
> Th'unfeeling for his own.
> (*Gray & Collins: Poetical Works*, 23)[8]

The obscurity of the pathetic scene forces a major praeteritic transfer of pathetic focus toward the speaker. Nothing is said directly about his situation, but, in a manner derived from Sentimental stance-gestures, the ostensible focus on the travails awaiting the Etonians points clearly back at the speaker, making a tender mystery of his suffering. 'all are men, / Condemn'd alike to groan'. Occasionality is only hinted at; something has happened to the speaker, but it is not clear what – and in fact, there is nothing in the poem that even claims, in so many words, either an occasional basis or a more specific complaint. Thus obscurity in narrative, in subject, and in visual perspective combine to create an impregnable lyric narrative – one which merely suggests, to anyone who wants to read between the lines, a autobiographical tale of suffering which is all the more credible because the speaker seems not to want to talk about it – but to have been spontaneously struck by the point as he gazed into the distance, uttering the poem (since spontaneous utterance is one of the conventions of Ode) in response.

For a poetics of this sort, the famous last line of the poem might serve as motto: 'Where ignorance is bliss, 'tis folly to be wise.' That is: when the poet can get more productive value from dissociation and alienation from the scene to be commemorated (from 'obscurity'), why would anyone want to know more, to move closer to the action?

Another important poem from Gray's 1742 experiments, 'Sonnet: On the Death of Mr. Richard West', exploits the dissociation of the mind of the speaker and the occasional landscape in an even more significant way. This text, along with the great 'Elegy' can claim to be the most direct ancestors of the Wordsworthian lyric: for in this modest poem, the occasion takes place only in the mind of the speaker, with absolutely nothing occurring in the visible world to show that there has even been an occasion. The disjunction between this and the more conventional funereal-occasional approach cannot be exaggerated; the central trope of the standard funereal poem is the hyperbolic grief of what Eric Smith called 'animate nature' (cited in Chapter 1). The seasons mourn the sad event; nations mourn it; in Dryden's poem 'Upon the Death of the Lord Hastings', even the very pustules which caused the death mourn it. In 'On the Death of Mr. Richard West', nothing except the 'I' mourns at all:

In vain to me the smileing Mornings shine,
And redning Phœbus lifts his golden Fire:
The Birds in vain their amorous Descant joyn;
Or chearful Fields resume their green Attire:
These Ears, alas! for other Notes repine,
A different Object do these Eyes require.
My lonely Anguish melts no Heart, but mine;
And in my Breast the imperfect Joys expire.
Yet Morning smiles the busy Race to chear,
And new-born Pleasure brings to happier Men:
The Fields to all their wonted Tribute bear:
To warm their little Loves the Birds complain:
I fruitless mourn to him, that cannot hear,
And weep the more, because I weep in vain.
                              (*Gray & Collins*, 23)

The poem divides sharply between the seen landscape and the mind of the speaker. In that mind, the occasion is occurring; in the landscape nothing has happened. The disjunction is sharp; the first four words imply, again praeteritically, that something is happening in the mind of the speaker, but the sentence rolls on with a list of apparently happy, conventional pictures of a sunny spring or summer morning. The reader has only those first four words, along with the funereal/occasional title, to qualify these happy scenes, which take up the remainder of the first quatrain. The fifth and sixth lines return to the mind of the speaker in a relatively calm, allusive manner, referring to the 'different Object' (the deceased) indicated in the funereal title. But the seventh and eighth lines make the disjunctive point sharply; '… in my Breast the imperfect Joys expire'. The landscape reasserts itself again; the third quatrain is devoted entirely to the happy landscape, with only the first word, 'Yet' to qualify the clause as the first four words of the poem qualify the first quatrain. The closing two lines simply return to the first term of the disjunction, the mind of the speaker; 'fruitless' and 'in vain' emphasize the fact that there is not, cannot be any resolution of the inner/outer disjunction. This is extraordinary in a funereal poem; it is even more extraordinary that Gray's radical technique here, which involves both the assertion of an independent and unverifiable mental occasion *and* the failure to impose any sort of resolution of unity on the mourning consciousness, should be so little appreciated.

The two innovations embodied in this compact poem imply a tremendously important transfer of poetic ground which Gray continues to exploit in the 'Elegy': the transfer of the funereal event from the grieving landscape to the mind of the speaker. If this can happen as the birds sing and the sun rises, as it does in 'Richard West', then it can happen anywhere. Was this not implied, anyway, in 'Eton College', with its opening motto and last stanza insisting on the right of the poet to commemorate what, when and where he pleases, simply on the basis of sensibility? And if this sensibility is, in Aristotle's phrase, 'a portable faculty', then it ought to be possible to generate a genuine funereal event wherever the speaker happens to be struck by the sort of unseen, unnoticed, private mental event which occasions 'Richard West'. This technical developmental tinkering with the mechanics of occasionality is the true origin of the 'Elegy'. The tinkering began with the title, which, in Gray's original plan, was even more radically casual in its relation to the dead who are ostensibly commemorated; Gray had titled the poem 'Lines Wrote …' and it was Mason who suggested the change to the more formal, traditionally commemorative 'Elegy Written …' in which not only the change of nouns, from the spontaneous 'Lines' to the finished-sounding 'Elegy' is matched by the diction shift from the enallage 'Wrote' to the more correct 'Written'.

Even after such taming revisions, the 'Elegy' is the single poem in the entire tradition which can claim to be epochal in itself – that is, uniquely important to the development of poetic technique. It is related to other works of the period, notably 'Night Thoughts' and 'The Grave' – but its innovation has been more influential than either of these, and its influence so basic that we hardly discern it, living as we do in the poetics it spawned.

The 'Elegy' premieres two revolutionary strategies: first, it blurs the funereal occasion in such a way that the 'occasional conformity' of the text cannot be checked or disputed by pedantic, suspicious readers; and second, it begins, in a quite subtle manner, the slow transformation of the speaker from mere occasioning device (i.e. the vehicle in whose mind the funereal occasion takes place) to focus of the occasion. The second tendency reaches a sort of climax in Cowper's 'Cast-away' and Wordsworth's Odes; the first is very widespread in the modern lyric. But the poem does more than this: its most remarkable feature is that it not only enacts the blurring of the poetic occasion from verifiable, public moments to dim, private ones – it also constitutes an argument for this transfer. It is this argument which is the basis for the view that Gray is presenting 'democratic' or 'egalitarian' views in the 'Elegy'. Gray, by all accounts, was a reclusive academic snob, who, despite his own modest birth, insisted on being thought of as a gentleman (Chalmers, 14: 139). Thus the democratic and egalitarian leanings, discerned by critics in the 'Elegy', seem rather improbable. Paul Fry's advice that we study 'poets as poets' is essential here; Gray's 'egalitarianism' is a way of opening up to the occasional poet a vast source of commemorable graves from which he was previously excluded.

The beginning of the poem is so well-known that it must be re-imagined:

> ELEGY
> WRITTEN IN A COUNTRY CHURCHYARD
>
> The curfew tolls the knell of parting day,
> The lowing herd wind slowly o'er the lea,
> The plowman homeward plods his weary way,
> And leaves the world to darkness and to me.
>
> (*Gray & Collins*, 34)

The title is in two parts. The first word, 'Elegy', is a generic marker intended to make certain claims (among them occasionality) and to promise (or narrow) the range of response (pleasurable sadness is the emotion suggested by this term for a mid-century reader). The second line of the title is distinct – this is a two-part title. This part of an eighteenth-century title invariably specifies the conditions under which the poem meets its generic requirements and implies a narrative which is underway when the poem proper begins. Here the narrative is only hinted at – Gray, along with Young, makes the narrative hint essential to the English lyric – but its most important feature is, again, *obscurity*. The indefinite article has never before had so important a role in an English poem: '… *A* Country Churchyard'. An earlier occasional poem would have gone to great lengths to tell the reader which churchyard, what day, who was there, and so on – but Gray, after all, is the poet who invents decontextualization. Thus the first level of obscurity the reader encounters is geographical. 'Written' – by whom? Someone has gone to this unspecified graveyard and come back with a poem – since the subtitle amounts to a deposition that the poem was, literally, written in that graveyard. But what is the relation of the agent behind the passive participle 'Written' to what he wrote? The eighteenth-century reader will insist on the delineation of some such relationship early in the poem, and Gray complies with the demand – but quietly, vaguely, in a hinted way. The first three lines of the first stanza do not mention the 'writer' at all; they consist of a suggestive list of things which are leaving the scene. The speaker appears only when these things – ploughman, cattle, the sun itself – have gone. The fourth line welds him to the notion of obscurity: 'And leaves the world to darkness and to me'. This is one of the wilder zeugmas in the history of English poetry; 'darkness' and 'me' are paralleled as the heirs of the sunset world.

The word 'me' at the end of the fourth line is all the reader will hear of the speaker of the poem. Gray's only attempt to fit the speaker into the context is thus a negative one – the speaker is not part of the day, not part of the work of this cattle-raising area, and is remaining on the gloomy scene as darkness falls. The speaker is not part of anything – in fact, the speaker doesn't know any of the people who are buried here. What a radical – and what an unfairly unappreciated – notion: to celebrate 'the unknown peasant'! – 'Unknown', not just to fame, but to the occasional poet himself! The job of the beginning of a funereal-occasional poem, as I have argued at length in earlier chapters, is to set out the claim of the poet to encompass the death in question. Gray does nothing, by conventional standards, to meet such a requirement. Yet, of all the violent reactions to his works, none, to my knowledge, accuses him of hijacking this funereal occasion. Clearly, Gray successfully carried out a major enclosure of valuable occasional property. How did he manage this? The answer must lie in the early stanzas; readers would not have gone on if these had not satisfied them. What do these stanzas do to allow the transfer of the 'Dead Souls' to Gray?

They blur the scene; first visually, by the coming of darkness ('and me'); and then *via praeteritio*, they speak of what is not, merely guessing rather than loudly claiming. Where other poets tried to grab the corpse, Gray lets the corpses float toward him, making their imagined deaths a scene encompassed in the mind of the alienated Gentleman visitor, a mental occasion. The first of these brilliantly subtle elements is the delineation of the speaker. Almost nothing is said of him; the word 'me' is literally the only direct reference to himself in the poem. But it is enough; any contemporary reader could and did know exactly what sort of speaker this is.

He is a gentleman; his diction, his leisure (loitering in the church-yard), his dissociation from the agricultural activities, and his sensibility (which is implied for the contemporary reader by the fact that he chooses to remain in the graveyard after dark) all mark his class.

Thus, by the end of the first stanza the reader has some idea of the implied narrative. But any contemporary reader would still have expected some relation between the speaker and the inhabi-tants, so to speak, of the churchyard. (This is the convention which, for example, allows readers of *The Man of Feeling* to be fairly sure that the woman wandering around the ruins on page five will be revealed to be the beloved of the deceased on page 100.) Gray chooses to turn the non-relation of speaker and dead into a remark-able dramatic asset. Instead of clearing, relations are blurred; and again, the first sort of blurring is literal, the loss of outline occa-sioned by the fall of night: 'Now fades the glimmering landscape on the sight …' (line 5). This is an important line in the minds of contemporary readers; this can be asserted with confidence because it is this line which forms the basis of the parody invented by Goldsmith, cited above: 'Mark the colours ere they fade.' Goldsmith grasps, consciously or unconsciously, that the idea of fading light is essential to Gray's poetry. In this darkness, distinc-tions vanish as they do at the end of the 'Ode on a Distant Prospect'. The speaker fades in as the starker light of day fades out of the scene; the obscure graves begin to phosphoresce in the absence of brighter lights. The blurring of speaker into subject occurs in the third to the fifth stanzas. The focus of the description, which has been outward over the rural landscape, now moves inward, to the churchyard where the speaker is standing – thus the subtle implication that the remainder of the poem is a mental event occurring in the speaker's mind. The speaker blurs distinctions even when moving in to focus on the dead; there are simply a number of places 'where heaves the turf in many a mould'ring heap'. No particular dead person is being celebrated. These dead are all equal – to the speaker, that is.

Even when the speaker begins the process of commemoration in the fifth stanza, the liability – unfamiliarity with the deceased – becomes a poetic asset, as the subject of a praeteritic description. The speaker tells us what 'no more' will happen: 'no more' occurs in lines 20 and 21, embedded in descriptions of generic rural pleas-ures. From the reminder of mortality the speaker moves back in time to guess what the accomplishments of these dead must have been. He does not know anything at all, for certain, about their lives – that would have been clear to the contemporary reader from the fact that he does not seek any one particular grave, and thus presumably has no relatives buried here. But his imaginative reconstruction of their virtues ('How jocund did they drive their team afield!' [line 27]) is therefore all the more impressive. It is also serving to transfer the field of this action from churchyard to speaker's mind – if these are strangers, then the scene of them 'driv[ing] their team afield' must be taking place in the mind of the speaker; he cannot be recalling a seen event. Sweet are the uses of obscurity; without one more word (after 'me' in line four) to remind the reader of the fact that all this is actually happening in the speaker's mind, the speaker encompasses the Dead Souls of every person mentioned into his own mind.

The speaker's first references to the dead to be commemorated are anything but respectful. Their introduction is as 'mould'ring heap[s]' in line 14; the next reference to them, in line 16, refers to them as 'rude forefathers of the village'. Not only does the speaker not know these dead; it does not sound, at least in the beginning, as if he much reveres them. 'Lowly', he calls these graves (line 20). But these first few references, which reverse the usual commemorative amplifying tropes, soon reveal their purpose. The speaker can claim these dead only because they are so obscure. He does not know them, but neither does anyone else who is capable of writing a funereal verse for them. The speaker emphasizes his claim to celebrate their obscurity by inventing opponents who personify traits of those higher on the social scale ('Ambition' line 29, 'ye Proud' line 37) who, in order to aid the proleptic defence, attack the commemoration of mere peasants (as MacPherson had actually done).

Gray, obviously, is not the first poet to point out the common mortality of rich and poor. The theme is a commonplace of Middle-English verse. Shirley's 'Glories of Our Blood and State', perhaps the best of the many earlier English poems on the theme, shares the focus of the 'Elegy' on the graves of peasants, using a complex metonymic parallel of agricultural and martial implements to show that peasant and knight lie equally still, at last, in the same ground. What is new in the 'Elegy' is Gray's subtle positioning of the speaker as the epideictic voice standing (literally) among the peasant graves, encompassing them and speaking for them against these imaginary aristocratic attackers. The notion of potential glories, obscure(d) gifts, is the argument used by the speaker in defending these peasants.

The poem, at this point (line 37) becomes more ambitious in its encompassing of the peasant graves; Gray turns the commemoration of unknown peasants into a theoretical defence of private occasions. This is the link with 'Richard West' and 'Eton College'; as the speaker of 'Richard West' experiences a private, invisible mental event, this speaker argues that an unknowable number of subjunctive glories reside beneath the soil of the churchyard; and as the speaker of 'Eton College' quickly assumes identity with the obscure occasion, so this speaker merges with the dead peasants against their imaginary attackers:

> Nor you, ye Proud, impute to These the fault,
> If Mem'ry o'er their Tomb no Trophies raise
> (lines 37–8)

As MacPherson said, this poem violates occasional rules because, in celebrating the obscure, it fails to supply the names and dates which the 'trophies' would offer; but Gray turns this violation into opportunity. Since there are no names, no trophies, no markers on these graves, the contents are public property, and their unknown attributes may be the subject of infinite speculation. This speculation is the form taken by the inevitable rhetoric of amplification which follows; what begins as the commemoration of sad obscurity (obscurity added to death proper as occasion of grief) turns, brilliantly, into a celebration of what these people did not do.

The four stanzas which execute this turn (stanzas 12–15) are the most easily recalled by the 'unsophisticated reader[s]' who admire the poem. The twelfth stanza begins, 'Perhaps in this neglected spot is laid / Some heart once pregnant with celestial fire'. The key words here are 'Perhaps' and 'neglected'; for the 'perhaps' is the product of the 'neglected'. What is neglected – what is obscure – yields what is unverifiable, undeniable – what is 'perhaps'. Since nothing is known, anything is useful to the poet, who has now cornered the market on these dead souls. Naturally, the next move of the new owner is to begin touting the dead souls which have come into his possession. And given the current of belief in 'giant ignorance' as the true source of invention – given the careers of such as Stephen Duck – why not argue that the real reservoir of 'celestial fire' is lying in peasant graves? Gray implies that obscurity is authenticity – not because he necessarily accepts this as a political or social fact, but because the Byzantine currents of literary technique and theory, interacting with each other over several generations, have led, inexorably, to such a conclusion.

Stanza fourteen, with its famous metaphors of lost gem and desert flower, is the climax of this argument. The metaphor itself is borrowed from Milton ('… This desert soil / Wants not her hidden lustre, gems and gold', *Paradise Lost*, II: 270–1), but Gray employs it in a much more cunning manner than did Milton; the churchyard of which the poet has taken possession is asserted to be priceless, in the strict sense; that is, its contents cannot now be evaluated.

Gray makes the most of his breakthrough in the lines which follow. He dares to assert that these nameless dead could have been the equals of Cromwell and Milton – a complex trope, given the debt of the poem to Milton's 'desert soil' metaphor. The mention of Cromwell turns Gray's argument back toward the dual use of obscurity, since Cromwell has, for the eighteenth-century literary culture, a dual nature, at once hero and regicide. These dead are at one moment (line 60) the equals of Cromwell and then, at the end of the line, his superiors: 'Some Cromwell guiltless of his country's blood'. The point about the virtues of obscure authenticity is made explicit in lines 65–8: '… nor circumscrib'd alone / Their growing virtues, but their crimes confin'd, / Forbad to wade through slaughter to a throne, / And shut the gates of mercy.…' Praeteritio becomes more than a trope here; it becomes a virtue.

This apotheosis of the unknown dead is itself only a tactical turn in Gray's complex strategy, for it is not the dead peasants themselves who will be the final 'corpse' commemorated in the poem. The latter part of the poem (lines 77–128) turns the occasion toward the commemoration of the 'Man of Feeling' who is the speaker and, paradoxically, the corpse of the poem. If the poem were about the peasants – if commemorating their death were the point – it would end at line 76: 'They kept the noiseless tenor of their way'. Instead the poem returns to its opening scene. From line 77 onward, the reader is reminded again and again that the vision of the dead peasants' lives was a flashback; a mental event taking place in the mind of the aristocratic visitor who, like a necromancer, summoned up these dead for his own ends.

Lines 77–84 shift instantly in time to the present tense and in scene to the churchyard:

Yet ev'n these bones from insult to protect
Some frail memorial still erected nigh,
 With uncouth rhimes and shapeless sculpture deck'd,
Implores the passing tribute of a sigh.

Their name, their years, spelt by th' unletter'd muse,
The place of fame and elegy supply;
And many a holy text around she strews,
That teach the rustic moralist to die.

(Gray & Collins, 37)

This is the scene which the visitor surveys – dominated by 'uncouth' versions of what he himself is now in a position to offer, in far more elegant form, to the dead peasants. Even the generic marker which begins the title is applied here to its 'uncouth' analogue, the crude verses scratched in headstones to commemorate the dead. The poem refers to itself here, places itself as a finer version of what the peasants' relatives – the usual suppliers of elegiac commemoration – are simply not equipped to supply (see lines 47–50). The trained elegist, the speaker of the poem, has now come to give a sort of second, finer funeral to these dead (a benevolent version of the Lord Jeffries figure in the Dryden-funeral legends). Lines 85–92 assert that this is indeed a desired, requested service (just as King's family gave its permission for the poets of *Justa Edovardo King II* to begin commemoration at the beginning of the volume):

For who to dumb Forgetfulness a prey,
This pleasing anxious being e'er resign'd,
Left the warm precincts of the chearful day,
Nor cast one longing ling'ring look behind?

On some fond breast the parting soul relies,
Some pious drops the closing eye requires;
Ev'n from the tomb the voice of Nature cries,
Ev'n in our Ashes live their wonted Fires.

(Gray & Collins, 37)

This is a ritual elegiac gesture, the permission-granting verse which usually occurs much earlier. It is certainly odd to find it here, late in the poem, and what is even odder is the intentional muddying of the referent. It seems to refer to the dead peasants who are the ostensible occasion of commemoration; but the beginning of the next stanza makes it clear that the visitor is the subject as well as the speaker of this commemoration:

> For thee, who mindful of th' unhonor'd Dead
> Dost in these lines their artless tale relate;
> If chance, by lonely contemplation led,
> Some kindred Spirit shall inquire thy fate,
>
> Haply some hoary-headed Swain may say,
> 'Oft have we seen him....'
> *(Gray & Collins*, 37)

Whose fate? That of the same 'being' whose fate is the occasion in '... Richard West': the speaker of the poem. The peasants are now the occasion of a second and greater occasion in the way that the death of West was the occasion of the second, greater occasion occurring via the collision of the speaker's turmoil and the serene landscape. This occasion is the most surprising turn of the poem, for the 'swain', whose ancestors are the apparent object of commemoration, becomes the speaker of an elegiac poem about the visitor who first mourned the 'swain's' ancestors in the churchyard. The implied narrative moves quickly here, but in a direction similar to other sentimental narratives (e.g. *The Man of Feeling*): the visitor now moves from flashback on the dead peasants' lives, to flash-forward to a moment after his own death, and places in the mouth of the 'swain' the narrative of his (the visitor's) death, as told in the 'uncouth' manner of the 'swain'. The narrative provided by this 'swain' is that of the person of sensibility who, like Harley in *Man of Feeling*, pines away from sheer excess of feeling, often after weeks of haunting some 'melancholy scene'.

The narrative of the death of this man of feeling is so compact that only readers already familiar with the outline of this paradigmatic death-narrative could grasp it; it is also so blurred, so purposely obscure in its use of pronouns and other referents, that Gray, who could be clear enough when he desired to be, must have chosen this obscurity. In this respect, it is a violation of the spirit of the poem to paraphrase its narrative so simply; this poem, like many others written by Gray, is designed to be unclear, especially in the matter of elegiac referent. Gray shifts referents freely in the latter third of the poem. He blurs and generalizes the referent by referring to 'some fond breast' to 'the parting soul' while still, apparently, talking about the peasants (line 89); but the next reference is even more confusing, since it begins in the first, then switches to the third person: 'Ev'n in *our* Ashes live *their* wonted Fires'. 'Their' cannot refer to the last plausible noun, 'Nature' (line 91) because of the number inconsistency. The first and third pronouns do not refer so much as suggest; and what they suggest is a shell-game of pronouns in which first and third persons, singular and plural, combine and blur. The result of the shell-game is that 'Thee' emerges from the chaos of pronouns as the subject of the last part of the poem. Broadly, the 'me' of line one becomes the 'thee' of line 93. This is the summit of a career-long technical obsession of Gray's; this is what he sought to do in the opening motto and closing stanzas of 'Eton College': to blur completely the occasion and the commemorating poet, in order to expand the poet's range by making every death potentially the catalyst of a mental occasion.

The shell-game happens very quickly; most twentieth-century readers are not even aware of it, preferring to recall the simpler pathos of the commemoration of simple peasants in the beginning of the poem. But contemporary readers would have been much more sympathetic to Gray's turn here, since sentimental aesthetics was, for all its vague metaphysics, a physical, almost materialistic theory of literature. Emotions worth having had physical effects; in moderate doses pathos-generated emotions had as effect the tear or the faint; in large doses their effect is weight loss, depression (pining away) and finally death. The fact that the visitor will himself need an epitaph before the 'Elegy' is over is a sort of testimony to the authenticity and force of his emotional reaction to the peasants' graves, and a kind of poetic justice for his usurpation of their occasion.

His death, described in the future tense, is nonetheless commemorated twice in the last part of the poem, first by the 'Swain' and then by the unnamed friends who do for him what he did for the peasants: provide a more noble and lasting monument. The accomplishment of the two epitaphs is like that enjoyed by the seventeenth-century poets who, spurning occasional rules and modesty as well, wrote their own elegies. Gray's two epitaphs focus on the death of the speaker, from two complementary angles, in a manner typical of sentimental literature: the first is a view from the outside, by a spectator who does not share the deceased's sensibility, while the second is the pathetically climactic inside view.

The view of the 'hoary-handed swain' is the outsider's view, a depiction of the movements of the doomed man of feeling's last days. The swain speaks for the current generation of peasants; his pronoun is 'we/us', and his narration emphasizes the gap between 'us' and 'him', the man of feeling. This is an important aspect of Gray's intricate play of identification and distinction; now, as the poem nears its end, the identification of visitor and corpses vanishes. This identification was necessary to the first stage of the poem, in which Gray was urgently concerned with grounding the occasion; now that this has been accomplished, it is necessary for him to bring the visitor back into focus and let 'the rude forefathers of the hamlet sleep' once more.

The swain's recital emphasizes the strangeness of the visitor's behavior, as seen by the peasants; rising early merely to see the sun rise (lines 98–100), then lying by the brook in the middle of the day (lines 101–4) or wandering the countryside experiencing emotions without apparent stimulus. This last activity is not only the most important marker of sensibility implied in the swain's narrative, but the most important for Gray, since it describes – from the view of an essentially uncomprehending speaker – the actual occurrence of a 'mental occasion':

> Hard by yon wood, now smiling as in scorn,
> Mutt'ring his wayward fancies he wou'd rove,
> Now drooping, woeful wan, like one forlorn,
> Or craz'd with care, or cross'd in hopeless love …
>   (*Gray & Collins*, 39)

The swain here describes the actions of the visitor and then attempts to account for them in his own simple way; the visitor must have been suffering from some private worry or a romantic reversal. The reader knows better; the reader knows that the visitor suffers ('suffered'?; 'will suffer'?; 'will have suffered'? – tense is intentionally problematic, though future-perfect is probably closest) from nothing more than the affecting landscape of the churchyard. This is a vital part of Gray's strategic movement in the poem. As in 'Eton College', Gray is concerned to prove that occasion need not involve a personal loss. The swain, who in essence stands for the older and stricter view of poetic occasionality, cannot accept the notion of someone suffering at the site of the graves of people unknown to him. Gray, however, is always, either explicitly (as in 'Eton College') or implicitly, as here, attempting to extend occasion according to Menander's motto that it is enough to be human to suffer, and thus to commemorate.

And if such suffering leads to death, as it does in the swain's tale of the visitor's sad end (lines 109–16), then the visitor's right to encompass the entire churchyard landscape has been affirmed in the most traditional manner – he himself will be buried, first among equals, in the churchyard itself. The death is handled quickly and obliquely in these lines; the swain's narrative is an outsider's, after all, and he cannot properly describe the pining away of the visitor. The last part of his narrative (lines 113–16) reemphasizes his exclusion from the event, in fact; he witnesses the funeral as an outsider, and cannot even read the inscription on the monument:

> The next [day] with dirges and in sad array
> Slow thro' the churchway path we saw him borne.
> Approach and read (for thou can'st read) the lay,
> Grav'd on the stone beneath yon aged thorn.

The parenthetical phrase '(for thou can'st read)' emphasizes the exclusion of the swain and his like from the funereal occasion which has become the centre of the poem. The phrase also serves to focus attention, via postponement, on the epitaph of the visitor, which is the end and climax of the poem. The swain, by asking the speaker to read to him this epitaph, frames it dramatically, and also emphasizes the shift in occasional pathos which Gray has subtly carried out through the length of the poem: the peasants, who were the ostensible focus of pathos, have now become mere respectful spectators at the graveside of the visitor. 'The Epitaph' itself is a masterpiece of obscurity and intentional blurring applied to traditional epideictic rhetoric:

The EPITAPH

Here rests his head upon the lap of Earth
A Youth to Fortune and to Fame unknown.
Fair Science frown'd not on his humble birth,
And Melancholy mark'd him for her own.

Large was his bounty, and his soul sincere,
Heav'n did a recompense as largely send;

> *He gave to Mis'ry all he had, a tear,*
> *He gain'd from Heav'n ('twas all he wish'd) a friend.*
>
> *No farther seek his merits to disclose,*
> *Or draw his frailties from their dread abode,*
> *(There they alike in trembling hope repose),*
> *The bosom of his Father and his God.*
>
> (*Gray & Collins*, 39)

In these lines, all is blurred into a paroxysm of pathos; the ground of the funereal occasion cannot be disentangled from the intentionally-blurred shell-game of persons, and the reader is invited to imagine him/herself as the corpse. The peasants are gone; the self is the focus of pity. Whose self? Gray does not want to make that clear. Making it as unclear as possible is in fact the point of the 'Epitaph'.

The first stanza of 'The Epitaph' (note the use of the definite article to avoid a name or pronoun) performs the last of the vital substitutions Gray has in mind: the application to the visitor of all the grounds of pathos first attached to the peasants. The visitor is described precisely in the terms first used about the 'rude forefathers of the hamlet': he, like they, is unknown 'to Fortune and to Fame' and, apparently, to learning as well ('Fair Science'). The meaning cannot be quite the same in the two cases; the visitor's learning clearly extends to literacy (his reading of the headstones in the early part of the poem makes this clear) and in fact, 'Science' is a term often used by sentimental authors to describe the aspect of learning they find dry or without resonance. But these are quibbles of a sort the deeply moved eighteenth-century reader would have been unlikely to make; that reader, prepared by the series of substitutions and by the *gradatio* of pathos, was meant to accept the broad grounds of similarity implied, not argue about degrees of difference between a sensitive young student and the true peasants. The broad similarities implied are all grounded in shared obscurity. The same obscurity which, in the early part of the poem, made of this country churchyard a sort of village common, which the visitor subjected to literary enclosure, now includes him – he has proved his sincerity and finalized his obscurity by dying and being buried among the objects of his earlier commemoration.

Rather than trying to 'clarify' this passage, the critic might usefully attempt to explicate and consider the uses of its essential lack of clarity. The obscurity of tense, referent and narrative is quite clear: the subject of 'The Epitaph' cannot simply be one of the peasants, as the swain's narrative makes it clear that it is the visitor (or at least one of a series of such visitors) who is being commemorated. This simply cannot be logically reconciled with the third line of the epitaph, 'Fair Science frowned not on his humble birth' unless the terms 'Science' and 'humble birth' are being used disingenuously, equating the relative obscurity (of birth) of a middle-or-upper-class youth with the outright obscurity of dead peasants. The identification is legitimate only as a mental event in its own right. This is implied somewhat less obliquely in the second stanza of the 'Epitaph', which uses the term 'Mis'ry' to refer to this outright obscurity which, by implication, lay several socio-economic levels below that of the visitor.

The last stanza seals the tomb with a single huge trope: an aporia. The form this trope takes is that of an imperative forbidding further inquiries ('No farther seek his merits to disclose'). The point of the imperative is clear; Gray's entire strategy here is the blurring of the lines between those who pity and those who have died – this is what makes it possible for him to wrench the emotive focus of the poem away from the dead to those who mourn them, who become, in the person of the visitor, the ones truly to be mourned. The poem unfolds this strategy in ever bolder stages; first asserting the right of the visitor to commemorate those truly dead peasants, then blurring the distinction between him and them, and then remaking that distinction in his favor, so that by the end of the poem, the peasant dead have become merely the occasion of the occasion, the stimulus for the more important event, the one which takes place in the mind of the visitor/reader.

6

Gray to Cowper: Cat to Cast-away via 'Night Thoughts'

Of the many modern English poems which descend directly from the 'Elegy', the one which exhibits the most remarkable evolution in the direct line is Cowper's famous 'Cast-away'. 'The Cast-away' is very close to the 'Elegy' in its basic strategy. But the 'Elegy' is not the only Gray poem which served Cowper as model; 'Cast-away' also derives, as will be argued below, from Gray's comic poem, 'Ode on the Death of a Favourite Cat, Drowned in a Tub of Gold Fishes'. The major difference in Gray's and Cowper's work is that Cowper, writing some time after Gray, must exaggerate the shifts Gray made. Gray's obscurity has served its purpose, shown the way in which the occasion could be usurped by that greater occasion: the mental event. Cowper, in 'The Cast-away', performs the usurpation in such a way as to emphasize what Gray had tried to make obscure: the wrenching of the occasional pathos from its ostensible object toward the mental occasion.

'The Cast-away' begins in exactly the same way as the 'Elegy': with the depiction of a sad scene in which one vital first-person pronoun has been deftly inserted. The 'Elegy' begins by mentioning that the exit of all others 'leaves the world to darkness and to me'; Cowper's poem gives the first-person pronoun only one line of the six-line opening stanza:

> Obscurest night involved the sky,
>   Th' Atlantic billows roar'd,
> When such a destin'd wretch as I,
>   Wash'd headlong from on board
> Of friends, of hope, of all bereft,
>   His floating home forever left.
> (*William Cowper: The Task*, 317)[1]

The elements are roughly the same as those in the first lines of the 'Elegy': darkness, the death of a person of low social rank (a sailor), emphasis on the obscurity of that person (no name given) and the placement of the first person deftly within that scene.

Cowper's strategy here, though clearly descended from Gray's, is less daring; Gray, in the 'Elegy' actually constructed an occasion out of nothing, while Cowper welds his mental event onto a public, verified one: the washing overboard of a sailor, described by Richard Walter in *A Voyage Round the World by George Anson* (1748). The middle of the poem is devoted exclusively to depiction of the sailor's long struggle against the elements, treading water in mid-ocean as he watches his storm-driven ship sail on. This part of the poem has been treated at length from a variety of critical angles, but rarely as a complex employment of funereal/occasional poetics. Cowper's method in writing about this death was that of the occasional poet looking for opportunity; he found an episode in a non-fiction source (Walter's narrative of Anson's voyage) and commemorated it. Cowper, a compassionate and deeply depressed individual, may well have felt grief or horror while reading Anson's account of the drowning sailor, but his employment of that death in a poem requires negotiation with cultural rules involving epideictic rhetoric, and it is Cowper's negotiation with these rules which is my concern here. Cowper's choice of this gloomy episode for commemoration is often described in psycho-biographical terms, as the product of his depression. But this sort of explanation can easily be used to dismiss complex poetic choices. There are many English poems written about drowning victims; the volume commemorating Edward King consists of nothing else. Unless we choose to explain those poems as the products of clinical depression, we should be wary of explaining Cowper's decision to commemorate a drowned man in purely psycho-biographical terms.

Like psycho-biography, religion has often been employed to explain the genesis of 'The Cast-away'. Cowper may well have been attempting to use the state of the sailor, alive yet doomed and utterly alone, as metaphor for the state of the 'Reprobate' in Calvinist theology, who suffers a sort of death-in-life due to being abandoned by God in much the way that the sailor is abandoned by his ship (like the Calvinist reprobate, the sailor is not damned for anything he has done; and the ship sails on by a larger necessity, not cruelty). But explaining eighteenth-century poetic techniques in terms of the theology of radical Protestantism is a complex business;

post-Reformation English poetry is in many respects the result, not merely the expression of this theology. Cowper might, or might not, have invented this poem if he had not been affected by Calvinist thought, but it seems unlikely that he could have invented it without the influence of Gray.

What is radically new in the poem is not its morbid subject or religious allegory, but rather two technical innovations: Cowper's emphasis on the dying, rather than on the death, of the sailor; and the related wrenching of the subject from the deceased to the mourner. The first aspect, the depiction of the feelings and actions of the doomed sailor, occupies the entire middle of the poem, stanzas three through eight (48 lines). The contributors to *Justa Edovardo King II* devoted very few lines to the actual process of drowning which King went through – the attempt to keep one's head above water, the slow loss of strength, the final sinking beneath the waves. In this, they are typical English elegists; only those elegies devoted to death in battle (which seems to have been thought an especially attractive process) spend much time on the process of slow death. In spending eight stanzas on the actual drowning of the sailor, Cowper is indeed doing something new. He does it in a way related to his overall goal, which is the transfer of the funereal occasion to himself. In focusing on the slow doom of the sailor, he is focusing on death as a mental event; and, like the visitor in the 'Elegy' – or thousands of Wordsworthian poems to come – this mental event occurs in the cranium of a single young Englishman isolated in a vast landscape (in this case, the vastest of all: the middle of the ocean).

The lesson taken from Gray, that the speaker must be absolutely isolated for the mental event to have free access, leads Cowper to celebrate, not only the Cast-away bobbing in the middle of the ocean but Alexander Selkirk, the original of Robinson Crusoe ('Verses supposed to be written by Alexander Selkirk'). In the beginning of that poem, Cowper naturally enough goes to the same effort to clear the scene, and to emphasize the pristine isolation of the speaker (Cowper, 273). Classically-minded critics, who have tended to deplore the alleged soft-minded romanticism which results in '[o]ur current overvaluing of pariahs, victims, and expellees of all kinds' (Fussell, 1972, 1), miss the point in treating technical innovations as lapses in poetic morality. Gray and Cowper may well have felt tender grief, or an empathetic sense of their own mortality, in thinking of the deaths they chose to commemorate; but it is also true that, consciously or unconsciously, they were able to value 'pariahs, victims, and expellees of all kinds' in part for reasons of craft – to value them as a source of good material, a good way to refract occasionality and expand the production of poems.

If the poem ended with the death of the sailor after his hopeless struggle, those critics who have found this poem to be simply a depiction of existential angst or Calvinist fatalism would have a stronger case; but in fact there are three stanzas following the death of the sailor (which occurs in line 47), and it is these stanzas which contain the major strategic movement executed by Cowper:

> No poet wept him: but the page
>   Of narrative sincere,
> That tells his name, his worth, his age,
>   Is wet with Anson's tear,
> And tears by bards or heroes shed
>   Alike immortalize the Dead.
>
> (Cowper, 319)

Just as in the 'Elegy' the first-person pronoun, so quietly introduced in the first stanza, becomes the true object of commemoration in the last part of the poem. Like Gray, Cowper names the original, funereal occasion as one not celebrated properly ('No poet wept him ...'). Gray made much of this theme in the 'Elegy' referring to the peasants as 'the unhonoured dead' (line 93) and emphasizing the crudeness and insufficiency of their memorials (lines 77–84). In fact, the end of Cowper's poem is virtually a point-by-point replication of the progression of lines 77–128 of the 'Elegy'. Where Gray mentions 'the tribute of a passing sigh' given to the rude stones which list 'their name, their years, spelt by the unlettered Muse', Cowper, after specifying that no poet 'wept' the sailor's death, mentions '... the page / Of narrative sincere, / That tells his name, his worth, his age ...' and adds that this page 'is wet with Anson's tear'. In both cases, the pattern is the claim that the death[s] in question went uncommemorated in the traditional manner, but were commemorated in some less 'poetic' but perhaps more sincere way – in the 'Elegy' by the crude headstones erected by other peasants, and in 'The Cast-away' by the recording of the incident by the commander of the expedition.

The issue at stake here is the place of the poetic text (the 'Elegy' or 'The Cast-away') in the epideictic process. Neither poet explicitly uses the inadequacy of earlier commemorative efforts to make space for his own work; both Gray and Cowper find the earlier, non-poetic efforts, respectively of peasant or explorer, adequate. Cowper makes the point more bluntly: '… Tears by bards or heroes shed / Alike immortalize the Dead'. Gray, as befits the founder of a subgenre, must be more complex and more subtle. Therefore he makes the adequacy of earlier efforts a part of his second-occasion strategy. The rude headstones erected for the peasants are adequately sincere – but their sincerity and touching crudeness lead (ll. 89–96) to the tears shed by the visitor ('Some pious drops the closing eye requires' l. 90). Thus, in Cowper, the tears – always an important physical proof of pathetic involvement in a work of sentimental literature – are already shed, by Anson; and, since Cowper makes a point of stating that such tears do 'immortalize the Dead' as effectually as any poet's 'tears in tune', the sailor's death would seem to be closed, as an epideictic event. In Gray, on the other hand, the tears shed by the visitor are the beginning of the second occasion – the death-by-empathy of the visitor himself. In Gray, therefore, the review of previous epideictic efforts merges smoothly into the second, mental occasion; in Cowper the apparent occasion – the sailor's death – is rather roughly jettisoned at this point. This jettisoning of the sailor is the truly radical movement of Cowper's poem, making explicit the movement of the occasion away from the commemorated event, and toward the repercussions of that event in the mind of the poet. And Cowper is explicit indeed about this in the final two stanzas of 'The Cast-away':

> I therefore purpose not or dream,
>   Descanting on his fate,
> To give the melancholy theme
>   A more enduring date,
> But mis'ry still delights to trace
>   Its semblance in another's case.
>
> No voice divine the storm allay'd,
>   No light propitious shone,
> When, snatch'd from all effectual aid,
>   We perish'd, each alone;
> But I beneath a rougher sea,
>   And whelm'd in deeper gulfs than he.
>   (Cowper, 319)

The corpse, which we have just seen vanish beneath the waves after six stanzas of hopeless struggle, simply drops from the picture in favour of the 'mis'ry' of the speaker. The shift derives from the 'Elegy', but in the earlier work this movement away from the ostensible objects of commemoration is a tricky and subtle one, performed, first of all, by supplying a narrative in which the sympathetic witness at the obscure death dies himself of grief, and second, by the continual shifting of referents, especially pronouns, until, as in 'Eton College', mourner and mourned are blurred together, sharing equally in the occasion.

Cowper, by contrast, makes the shift as clear and abrupt as possible. His penultimate stanza makes a point of discarding the claim of traditional elegies to originate in epideictic purpose; he does not want 'to give the melancholy theme / A more enduring date ...' Cowper even mocks this hoary epideictic claim by using the verb 'Descanting', – an elaborate and rather fussy word, out of keeping with the rough diction of the rest of the poem – to describe the elegiac claim to epideictic utility.

At this point the poem is praeteritically listing claims which do not apply; there has not been any positive claim about what the poem is meant to do. In the closing couplet of the penultimate stanza, Cowper begins to make such a claim:

> But mis'ry still delights to trace
> Its outlines in another's case.

With these lines, the hidden first-person speaker returns suddenly. The pronoun 'I' itself has not appeared, and will not until the climactic moment at the very end of the poem, but its stalking-horse in this couplet is the indefinite possessive pronoun 'another's'. The 'another' mentioned here is, of course, 'I'.

The conclusion of the poem is thus the carefully prepared introduction of the 'I'. This appearance is delayed even longer; pronouns are absent from the beginning of the last stanza, which simply recapitulates the sad ending of the tale. The first two lines refer clearly to the sailor's plight ('storm' and 'light'). But the middle lines of the stanza blur the narrative context in a way which seems to be derived from Gray's technique: 'When, snatch'd from all effectual aid, / We perish'd, each alone ...' The participle 'snatch'd' has no particular nautical flavour, and the sense that the narrative is blurring is confirmed by the surprising appearance of the first-person plural pronoun, 'We', – the plural blurring the line between sailor and 'I'.

Cowper's technique is so similar to Gray's in its general shape that its dissimilarity in poem-ending strategy is all the more remarkable. Both tactical plans have the same strategic goal: the generation of tremendous pathetic effect from the 'unhonoured' death of an obscure object (peasants, sailor) – and then the transfer of as much of that occasionally-grounded pathos as possible to an unoccasioned, ungrounded self-referential pathos. Cowper's design for the transfer is both more daring and less original than Gray's; Cowper's occasion is real, Gray's invented; Gray merges pseudo-occasion and secondary mental occasion, while Cowper moves from one to the other as sharply and bluntly as possible. Cowper's pronoun switch ('he' to 'I') is sudden and surprising; Gray's (which is too blurred to be re-summarized here) is as smooth and murky as Gray can make it.

Cowper's bluntness is related to his delay of the surprise pronoun transfer until the very end of the poem. This delay is essential to his plan. If 'The Cast-away' were even one stanza longer, the poet would have to face the occasion-centred reader's inevitable demand: 'Oh? What happened to you that was so much worse than being left to drown in the middle of the ocean?' By cutting off the text with the massive aposiopesis, Cowper forces the reader to guess. The unseen catastrophe is portrayed metaphoric- ally ('rougher sea'), which adds to the vagueness – presumably the catastrophe was not actually a nautical one, so the terms here cannot be taken literally. They intentionally offer no hint at all of the circumstances of Cowper's greater disaster. The assertion is there, at the very end, to be taken or left. Like Edward Young, Cowper has realized how sweet are the uses of obscurity of another sort – the sort which derives from purposely giving partial, suggest- ive information about an alleged private occasion. This is another strain of grounding which enters the English lyric as a means of confronting the constriction of invention: the rhetoric of aporia and aposiopesis; the rhetoric of the hint, the voice which is simply too deeply moved to tell the full story.

Cowper exploits this aporaic obscurity in many of his other late poems. The well-known 'Hatred and Vengeance, My Eternal Portion' is a dramatic case; most editors have added an occasioning title, 'Lines Written During a Period of Insanity' – but Cowper left the poem untitled (Sambrook, in Cowper, 239). The addition of this

occasioning title suggests later editors' anxiety at the unsubstan-
tiated claim in the poem. The title turns out to be the most
forthcoming part of the poem in terms of information on its occa-
sioning basis; without this title, the poem consists of dire aporia:

> Hatred and vengeance! my eternal portion,
> Scarce can endure delay of execution,
> Wait, with impatient readiness, to seize my
> > Soul in a moment.
> > > (Cowper, 239)

The reliance on aporia concerning the actual self-referential cata-
strophe means that the poem requires another narrative which *can*
be told, and believed by readers, just as 'The Cast-away', which
has as its desired subject the afflictions of its speaker, requires a
stalking-horse, non-fictive story about the death of the sailor. The
story Cowper picks is a scriptural one this time: that of Judas, most
abhorred figure in the New Testament. Once again, Cowper's
strategy is to devote the middle of the poem to this story, the
outlines of which are known and accepted by all readers, and then
suddenly turn back, in the last stanza, to the literally unspeakable,
worse damnation suffered by the self:

> *Him* the vindictive rod of angry justice
> Sent quick, and howling to the center headlong;
> I, fed with judgments, in a fleshly tomb, am
> > Buried above ground.

This scripturally-grounded story can then be used as the first
term of a *commutatio,* a figure relying on the Aristotelian major
topos of the Greater and Less, to praeteritically imply the true
horror which has happened to the speaker. This poem, written over
20 years before 'The Cast-away', shows Cowper's reliance on
Gray's basic occasion-transfer technique, combined with horrific
aporia, as his basic pathos-generation device. Again the poet seeks
the worst imaginable story, the name which is associated with
absolute despair (lost sailor, lost soul) and again he simply asserts,
at the end of the poem, that something worse – something so terri-
ble it cannot be named – has happened to him.
This strategy, which can be traced from Young, through Cowper,
to Wordsworth, ends in the complete equation of the poet's ethos

and the intensity of the reader's emotional response. Chalmers says as much in the conclusion of his capsule biography of Cowper:

> But what adds a peculiar charm to Cowper is, that his language is every where the language of the heart. The pathetic, in which he excels, is exclusively consecrated to subjects worthy of it. He obtrudes none of those assumed feelings by which some have obtained the character of moral, tender, and sympathetic, who in private life are known to be gross, selfish and unfeeling. In Cowper we have every where the happiness to contemplate not only the most favourite of poets, but the best of men.
>
> (Chalmers, 18: 602)

Cowper's work is defined by Chalmers in this passage as pathos grounded in ethos – feelings which can be accepted because the poet has made of his own life their occasion. This is one of the more important implications of the mental event as occasion; the most convincing mental event – the one most difficult to fake – is an incapacitating mental illness. Chalmers, having detailed, in his biography, the many years Cowper spent in a state of what would now be termed clinical depression, ends with this passage telling the reader that Cowper can be trusted because his horrific life is a testimony to the validity of his poetic ethos.

Cowper owes to Gray the other major pathos-generating occasional device in his arsenal: the animal elegy. The animal elegy is an ancient genre, but its mid-eighteenth-century flourishing is a natural product of the course of generic innovations Gray pursued in the 1740s. As in all his work of that time, Gray is experimenting, in his animal elegy, with ways to broaden and blur the occasional basis of lyric poetry by celebrating beings too low on the social scale to merit commemoration. During the same year he began the 'Elegy', Gray wrote an influential elegiac poem commemorating a being even lower in the 'Great Chain' than a peasant: an animal. This is why the 'Ode on the Death of a Favourite Cat ...' made such an impression – and such an ambivalent one – on Gray's contemporaries. Its relation to the 'Elegy' in expanding the range of commemorable objects was felt, unconsciously, as part of the current of value-reversal involving the Homeric model and the superiority of 'Giant Ignorance' over nice judgement.

Gray's experimental move downward toward obscure objects of commemoration is played seriously indeed in the 'Elegy' but must be played, at least superficially, for laughs in the further downward extension, to an animal as elegiac object, in the 'Ode on the Death of a Favourite Cat …' The poem is typical of an extended-occasion work in that the first title, 'ODE' marks it as occasional in a manner less strict than an 'Elegy', and in the way in which the subtitle which follows refines and specifies the claim to occasionality:

> Ode
> on the Death of a Favourite Cat,
> Drowned in a Tub of Gold Fishes

The claim to an actual occasioning event (the cat's drowning) is made here, and only here, because Gray is not really expecting to generate epideictic pathos as he is in the 'Elegy'. Gray may not have cared to risk serious pathetic rhetoric on so slim an occasional basis – not that the audience would doubt the reality of the cat's drowning, but they would probably be unmoved by it. Gray devotes the rest of the poem to what is, at least superficially, a comic allegory on greed and its consequences.

But at least one important reader did not see it so – William Cowper used the central device developed here as the dramatic focus of 'The Cast-away'. 'The Cast-away' is basically a recombination of the elements of two of Gray's occasional experimentations: the 'Elegy' and the ode on the cat's death. From the 'Elegy' he takes the idea of an uncommemorated death, a death of one so lowly his name is not even employed in the poem; from the cat's-death ode he borrows the idea of drowning slowly, all alone. The debt to Gray's 'Ode' is clear. Here is Gray's stanza on the cat's watery death:

> Eight times emerging from the flood
> She mew'd to ev'ry watery god,
>   Some speedy aid to send.
> No Dolphin came, no Nereid stirr'd;
> Nor cruel Tom, nor Susan heard;
>   A Fav'rite has no friend!
>   (*Gray & Collins*, 28)

Gray emphasizes the cat's protracted struggle against drowning and the iteration of the aid which failed to arrive. Cowper pursues the same strategies in 'The Cast-away', first, the emphasis on protracted struggle against drowning:

Not long beneath the whelming brine,
  Expert to swim, he lay;
Nor soon he felt his strength decline,
  Or courage die away;
But waged with death a lasting strife,
Supported by despair of life.

He shouted; nor his friends had failed,
  To check the vessel's course....
                    (Cowper, 317)

In Cowper's poem, as in Gray's, the elegiac subject is abandoned
in water; in both, the subject struggles against the water and calls
for help; in both, there is no help. This is the point of Gray's cat
story, as Cowper assimilated it. One can see in his expansion of
Gray's iteration of failed salvations the importance he attached to
this aspect of the story:

No voice divine the storm allayed,
  No light propitious shone....
                    (Cowper, 319)

This is Cowper's treatment of Gray's ostensibly comic lines, 'No
dolphin came, no Nereid stirred, No cruel Tom, nor Susan heard;'.
Cowper not only derived the possiblity of dramatizing the drown-
ing of an obscure being from Gray; in his 'Epitaph on a Hare' he
also employed Gray's basic experimental model in the ode on the
cat's death, the use of animals as elegiac subject. And, just as he
took the comic drowning in that poem and made it a serious elegiac
occasion in 'The Cast-away', he takes the comic notion of animal
elegy and makes it a matter of real pathos.

In this poem Cowper unites all the lessons he has learned from
Gray and even adds one which he will pass on to Wordsworth. The
first stanza derives directly from Gray's reversal of elegiac subject in
the 'Elegy'; like Gray's poem, it is at pains to point out the way in
which the subject of this elegy is not suitable for commemoration:

Here lies, whom hound did ne'er pursue,
  Nor swifter greyhound follow,
Whose foot ne'er tainted morning dew,
  Nor ear heard huntsman's hallo',
                    (Cowper, 292)

The tortured syntax of the stanza emphasizes this praeteritic reversal. The stylized headstone-phrase 'Here lies' usually calls for the proper noun to follow immediately. Instead, the rest of the stanza digresses to tell what this hare did not do. The proper noun in question, 'Tiney', is postponed until the beginning of the second stanza, as the reader is told that the so-far-unnamed hare did not do even the limited number of martial or heroic things of which a hare is capable: did not flee the hounds, did not wander the woods, did not fear the huntsman. This sets the elegiac subject apart, not just from the aristocratic warriors usually commemorated, but even from the likes of Pope's pheasant in 'Windsor Forest' and Gray's cat, who in their way died heroic deaths. This is a domestic rabbit, in every sense, with nothing but its comic truculence to give it a Homeric status. The second and third stanzas continue the praeteritic iteration of Tiney's non-qualities in the Gray fashion; he was *not* friendly, grateful or otherwise endearing:

> Old Tiney, surliest of his kind,
>   Who, nurs'd with tender care,
> And to domestic bounds confin'd,
>   Was still a wild Jack-hare.
>
> Though duly from my hand he took
>   His pittance ev'ry night,
> He did it with a jealous look,
>   And, when he could, would bite.
>   (Cowper, 293)

But Cowper, true to his model, has done something very important in this praeteritic disavowal: he has found a way to insert, quietly, the key first-person pronoun: '… duly from my hand he took …'. As so often in poems of this genealogy, there is only one mention of the 'I' in the beginning of the poem; but it is enough to suggest the later refraction of the poem from its ostensible subject to the sensibility which apprehended that subject; the 'I'. Rachel Trickett[2] points out Cowper's (and Wordsworth's) habit of employing animals as topics in a way connected with the effort to dispel the author's depression. Cowper actually employs the hare as an ostensible subject to point the occasion back toward the 'I'. Thus the pathos-to-ethos design common to all Cowper's and Gray's work.

This refraction toward the poet is effected by an intentional accumulation of inadequate elegiac material in the middle stanzas:

His diet was of wheaten bread,
    And milk, and oats, and straw,
Thistles, or lettuces instead,
    With sand to scour his maw.

On twigs of hawthorn he regal'd,
    On pippins' russet peel;
And, when his juicy salads fail'd,
    Sliced carrot pleas'd him well.
                    (Cowper, 293)

The rhetorical effect of these stanzas is to convince the reader that the rabbit is so insignificant that he cannot be the real subject of the poem. Two stanzas on the rabbit's preferred foods (which are followed by two more on his play habits); these catalogues are as far from traditional commemoration as it is possible to go. And, in order that the reader be certain to notice this designed insignificance, the prosody becomes mechanical and dull, and the diction drops sharply; lines like 'And milk, and oats, and straw' followed by 'Thistles, or lettuces instead' are so loudly banal that they inevitably refract meaning away from themselves and toward the ethos of the speaker.

Like other Cowper poems employing a humble ostensible subject, this one effectively ends, in terms of that subject, several stanzas before the real ending of the text. In this case, the ending – marked as such by the summing up of Tiney's lifespan, 'Eight years and five round-rolling moons' comes three stanzas before the real end, and, as in 'The Cast-away', introduces the real ethos-subject. This latent subject comes through immediately after the jettisoning of the ostensible subject, in the concluding stanzas of the poem:

I kept him for his humour' sake,
    For he would oft beguile
My heart of thoughts that made it ache,
    And force me to a smile.

But now, beneath this walnut-shade
    He finds his long, last home,
And waits, in snug concealment laid,
    Till gentler Puss shall come.

He, still more aged, feels the shocks

From which no care can save,
And, partner once of Tiney's box,
Must soon partake his grave.
                    (Cowper, 294)

We learn in these lines that the speaker kept the rabbit because it was useful in times of depression. The depression is described only by a hint (the great lesson Cowper had picked up from Young): '… beguile / My heart of thoughts that made it ache'.

That is the only explicit reference to the latent 'I'. The poem returns to its ostensible subject, moving (like the 'Elegy') to the future-tense grave-scene, and then moves on from this rabbit to another, 'still more aged …' who will also, in the course of things, soon die. The move from 'Tiney' to the speaker, and then, interestingly, away again to yet another elegiac subject – this one also a rabbit and, apparently, not even in danger of death at the moment of writing – reflects Cowper's innovative employment of purposely innapropriate subjects for pathos, precisely so that that pathos may refract more powerfully toward the real object of reader sympathy, the 'I'. Cowper's fondness for animal pathos (he has three poems about bullfinches alone) has often been ascribed to an increasing sympathy for animals in English culture, and it does at least parallel that development; but it seems rather to make use of it, using creatures only recently seen as potential vessels of pathos as effective substitutes or, to mangle Eliot's term, 'objective *non*-correlatives' of the speaker's ethos.

Cowper's experiments with purposely inappropriate commemorative subjects went even further than the animal elegy. In 'The Task', he uses a common invention-reattributing design of early-eighteenth-century personal verse to demonstrate the extraordinary sensitivity of the ethos which is his only real subject. It seems to me that the descriptive poetry of 'The Task' is intentionally awkward; here, as in the animal poems, it is not the appropriateness but, on the contrary, the wild and obvious inappropriateness of the ostensible subject which is the point. For refracting mirror, Cowper allows a 'volunteer from the audience', as it were, to choose … a sofa. The choice of this homely article of furniture completes the downward movement of the occasioning object, while the attribution of that choice to another not only emphasizes the poet's non-responsibility for the invention but acts as a challenge, a proof of skill or sensibility. The choice is not as random or original as it seems; at least as far back as *le Lutrin,* and extending through *The Dispensary* and *Rape of the Lock,* the use of disproportion between object and sensibility has been employed by European mock-epic poets, while the sofa itself was used as framing device in the famous eighteenth-century pornographic novel *Le Sopha.* Cowper, of course, does not use the sofa in the disrespectful, humorous manner of his French models, but disproportion is as essential to his method as to theirs. The first line of this huge poem, in which Cowper contrasts it to his earlier and equally massive works on more grand moral topics, makes clear the importance of the disproportion:

> I sing the sofa. I, who lately sang
> Truth, Hope and Charity, and touch'd with awe
> The solemn chords, and with a trembling hand,
> Escap'd with pain from that advent'rous flight,
> Now seek repose upon an humbler theme....
> (Cowper, 57–8)

Cowper goes out of his way, in these lines, to emphasize the unnaturalness of a sensibility as pious and abstracted as his own descending to such a theme; and the primacy of that self, that 'I'. This very long poem not only begins with that pronoun but repeats it in a prominent anaphora at the beginning of the second sentence, and goes on to place both the low and high topics entirely within an ethos-context. Even punctuation aids the oxymoronic rhetoric here; instead of the colon, comma and semi-colon which are his preferred punctuations, Cowper lets the first, disjunctive, four-word sentence end with a flat full stop. The theme of this disjunctive style is the tension between high sensibility and low topic; thus occasionality comes to the fore as the reattributive explanation for the descent of the 'I' to such a topic. This is the aim of the next two lines of the poem:

> The theme though humble, yet august and proud
> Th'occasion – for the Fair commands the song.
> (Cowper, 58)

The occasion, that is, is a request; and the request comes from 'the Fair' – who, according to gender convention of the period, may be excused for preoccupation with household goods. The reattribution of the occasion here only reinforces the point made at length in Cowper's prose 'Advertisement' to the poem, which prefaced the 1785 edition:

> The history of the following production is briefly this. A lady, fond of blank verse, demanded a poem of that kind from the author, and gave him the SOFA for a subject. He obeyed; and having much leisure, connected another subject with it: and pursuing the train of thought, to which his situation and turn of mind led him, brought forth at length, instead of the trifle which he first intended, a serious affair – a Volume.
>
> (Cowper, 55)

The reattribution is all; the poem may be infinitely extended once its ground in the lady's request is set, and its germination in the 'train of thought' and 'turn of mind' established as the fruit of this occasioning. Perhaps this more solid occasional strategy is the reason that 'The Task' is remembered when Cowper's blank-verse 'volumes' on Hope, Truth and Charity are forgotten. In those poems, the abstract topics were introduced directly, without the occasional grounding of 'The Task'. 'Charity', for example, begins with an apostrophe to the abstraction itself, to which the poem is then attributed. The author is then 'impell'd' to write in praise:

> Fairest and foremost of the train that wait
> On man's most dignified and happiest state,
> Whether we name thee Charity or love,
> Chief grace below, and all in all above,
> Prosper (I press thee with a pow'rful plea)
> A task I venture on, impell'd by thee:
> O never seen but in thy blest effects,
> Or felt but in the soul that heav'n selects;
> Who seeks to praise thee, and to make thee known
> To other hearts, must have thee in his own.
> (*The Poems of William Cowper*, 1: 337)[3]

The common elements of this poem and 'The Task' are clear; even the key term, 'task' is used by Cowper to describe his work, in this introductory passage. But the grounding Cowper sketches here turns into a discussion of its shortcomings; Cowper says twice (the seventh and tenth lines) that he cannot demonstrate the validity of the grounding theme unless the reader already believes in it. This is the sentimental aporia, a key trope; but its intensity here is related to the weakness of the apostrophic/reattributive method Cowper chose. Here, as in 'The Task', the poem is re-attributively the responsibility of 'the Fair'; but 'the Fair', in this case, is a Goddess, and worse yet, a pagan one uneasily crowning a poem on a Christian theme. Thus when Cowper claims to be 'impell'd by thee [Love]' he is going through the motions of invocation. The theme remains as abstract as before; the poem is essentially a very long meditation without any apparent dramatic grounding.

Thus the method of 'The Task'. 'The Fair' becomes a real woman; the 'task' moves down many, many levels of idealization; and as a result, the entire seemingly endless work is given a glaze of occasionality. It is important in attaining this glazing effect that Cowper not choose his subject – that was the drawback of the poems on Hope, Charity and Truth. They appear to be the products of premeditation – and premeditation, or rather the appearance of it, is the dread enemy of the mental occasion.

The reliance on the sort of rhetorical devices found in the beginning of 'The Task' reveals Cowper's debt to another teacher: Edward Young. It was Young who, along with Gray, furnished the largest component of Cowper's technique. Young's single extraordinary success was far more narrowly grounded than Gray's broad innovations; but within that narrow range, Young was an important innovator. Young produced two texts of great importance in the development of occasion-grounded mental-event poetics: his enormous poem 'The Complaint, or Night Thoughts', and his prose essay on originality in literature, 'Conjectures on Original Composition'. Young's one great poem has been remembered not by its first title, 'The Complaint', but simply as 'Night Thoughts', because it was popularly understood as a great representative of the nocturnal poetics which constitute a major subgenre within the post-Reformation English literary world.[4] But while 'Night Thoughts' owes much to earlier nocturnal meditations, particularly Thomas Parnell's 'Night Piece: On Death', it differs from them, and shows its affinity with other vital mid-century work, in its employment of occasional manipulation on a template of obscurity. Because of the hints of occasion Young employed, the impact of 'Night Thoughts' was much greater and more enduring than that of Parnell's work. Parnell's 'Night-Piece on Death' does not go through the hidden-occasion technique employed by Young, but does employ the device of insomnia as mental occasion which precipitates the actual composition of the poem (still in use in the twentieth-century by ethos-occasioned writers, as in Céline's oft-repeated claim that if he had been able to get any sleep, he would never have written a line.) The beginning of the 'Night-Piece' quickly establishes a scene of troubled insomniac musing:

> By the blue taper's trembling light,
> No more I waste the wakeful night,
> Intent with endless view to pore
> The schoolmen and the sages o'er ...
> (Chalmers, 9: 364)

The poem then becomes a meditation on mortality; as such both Blair's 'Grave' and Young's 'Night Thoughts' clearly derive from it, but this only underlines the fact that it was not the moral content of Young's masterpiece which led to its success (since no such popular enthusiasm greeted Parnell's work). It was the one element which Parnell does *not* exploit: the hidden occasion.

The progression from Gray to Young seems almost fated; as Gray is the poet of twilight, Young is the poet of the night. Night and the 'I' come into their own, as the first stanza of the 'Elegy' foretold ('... leave the world to darkness and to me.'). Like the 'Elegy', Young's poem works by turning out the light. In his darkness, as in Gray's falling dusk, the poet can move more easily, asserting with less fear of contradiction the claim of occasional truth. 1742 deserves to be remembered as the real 'Year of Wonders' in modern English poetics; for in that year, even as Gray was writing his most revolutionary texts, and Robert Blair was completing 'The Grave', Edward Young began publishing 'Night Thoughts'. In such a work, beginning is everything. As I have implied throughout this study, in any work attempting to ground itself in any sort of literal belief, beginnings are crucial. The beginning of the truth-grounded poem usually establishes its claim as a non-fictive narrative, and thus, as occasionality mutates via sentimental response toward the modern poem, its claim as a pathos-object. 'Night-Thoughts' is 10 000 lines long, but its structure is simple: it consists of two parts, of unequal length but equal importance. The first is the introductory prose note; the other is the 10 000-line poem itself.

The introductory note is very brief:

THE COMPLAINT
OR
NIGHT THOUGHTS
———
PREFACE

As the Occasion of this poem was *Real,* not *Fictitious;* so the
Method pursued in it, was rather *imposed,* by what sponta-
neously arose in the Author's Mind, on that Occasion, than
meditated or *designed.* Which will appear very probable from the
Nature of it. For it differs from the common Mode of Poetry,
which is from long Narrations to draw short Morals. Here, on the
contrary, the Narrative is short, and the Morality arising from
it makes the Bulk of the Poem. The Reason of it is, that the Facts
mentioned did naturally pour these moral Reflections on the
Thought of the Writer. [italics in original] (*Night Thoughts,* 35)[5]

This preface appeared only when 'Night the Fourth' was issued
in March 1743, but its survival as an integral part of the text testifies
to its importance. As it appeared in the March 1743 printing of
'Night the Fourth', the preface consisted of the paragraph cited
followed by this one:

It is evident from the *First Night,* where three Deaths are
mentioned, that the Plan is not yet completed; for only two of
those three have yet been sung. But since this *Fourth Night*
finishes one principal and important Theme, naturally arising
from all three, *viz. the subduing our fear of death,* it will be a proper
pausing Place for the Reader, and the Writer too. And it is uncer-
tain whether Providence, or Inclination, will permit him to go
any farther. (*Night Thoughts,* 35)[6]

The reasons for the deletion of this second paragraph are clear; it
fits only at the halfway point of the poem, and uses Young's char-
acteristic technique – dark hints of autobiographical factors welling
up in (as) the text – to make a point which no longer applied when,
after all, 'inclination' or ambition went so far as to permit him to
write five more Nights, the last and ninth the longest of all.
This brief introductory note is one of the more important ancil-
lary prose texts in the history of the English lyric. Every word is
charged with meaning. Young's strategy in this Preface rests on

two interlocking claims: the occasional basis of the poem and its abstract, non-narrative form. The first claim is made directly and without elaboration: 'the Occasion of this poem was *Real,* not *Fictitious'.* The antithesis between 'real' and 'fictitious' is an emphatic device, as Young's use of italics makes clear. The reader, having absorbed this assertion, would expect some explication of the occasion in question – but that is the very last thing Young wants to provide. Young, like Gray, was driven by the harsh spotlight of the demand for occasional truth to seek the uses of obscurity; but his obscurity is simpler than Gray's, and relies on the claim of occasional validity, followed, as here, by no details whatsoever. Instead of detailing the occasion, Young instantly moves to the second, interlocking ('As/so') antithetical claim: 'As' the poem is grounded in a real occasion, 'so the Method pursued in it, was rather *imposed,* by what spontaneously arose in the Author's Mind on that Occasion, than *meditated* or *designed.'* An extraordinary statement; the poet claims, at the beginning of a 10 000-line work of blank verse, not to have 'meditated' or 'designed' the work. Who did, then? The unspecified occasion itself. This is the logic of Young's argument: the occasion produced the poem via its effect on the author's mind. The poet's part was to transcribe, in a sort of automatic writing, what the interaction of occasion and mind produced – that is, to transcribe a mental occasion.

This occasion is never described in the 'Advertisement', nor, for that matter, at any point in all nine of the lengthy 'Nights'. At some points in the poem, Young hints that he lost three loved ones within a short space of time, but he wisely declined to be any more specific. Instead, as he does in this prose 'Preface', Young moves quickly from outer-world occasion to mental occasion and then to a description of one of the 'results' of this second, mental occasion: the amorphous structure of the poem. Employing another in this chain of antitheses, Young contrasts his work with what he claims is the norm for poetry; while most poems 'from long Narrations … draw short Morals', in this work 'the Narrative is short, and the Morality arising from it makes the Bulk of the Poem'. In fact the narrative is not merely 'short', but is intentionally left out, and a powerful aporia installed in its place. It is part of the implication of non-premeditation, of automatic writing, that Young, the author, can so describe his work, as if noting a feature he was seeing, with surprise, for the first time. Having made this note, he drives home the implication of non-premeditation, by saying that 'the Reason of it is, that the Facts mentioned did naturally pour these moral Reflections on the Thought of the Writer'. This sentence repeats Young's assertion about the reactive process of composition; 'The Facts mentioned', that is the occasion 'did naturally pour' – the occasion is the active agent in the sentence, and the verb, 'pour', implies that the author is a mere vessel: '… on the Thought of the Writer'. The 'thought' of the author is here an indirect object. The agent/subject is the original occasion; that occasion precipitates a host of 'moral Reflections' in a sort of automatic chemical reaction. This precipitate is then 'poured' into the author's passive mind and then onto the page.

As this passive version of composition implies, Young wishes to avoid the imputation of invention. 'Unspecified' is the key to this occasion. 'Here … the narrative is short …' indeed; but its power over readers was all the stronger for its tantalizing aporiac presentation. If Young had been banal enough to say, 'X, Y and Z happened to me, and I thought I would pass along some reflections on these events' the 'Night Thoughts' would be forgotten; instead, his wonderfully wily presentation made every reader feel like a code-breaker, reading between the lines for a true story so terrible it could only be revealed hint by hint. This technique is borrowed from the early novelists; as Stewart has shown, memoir-novelists had made good use of this sort of narrative obscurity in using apparent code names and frightened-sounding omissions ('The town of D_____', 'Old Baron K_____ff' and so on). Young, whose overall grounding techniques are much more novelistic than the specifically poetic means developed by Gray, manages to bring this much of romanesque illusion-strategy successfully into the lyric repertoire.

Young's hint of a real-life tragedy was a far more successful grounding device, but also a more risky one, since it seems unlikely he could have produced any actual tragedies to offer as occasional basis for the poem. Had he been forced to specify the nature of that momentous event, he would have been in some trouble; for Young, like Gray and Cowper, was a typical example of the school-bred poets who led very uneventful, placid lives. To readers eager to believe in the occasional basis of the 'Night Thoughts', the very obscurity of Young's life made it possible that something had happened to him; for who would have known? The occasional assertion made in the first sentence of the 'Preface' could not be contradicted (or confirmed, either), because its terms are so vague that there is nothing to contradict.

The poem is divided into nine sections, nine 'Nights'. The stated subject of 'Night the First' is 'Life, Death and Immortality'. This seemed, to the eager cryptographer-readers Young had tantalized with vague hints of tragedy, to promise some answers. Anything with the word 'Death' in it would be likely, especially after the hints of the 'Preface', to offer some data on the death[s] in question, the occasioning death[s]. But there is no immediate payoff. Instead, the first lines of the first 'Night' begin with a description of insomnia. Insomnia here functions as yet another anti-premeditation device; the author, far from trying to impose a literary product on the reader, was merely trying to sleep; the text is the product of his failure, caused – precisely like insomnia – by the physical by-products of morally-charged memories. This is implication of the first lines of the poem:

> Tir'd Nature's sweet restorer, balmy *Sleep!*
> He, like the World, his ready visit pays
> Where Fortune smiles; the wretched he forsakes;
> Swift on his downy pinion flies from Woe,
> And lights on Lids unsully'd with a Tear.
>   From short (as usual) and disturbed Repose,
> I wake: How happy they, who wake no more!
>   (Young, 37)

The present-tense description of the moment of waking adds to the ethos of spontaneity which Young desires above all, while the apparently spontaneous, bracketed interjection, '(as usual)' broadly hints that this is far from the first time the author has so awakened. The turn to the sermonic, general voice is done by the next phrase, '... How happy they, who wake no more!' The reader, led by the 'Preface' to expect autobiographical revelations, expects this periphrastic mention of the dead to lead to the revelation of the poem's funereal occasion; instead, Young, borrowing from Hamlet's soliloquy, slides, via epanorthosis, to the fear of the after-life ('Yet that were vain, if dreams infest the grave') and quickly back to the vaguely-implied occasion:

> I wake, emerging from a sea of Dreams
> Tumultuous; where my wreck'd desponding Thought
> From wave to wave of *Fancy'd* misery,
> At random drove, her helm of reason lost.

> Though now restor'd, 'tis only Change of pain,
> (A bitter change,) severer for severe.
>
> (Young, 37)

The speaker, using a shipwreck metaphor, places the terror of bad dreams in a lesser/greater topos, with the terrors of waking occupying the place of the greater. What makes this *commutatio* so remarkable is that, like the one Cowper deploys at the end of 'The Cast-away', Young's *commutatio* never reveals what this greater waking fear involves. The reader is thus drawn to keep reading, hoping to collect enough narrative clues to piece together a coherent story. Young, well aware of the eager audience's tendency to sift large volumes of poetry for such clues, continues scattering them bit by bit, never quite giving away the occasion. In this way, he provides epideictic grounding to a huge expanse of blank verse. General and particular themes, public sermon and private, implied lament, weave together throughout these lengthy 'Nights'. Generally speaking, Young keeps the same ratio of these elements throughout all nine 'Nights'. The Sermon – the generalized preaching of morality – is by far the bigger chunk of the poem, at least 9000 of the 10000-odd lines. But the much smaller element, the implicitly occasional lament, is at least as important as the sermonic (and in fact, since this element is uniquely responsible for the success of 'Night Thoughts', it could claim to be the more important of the two.)

The putatively occasional element is usually placed in tantalizing positions, at the very beginning or ending of a long sermonic passage, as in this passage from 'Night the First' which depicts the insomniac speaker's perception of the darkness around him:

> *Night,* sable Goddess ...
> ... and Darkness, how profound?
> Nor Eye, nor list'ning Ear, an object finds;
> Creation sleeps. 'T is as the general Pulse
> Of life stood still, and Nature made a Pause;
> An aweful pause! prophetic of her End.
> And let her prophecy be soon fulfil'd;
> Fate! Drop the Curtain; I can lose no more.
>
> (Young, 37)

The hint of a real-life occasion occurs in the last phrase of the citation: 'I can lose no more'. It, like the rest of these early hints, seems to suggest a death or deaths as occasional basis of the poem. But the suggestion is all the reader gets; the next line returns to the generalizing, sermonic voice with an apostrophe to *'Silence* and *Darkness'*. The first half of 'Night the First' does no more than maintain the succession of parenthetical aporiac phrases promising occasional revelation. The phrases containing the promise begin to occur at intervals of a hundred lines, as if Young thought the audience needed fresh hints at that interval if they were to continue reading. The phrases which hint at occasionality are as regular in their rhetorical structure as in their placing; most are parenthetical epanorthoses which seem to be forced out of the speaker (again the implication of unpremeditation) who seems to want to hide his suffering:

> … O lead my Mind,
> (a Mind that fain would wander from its Woe)
> Lead it through various scenes of Life and Death …
> (Young, 38)

This typical interruption links two sermonic passages by seeming to slip and offer a glimpse of the tormented speaker's thoughts. The speaker hints at his 'Woe' in the parenthetical correction, halting the sentence to modify the noun 'Mind' into one which wants to avoid its private suffering. The imperative sentence then goes on its way ('Lead it through various scenes …') as if the shaken speaker has recovered himself and forced himself to go on with his pious abstractions. Thus the meaning of the imperative sentence – the prayer to have the mind 'led' away from its own, occasional troubles – is reproduced by the rhetoric of the passage, with its apparently unwilled interpolations of private suffering, deftly placed between general, sermonic stretches.

This is the way Young 'allows' his intricate, disingenuous 'confessions' to come tumbling out: as momentary lapses in the iron self-control of a speaker determined not to reveal the 'real, not fictitious' occasion he promised the reader. The sententia leads, again and again, to the aporiac exclamation:

> Night-visions may befriend (as sung above):
> Our *waking* Dreams are fatal. How I dreamt
> Of things Impossible? (Could Sleep do more?)

> Of Joys perpetual in perpetual Change!
> Of stable Pleasures on the tossing Wave....
> (Young, 41)

The generalization about the evils of fancy gives way, as if involuntarily, to the confessional exclamation 'How I dreamt / of things Impossible?' Again the reader expects Young to tell all, in this moment of pain; but of course, that would be 'fatal' indeed, and so the revelation blurs again, ending in implications of mortality as vague as those 'sung above'.

Young first reveals details of his supposed tragedy halfway through 'Night the First'. The hint, which is vague enough, was yet sufficiently specific to send many avid detective-readers looking for its autobiographical basis:

> Death! Great Proprietor of all! ...
> ... why exhaust
> Thy *partial* Quiver on a Mark so mean?
> Why, thy *peculiar* rancor wreck'd on me?
> Insatiate Archer! could not One suffice?
> Thy shaft flew thrice, and thrice my Peace was slain;
> And thrice, e're thrice yon Moon had fill'd her Horn ...
> (Young, 42)

This passage seems to suggest that Young had witnessed three deaths (presumably of persons close to him) in less than three months. So, at any rate, contemporary readers interpreted it; and the seriousness with which they investigated this hint is one of the most telling proofs of the importance of Stewart's 'literal belief' to ethos-centred modern English poetry.

Sir Herbert Croft's *Life of Young*, aware of the popular curiosity about Young's alleged three tragedies, takes as its first task the defusing of readers' expectations. Croft – who, as author of *Love and Madness*, a sensationalized dramatization of Chatterton's career, had a hand in the poetics of authenticity himself – devotes almost the entirety of his biography of Young to calming down readers excited by the hinted confessions of 'Night Thoughts'. Such readers could quickly become offended when they happened to encounter the author of 'The Complaint' in company; expecting to find a melancholy hermit, they were disgusted to find a cheery, witty cleric:

Young's cheerfulness in company, indeed, quite offended the more solemn of his admirers, who wished the author of the *Night Thoughts* to behave always in character with his poem…. [One admirer], we are told, 'was much disappointed in his conversation. It appeared to her light, trifling and full of puns'. (Forster, 278)

Croft's task as biographer was to negotiate some truce between Young's admirers, who expected this sort of demonstrable melancholy, and the actual narrative of the *Life of Young* – the simple tale of a bland, well-meaning clergyman to whom virtually nothing, good or bad, had ever happened. Croft's introductory letter, appended to his *Life of Young*, deals immediately with the relation of Young's life and work:

Of great men, something must always be said to gratify curiosity. Of the illustrious author of the Night Thoughts much has been told of which there never could have been proofs; and little care seems to have been taken to tell that of which proofs, with little trouble, might have been procured. (Chalmers, 13: 339)

Croft is speaking here of the attempts made by readers to derive the life from the work; to puzzle out Young's troubles from the hints in 'Night Thoughts'. But two pages later, Croft reveals the literary trait that made it inevitable that readers would try to track down the biographical basis of Young's hints:

The affectionate mention of the death of his friend Harrison … at the close of this poem ['Epistle to … Lord Landsdowne'] is an instance of Young's art, which displayed itself so wonderfully some time afterwards in the Night Thoughts, of making the public a party in his private sorrow. (Chalmers, 13: 341)

As Croft states, the essence of 'Young's art' lay in 'making the public a party in his private sorrow'. It was, of course, in the 'Night Thoughts' that this 'art' reached its peak, but the 'Night Thoughts' are a late production, and, as Croft reveals, Young's artful use of 'private sorrow' predates that work by decades. Croft finds it in Young's poem on the death of Addison (1719):

In 1719 [Young] lamented the death of Addison, in a letter

addressed to their common friend Tickell. For the secret history of the following lines, if they contain any, it is now vain to seek:

> *In joy once joined,* in sorrow, now, for years –
> Partner in grief, and brother to my tears,
> Tickell, accept this verse, thy mournful due.
> (Chalmers, 13: 345; italics in original)

This is clearly an early version of the hinted-occasion technique deployed at such length in the 'Night Thoughts'. 'In joy once joined ...' is indecipherable even to Croft. Here Young is able to use a different convention to supply slight hints: his disingenuous convention of carrying on a verse conversation with Tickell makes it possible for him to refer quickly and obliquely to a shared past, as to a good friend. The reader must guess (is meant to guess).

These hinted-occasionals did not form the bulk of Young's early work; most of his youthful poems were flattering panegyrics, occasional in a straightforward and (in the view of later readers of the 'Night Thoughts') uninteresting way. Croft says of these works that 'If Young must be acknowledged a ready celebrator, he did not endeavour, or did not choose, to be a lasting one.' (Chalmers, 13: 347) It was the manipulation of 'private sorrow' and the occasion which alone made Young a poet his contemporaries wanted to read. As Croft says,

> In 1734 ... [Young] now appears to have given up all hopes of overtaking Pindar, and perhaps at last resolved to turn his ambition to some original species of poetry. This poem [Young's final 'public' poem] concludes with a formal farewell to Ode, which few of Young's readers will regret ...
>
> In a species of poetry altogether his own, he next tried his skill, and succeeded. (Chalmers, 13: 351)

This new 'species of poetry' is the 'Night Thoughts'; and Croft's manner of introducing it in his 'Life of Young' is significant. The passage is a long one, but important enough to quote in full:

> Of his wife [Young] was deprived in 1741. [Mrs. Young] had lost, after her marriage with Young, an amiable daughter, by her former husband, just after she was married to Mr. Temple, son of Lord Palmerston. Mr. Temple did not long remain after his wife,

though he was married a second time.... Mr. and Mrs. Temple have generally been considered as Philander and Narcissa [of 'Night Thoughts']. From the great friendship which constantly subsisted between Mr. Temple and Young, as well as from other circumstances, it is probable that the poet had both him and Mrs. Temple in view for these characters; though at the same time some passages respecting Philander do not appear to suit either Mr. Temple or any other person with whom Young was known to be connected or acquainted, while all the circumstances relating to Narcissa have been constantly found applicable to Young's daughter-in-Law.

At what short intervals the poet tells us he was wounded by the deaths of the three persons particularly lamented, none that has read The Night Thoughts (and who has not read them?) needs to be informed.

> Insatiate Archer! could not One suffice?
> Thy shaft flew thrice; and thrice my Peace was slain;
> And thrice, e're thrice yon Moon had fill'd her horn.

Yet how it is possible that Mr. and Mrs. Temple and lady Elizabeth Young could be these three victims, over whom Young has hitherto been pitied for having to pour the 'midnight sorrows' of his religious poetry; Mrs. Temple died in 1736; Mr. Temple, four years afterwards, in 1740; and the poet's wife seven months after Mr. Temple, in 1741. How could the insatiate Archer thrice slay his peace, in these three persons, 'ere thrice the Moon had fill'd her horn'?

But in the short preface to The Complaint he seriously tells us, 'that the occasion of this poem was real, not fictitious; and that the facts mentioned did naturally pour these moral reflections on the thought of the writer'. It is probable, therefore, that in these three contradictory lines the poet complains more than the father-in-law, the friend, or the widower. (Chalmers, 13: 351–2)

Croft's preferred method of construing the crucial 'insatiate Archer' passage of the poem is that of literal belief; he immediately begins looking for correspondences between the life and the work. He has no doubts about the nature of the occasions he is seeking: three deaths. But when Croft (like many another devoted reader of 'Night Thoughts') looks for the biographical proofs he needs, they cannot be found. The only death which seems, at first, to fit the bill is that of Young's wife in 1741, just before the poem is begun. But where are the other two deaths? The only ones Croft can supply are those of Young's wife's daughter by a previous marriage and her husband. The grown, married daughter of a previous marriage is not quite the close relative Croft and other readers eager for occasional grounding would have liked to find undergirding the massive epideictic pathos of the 'Night Thoughts'; but someone, some real, verifiable death, must be found, and she seems closest. A third death is still required, however, and for this Croft can only offer a very dubious nominee: Mr. Temple, the husband of the wife's-daughter-by-a-previous-marriage. Adding to the weakness of Mr. Temple's candidacy is the fact that, having lost that particular Mrs. Temple, he managed to find time to marry a new Mrs. Temple, unrelated to Young in any way, before dying himself.

This is not the sort of basis trusting readers had in mind, but it could have offered some sort of occasioning foundation to the text, were it not for the fact that Young, seeking to amplify the pathetic effect of his hinted tragedy, made the basic error of specificity. He names a precise, if grandly-phrased, period of time in which the three tragedies occurred: 'ere thrice yon Moon had fill'd her horn.' – that is, in less than three months time.

This is the last straw for Croft's dogged attempt to ground the text to his satisfaction. Death-dates can be easily checked, and these simply do not check out. Croft's puzzled tone, in explaining the discrepancies, refers directly to the all-important 'Preface', demonstrating the powerful impact such a direct assertion must have had on many readers less acclimated to the literary game than the professional, Croft.

But even for Croft, there is clearly something lost when the occasional foundation falls away. There is a bitterness, born of the consequences of a poetics founded on the truth/lie antithesis, in Croft's final antithetical apportioning of Young's motive powers in creating the 'Night Thoughts': 'in these contradictory lines the poet complains more than the father-in-law, the friend, or the widower'. Croft's awareness of the loss of pathetic effect his embarrassed revelation is likely to have on the 'unsophisticated reader' is clear; he attempts to blur, on his own, the occasional claims Young had made too clear:

That domestic grief is, in the first instance, to be thanked for these ornaments to our language, it is impossible to deny. Nor would it be common hardiness to contend, that worldly discontent had no hand in these joint productions of poetry and piety. Yet am I by no means sure that, at any rate, we should not have had something of the same colour from Young's pencil ... In so long a life, causes for discontent and occasions for grief must have occurred. It is not clear to me that his Muse was not sitting upon the watch for the first which happened.

... Still, is it altogether fair to dress up the poet for the man, and to bring the gloominess of the *Night Thoughts* to prove the gloominess of Young ...? (Chalmers, 13: 352–3)

Croft's evident anxiety about the ethics of a faked occasion leads him to ask this crucial question. Is the ethos of the poet the ground of authenticity? Must it not be, when the ground of straightforward occasionality – which Croft, reluctantly, has just disproved – is removed? Croft, writing on the cusp of an historical shift from 'worldly discontent' (public occasion) to mental occasion, turns to the ethos of the poet as ground for validity. Young's poem itself is designed to blur the line between these two kinds of occasional grounding; Young's only mistake – and it should be remembered that Young is an experimental poet, working in what Croft rightly calls 'a new species of poetry' – was to be too specific in hinting at the nature and timing of the outward occasions which triggered the mental one. But Croft knows well that contemporary readers are not ready to accept a purely mental occasion:

Readers I know there are of a strange turn of mind, who will hereafter peruse the Night Thoughts with less satisfaction; who will wish they had still been deceived; who will quarrel with me for discovering that no such character [existed]. (Chalmers, 13: 353)

Two of the dead hinted at by Young in 'Night the First' are named at last: they are Philander (supposedly Mr. Temple) and Narcissa. Philander is the first of the three victims whose fate is discussed in 'Night the First'; an apostrophe to him follows the discussion of earthly happiness:

> Mine dy'd with thee, *Philander*! thy last Sigh
> Dissolv'd the charm; the disenchanted Earth

> Lost all her Lustre; where, her glittering Towers?
> (Young, 46)

According to the tantalizing alternation Young has pursued
throughout the poem, this momentary revelation of personal grief
lasts only a line; '... where, her glittering Towers?' and leads,
naturally, back to a generalized, sententious passage. But the hint
of autobiographical basis returns; after sententia comes occasion,
blurred hints about Philander's death:

> ... O how Ambition flush'd
> Thy glowing cheek? Ambition truly great,
> Of virtuous Praise: Death's subtle seed within,
> (Sly, treacherous Miner!) working in the Dark,
> Smil'd at thy well-concerted scheme, and beckon'd
> The Worm to riot on that Rose so red,
> Unfaded e're it fell; one moment's Prey!
> (Young, 46)

The hints of a narrative are fairly strong (by the standards of
'Night Thoughts') here: Philander was apparently an ambitious,
noble young man who died in some sudden way. These hints,
which must suffice the reader for the rest of the poem, are as close
to a specific grounding as Young is willing to get. For the remain-
der of the poem, the apostrophes to the dead and the exclamatios
their memories summon up are the only reminders of occasional-
ity, except for the one living character: Lorenzo. Lorenzo is the
most frequently invoked character of the poem; he is designed to
link the occasional and the didactic themes by providing a living
auditor, a survivor as it were of the 'domestic grief' which has over-
whelmed the speaker, an auditor to whom all Young's pious advice
may be apostrophically addressed. After the other characters have
dropped out of the poem in 'Nights' four through nine, it is only
Lorenzo who is left to provide even the hint of the wash of occa-
sionality in which Young tries to moisten his otherwise dry,
didactic poem. 'Lorenzo', the name itself, is invoked (in italics) at
the beginning of each new passage, on the average of once every
fifty lines, throughout the entire poem. The invocations are largely
alike, as this small sample will show:

For what calls *thy* Disease *Lorenzo?* not
For *Esculapian*, but for *moral* Aid.
                    (Young, 52)

Lorenzo, more than miracles we want!
Lorenzo – O for Yesterdays to come!
                    (Young, 59)

But, here, *Lorenzo,* the Delusion lies …
                    (Young, 62)

Lorenzo! pardon what my Love extorts,
An honest Love, and not afraid to frown.
                    (Young, 65)

The Vale of Death!…
… Fit Walk, *Lorenzo,* for proud human Thought!
                    (Young, 79)

Lorenzo! no, the Thought of Death indulge …
                    (Young, 81)

For the twentieth-century reader, it is clear enough that 'Lorenzo' is simply an occasioning and vivifying trope Young uses to recontextualize a sprawling didactic text which would otherwise lose even the most dedicated readers. Even with 'Lorenzo's' help, Croft implies that readers were much more excited by the first four 'Nights' than the latter five (Chalmers, 13: 352). But the running apostrophe to 'Lorenzo' worked for the contemporary audience; they thought him, like 'Philander' and 'Narcissa', an actual person whose hidden identity could be successfully deduced from the textual evidence. Naturally, then, readers certain that the occasional basis of the poem was as clear and straightforward as Young declared it to be in his 'Preface' went looking for the identity of Lorenzo, the somewhat dissolute young man who is implicitly characterized by the speaker's admonitions to him, as represented by the sample above.

The implied relationship between the speaker and 'Lorenzo' led most readers to the judgement that Lorenzo had to be Young's son, Frederick. Croft, uneasily pursuing his ethos-as-occasion explanation of Young's narrative discrepancies, concedes that Young's

contemporaries believe … that [Frederick Young's] debauched and reprobate life cast a Stygian gloom over the evening of his father's days ... and succeeded at last in bringing his 'gray hairs with sorrow to the grave'. (Chalmers, 13: 353)

The intensity with which readers had made this awkward identification is indicated by the vehemence with which Croft, in his 'Life of Young', tries to refute it. But Croft is aware that, in doing so, he may spoil the pleasure of the text for those readers who demand occasional grounding:

> Readers I know there are of a strange turn of mind, who will hereafter peruse the Night Thoughts with less satisfaction; who will wish they had still been deceived; who will quarrel with me for discovering that no such character as their Lorenzo ever yet disgraced human nature, or broke a father's heart. Yet would these admirers of the sublime and terrible be offended, should you set them down for cruel and for savage. (Chalmers, 13: 353)

Of course the reader who is insistent on occasional grounding would be intimidated by the charge of coldheartedness; such a reader is also likely to be the sentimental reader, who shares with the occasionally-grounded reader an insistence on the epideictic and cathartic aspects of the reading experience. To call such people cruel would not merely offend, but astonish them; they are the people of sensibility. They merely want assurance that they have not been fooled; that they do have something real to weep over. Thus MacKenzie's sardonic/sentimental axiom that 'one is ashamed to be pleased with the work of one knows not whom', cited above.

By creating this dilemma, this fundamental collision between occasional and sentimental poetics, Croft tries to wean the sentimentally-inclined reader away from the requirement of occasional/autobiographical truth in responding to 'Night Thoughts'. Yet even Croft, unhappily aware that Young has faked or at least altered some of the essential occasional bases of the poem, is loathe to abandon the notion that Lorenzo must be some real person, someone close to the author. A son is simply too close; that would be nightmare, not sentiment. Moreover, as Croft points out, the dates simply do not add up to an identification of Frederick as 'Lorenzo'; 'Young's child [Frederick] was not born till June 1733. In 1741 this Lorenzo, this finished infidel ... was only eight years old'. (Chalmers, 13: 354)

But after having cleared the son of being 'Lorenzo', Croft cannot abandon the idea of occasional grounding altogether; he adopts, in a remarkable way, the manner Young developed in the 'Night Thoughts' he blurs, while seeming to reveal, biographical implications. At one point, Croft hints that the elusive 'Lorenzo' was a friend of Young's during a youthful, dissolute period, and then seems to hint that Young is addressing his own, younger self – and then returns, rather inconsistently, to the idea that Lorenzo was, in fact, Young's son, who is this time implicated in minor offences.

Borrowing his subject's favourite technique, Croft ends with an aporia, hinting to Samuel Johnson, who solicited Croft's account of Young, that the truth is too terrible to tell:

> He who is connected with the author of the Night Thoughts, only by veneration for the poet and the Christian, may be allowed to observe, that Young is one of those, concerning whom, as you remark in your account of Addison, it is proper rather to say 'nothing that is false than all that is true'. (Chalmers, 13: 357)

Thus the biographer, attempting at first to confirm the autobiographical grounding of the poem and finding no evidence with which to do so, is led by a tortuous series of alternative explanations back to the technique which proved successful in grounding the poem itself: the broadly-hinted aporia of a 'domestic grief' too terrible to be told in full. This is Young's great contribution to the emergent poetics of the mental occasion. Its strength is its ability, evident in the 'Night Thoughts', to provide a sort of glaze of occasional urgency to what must strike the twentieth-century reader as a numbingly boring sermonic text. The drawback of the hinted-occasion technique is akin to that of the found-text method: the problem of verifiability. Young's method is not quite so vulnerable to the researches of scholars as was that of the forgers of fake 'ancient' texts, MacPherson or Chatterton; but Young did clearly go too far in specifying not only the number and interval of the three tragedies but their nature: three deaths. Death, while the most traditional and pathos-charged of occasioning events, is also by its nature the most easy to verify – or disprove. As Croft's embarrassed account makes clear, the failure to find the deaths in question in the record seriously damaged the pathetic impact of the 'Night Thoughts'.

The tactic to which Croft, and other committed admirers of Young, resorted when straightforward occasional grounding for the 'Night Thoughts' could not be found, is a significant one: in place of solid biographical verification of the occasional claims of the poem, readers emotionally committed to its authenticity resorted to 'urban legends' re-grounding the ethos of the author, making Young's gloomy nature a mental event – depression as occasion. Croft records two interesting examples. First, he offers this gothic anecdote:

> When Young was writing a tragedy, Grafton is said by Spence to have sent him a human skull, with a candle in it, as a lamp; and the poet is reported to have used it. (Chalmers, 13: 352)

The skull (not likely to have been displayed by the pious and ambitious Young) functions in Croft's biography as a replacement for the missing three corpses. It relocates the authenticity of the occasion in a mental event (a predisposition toward the macabre), an ethos. Croft follows this anecdote with another:

> What [Young] calls the *true* Estimate of Human Life, which has already been mentioned, exhibits only the wrong side of the tapestry; and, being asked why he did not show the right, [Young] is said to have replied, that he could not. By others it has been told me that this was finished; but that, before there existed any copy, it was torn in pieces by a lady's monkey. (Chalmers, 13: 353)

This legend reveals a strange anxiety among Young's readers; they clearly would like to believe him utterly morbid and incapable of writing anything other than the depressing 'Night Thoughts', because, if the morbid tone of the poem could be grounded in the author's depressive tendencies, then the authenticity of the poem is restored, without the necessity of dead relatives. But at the same time, they hoped that their favourite author *did* write a happier version of the world, but that this redeeming text was ripped apart by 'a lady's monkey' – an animal proverbially associated with Satanic mischief. The monkey is a great invention in its own right; it satisfies both desires, since it suggests that Young wanted to offer a redemptive vision, but was simply not fated to do so.

The genesis of all these tales is the readers' desire to find a new ground for the poem. This reader anxiety is proof that Young's occasioning technique, though influential and important, was not quite perfected. His readers actually led the way with the legends about skulls and monkeys: they transfer authenticity toward ethos, and away from funereal occasions.

The innovations developed in the realm of occasioning ethos spread quickly through English poetic culture. William Shenstone, a typical product of the emergent ethical poetics, exemplifies, in his elegies and his 'Essay on Elegy' (Chalmers, 13: 263), the new method of grounding the text in the biography, without the need for specific, verifiable events. Shenstone's life shares with those of Young, Gray and Cowper a tone of respectable uneventfulness. It may be that this sort of uneventful respectability had a part in stimulating the development of the mental occasion as poetic grounding; in lives circumscribed by polite learning, country walks, and adherence to the sterner virtue which the aging century demanded, mental events were often the only ones available for commemoration. Johnson puts the matter politely in saying of Shenstone that 'His life was unstained by any crime', while Gray, in a typically acute and cruel letter, stresses the mixture of dulness and ambition which defined Shenstone's life:

> Poor man! he was always wishing for money, for fame, and other distinctions: and his whole philosophy consisted in living against his will in retirement, and in a place which his taste had adorned, but which he only enjoyed when people of note came to see and commend it: his correspondence is about nothing else but this place and his own writings, with two or three neighboring clergymen, who wrote verses too. (Chalmers, 13: 259)

This is a life characterized by the very feature which Shenstone emphasizes in the essay on elegy: the development, for literary presentation, of a stylized 'sensitive' ethos intended to serve as the grounding of elegiac poetry (an ancient *topos* whose successive incarnations in English literature are traced in detail by Williams in *The Country and the City*). According to Gray, Shenstone's hermitage was torment to him unless there was someone there to see it. This oxymoronic ethos – a secluded retreat which must have witnesses – is one example of a phenomenon which seems to characterize the work of the mid- to late-century in England: as poetry turns toward ethical grounding, the work gives way to the life, and effort to circumvent occasional requirements is devoted, more and more, to the polishing, and presentation for others' contemplation, of a suitable ethos. This is the constant theme of the young Boswell's journals in London and Holland during the years 1762–1764. Boswell leaves Edinburgh for London and salutes an ancient landmark, watching himself do so and recording the action as if he were himself 'The Man of Feeling', as if his life were already translated into literary narrative:

> I ... bowed thrice before Arthur Seat, that lofty romantic mountain on which I have often strayed in my days of youth [n.b. Boswell is twenty-two], indulged meditation and felt the rapture of a soul filled with ideas of the magnificence of GOD and his creation. Having thus gratified my agreeable whim and superstitious humour, I felt a warm glow of satisfaction. Indeed, I have a strong turn of what the cool part of mankind have named superstition. But this proceeds from my genius for poetry, which ascribes many fanciful properties to everything. This I have great pleasure from; as I have now by experience and reflection gained the command of it so far that I can keep it within just bounds by the power of reason, without losing the agreeable feeling and play to the imagination which it bestows. I am surely much happier in this way than if I just considered ... Arthur Seat as so much earth and rock raised above the neighbouring plains. (Boswell, *London Journal*, 41–2)

'I am surely much happier ...' – phrases like this, self-referential and meant to be reassuring, recur endlessly in Boswell's journals, reflecting the desperate concern of the aspiring mid-century literary contender with maintenance of his ethos. Boswell goes to some lengths to make his good-byes to Edinburgh look like those of a man of sensibility; but even so, he must endlessly reassure himself that he is in fact such, and not part of the much more numerous and insensible 'cool part of mankind'. For thousands of aspiring geniuses like Boswell, ethos, and not production of literary work, defines the literary man. 'Am I not a genius?' is Boswell's constant, insatiable question in his youthful journals; and it is not quite the rhetorical question it seems. When belief in the poet's ethos has been secured, any poems backed by that ethos are assured of success. Belief in the text precedes the reading of it; belief in the text, by 1750, is a matter of ethos.

Shenstone's life and works reflect the change. Shenstone promises the reader, 'Elegies Written on Many Different Occasions', but the innovation which Shenstone reveals in the poems and defends in the 'Prefatory Essay on Elegy' attached to the text is the redefinition and expansion of 'occasion'; from a public event to a private, mental one, of which the elegy is the 'effusion'.

Shenstone's essay begins by redefining elegy away from funereal occasion and toward the mental event or pathetic effect associated with it. The occasion proper, in this new definition, is simply the original, antique, precipitate cause of an elegy:

> I think we may conclude … that elegy, in its true and genuine acceptation, includes a tender and querulous idea: that it looks upon this as its peculiar characteristic, and so long as this is thoroughly sustained, admits of a variety of subjects; which, by its manner of treating them, it renders its own. It throws its melancholy stole over pretty different objects; which, like the dresses at a funeral procession, gives them all a kind of solemn and uniform appearance. (Chalmers, 13: 263)

Shenstone's effort here is clearly the transfer of the definitive elegiac component ('its peculiar characteristic') from subject (mourning) to tone ('tender and querulous'). The second half of the cited paragraph reiterates this notion in several ways, ending with the trope of the funeral procession as mere 'dresses' – a manner of dressing any subject whatever so that it looks like what is associated specifically with death. Shenstone's anxiety over the scope of elegy is clear:

> It is probable that elegies were written at first upon the death of intimate friends and near relations; celebrated beauties, or favourite mistresses; beneficent governors, and illustrious men…. After these subjects were sufficiently exhausted, and the severity of fate displayed in the most affecting instances, the poets sought occasion to vary their complaints. (Chalmers, 13: 263)

In this 'historical' passage, Shenstone describes, not the progress of elegy from Greece to the present but the history of elegy in his own time. Like many another literary historian, he projects changes taking place in his own lifetime backwards to antiquity, and then explains current evolutionary developments as a reassuringly slow march from ancient to modern. What Shenstone means to do here is to give the expansion of the occasions available to the elegist 'the glamour of antiquity'; he fixes the narrow occasional poetics at the earliest stages of antiquity (when in fact it had reigned most strongly in the seventeenth century). Shenstone then states quite directly that it was the 'famine of occasions' in the late seventeenth and early eighteenth century which drove the elegists to seek new topics: 'After these subjects were sufficiently exhausted … the poets sought occasion to vary their complaints'. As a description of elegiac rules over the millennia, this is wrong; but as a summary of changes taking place circa 1750, it is concise and accurate. Even the verbal form Shenstone chooses is resonant with meaning: the poets 'sought occasion to vary their complaints'. That is: the mid-eighteenth-century poets sought unturned occasions – dying peasants, dying animals, and most of all the ephemeral mental states these new-modelled occasions produce.

Shenstone goes on to give his artificially periodized version of the mid-century's progress in seeking new occasions:

> … the next tender species of sorrow that presented itself, was the grief of absent or neglected lovers. And this indulgence might indeed be allowed them; but … they were not contented. They had obtained a small corner in the province of love, and they took advantage, from thence, to overrun the whole territory. They sung its spoils, triumphs, ovations and rejoicings, as well as the captivity and exequies that attended it. They gave the name of elegy to their pleasantries as well as lamentations; till at last, through their abundant fondness for the myrtle, they forgot that the cypress was their peculiar garland. (Chalmers, 13: 263)

Again, this 'history' actually describes changes which are occurring within Shenstone's lifetime. Shenstone says that poets, presumably hoping for an added epideictic charge, applied the term 'Elegy' to love poetry ('pleasantries'). This, he implies, was a misapplication of the term. This seems odd, since Shenstone's evident intention is to expand the range of the term 'elegy'; but in fact, his definition is tonal, and thus he can say with at least some consistency that 'pleasantries' are not fit to be called elegy. (They are, as it were, too 'pleasant'.) This is his next assertion:

> In this it is probable that [poets] deviated from the original design of elegy; and it should seem, that any kind of subjects,

treated in such a manner as to diffuse a pleasing melancholy, might far better deserve the name, than the facetious mirth and libertine festivity of the successful votaries of love. (Chalmers, 13: 264)

This is the crucial distinction: any text which has the proper physical effect on the reader (since the emergent ethos-sentimental poetics demands measurable physical response to pathetic efforts) is worthy of being termed an elegy. Subject, as such, is not a criterion; tone and physical effect are the only valid criteria. This is the reason he places the odd adjective 'successful' before the excluded category, 'votaries of love'. A successful 'votar[y] of love' will not possess the necessary 'sadful' ethos, and must thus be excluded from the elegists' ranks. A failed lover, on the other hand, is presumably welcome to be called an elegist. In this tonal/ethical criterion for the claim of mutated occasional grounding can be seen the beginnings of the stereotype of the modern poet: an isolated, depressed wanderer experiencing an unending chain of mental events united by their unvarying depressiveness.

Shenstone in fact divides his new-modelled elegy from older, dramatic forms, via a public/private antithesis: 'Epic and tragedy chiefly recommend the public virtues; elegy is of a species which elevates and endears the private'. (Chalmers, 13: 264) This is the link between Gray's, Young's and Shenstone's convergent poetic insights; the elegy, for all three, has become the form which celebrates the obscure – whether the obscure be defined as those people, like Gray's peasants, who are socially obscure; or as those events which, like Young's elusive threesome of terrible, private griefs, are narratively obscure; or as Shenstone's retirement to the obscurity of a country retreat, where the mental events of a circumscribed and outwardly eventless life may be celebrated at length. Shenstone defines the style of this celebration of obscurity by employing again the telltale metaphor of mourning dress:

As to the style of elegy … [i]t should imitate the voice and language of grief, or if a metaphor of dress be more agreeable; it should be simple and diffuse, and flowing as a mourner's veil. A versification therefore is desirable, which, by indulging a free and unconstrained expression, may admit of that simplicity which elegy requires. (Chalmers, 13: 264)

Shenstone has already referred, in the second paragraph of the 'Prefatory Essay on Elegy' to funeral dress, calling elegiac tone a 'melancholy stole' which deepens pathetic effect 'like the dresses at a funeral procession'. Here he demonstrates the importance of this metaphor by using it again ('flowing as a mourner's veil') and by identifying the metaphor as such ('if a metaphor of dress be more agreeable') before offering it to the reader, as if to make sure that no reader could miss his point. The metaphor is indeed a crucial one. Shenstone's first argumentative move in the 'Essay' is to detach elegiac *tone* (grief) from elegiac *subject* (death). The metaphor of funeral dress does exactly the same thing in metaphorical terms: it detaches the pathos of the epideictic/funereal occasion from that occasion itself. This is what Gray's 'Elegy' does as well; and this is the great achievement of the 'Night Thoughts'; and of Blair's 'The Grave'. All these poems, by various means, borrow funeral dress, as it were, without having to wait for a real, public occasion.

Shenstone's prescription of ordinary English diction (which is what he means by 'style') is an important part of the prescription for an ethos-centered, mentally-occasioned lyric. He identifies this diction, in the passage cited above, as contributing to the feeling of occasionality – as part of the mourner's dress. By imitating the unpremeditated grieving effusion of the mourner, this simplified, home-grown diction helps to attribute the poem to an occasion, however obscured, and thus makes for 'that simplicity which elegy requires'.

Shenstone finally turns his prescriptions back toward his own work, ending with a self-referential testimonial reminiscent of Young's – and even more, of Wordsworth's:

> The author of the following elegies entered on his subjects occasionally, as particular incidents in life suggested, or dispositions of mind recommended them to his choice. If he describes a rural landscape, or unfolds the train of sentiments it inspired, he fairly drew his picture from the spot; and felt very sensibly the affection he communicates. If he speaks of his humble shed, his flocks and his fleeces, he does not counterfeit the scene, who, having (whether through choice or necessity is not material) retired betimes to country solitudes, and sought his happiness in rural employments, has a right to consider himself as a real shepherd. The flocks, the meadows, and the grottoes, are his own, and the embellishment of his farm his sole amusement. As the sentiments

therefore were inspired by nature, and that in the earlier part of his life, he hopes they will retain a natural appearance …(Chalmers, 13: 265)

This testimonial to the ethos undergirding the poems fits so well with Gray's bitter depiction of Shenstone's literary life that it amounts to a corroboration of Gray's implication that Shenstone had staged his retreat to the countryside as a prop to his poetic ethos, and that Shenstone actually pined in frustration when there was no one to witness his ethos. Shenstone first claims, in the direct prefatory way pioneered by Young, that every one of his poems is in fact grounded in an occasion. But Shenstone immediately qualifies this assertion by redefining occasion; first he names 'particular incidents' and then adds 'or dispositions of the mind' as categories of grounding occasion. The provision of 'dispositions of the mind' as basis of occasion is of course what is new in this definition – the provision of the mental event as an occasion in itself, no longer (as in Young's and Gray's works) listed as a secondary, stimulated occasion provoked by an actual event (a visit to a graveyard, for example) but as a complete foundation for occasionality in itself. The only secure landscape the mid-century poet could find in which to experience unassailable poetic occasions was intra-cranial space. Shenstone, a second-generation poet of the mental occasion, thus makes explicit the tendency which had been visible in the greater works which just preceded his own.

Ethos, in Shenstone's case, means something like literal, as well as figurative enclosure – private ownership of the rural setting in which the new elegies are to be produced. In his 'Essay' he claims all the occasions which may take place on his own land, much like a lord claiming the right to hunt all the game animals which might subsist on his grounds; the 'shed … flocks … fleeces' are his own, Shenstone says – and he means this in the most literal, legal sense. Gray's emphasis on Shenstone's literary motivations for withdrawing from society is amply confirmed by Shenstone's shrill insistence on his seigniorial rights to play the 'swain'. He even argues that he has the right to pen true pastoral because he is himself a shepherd. This is the most interesting and bizarre part of the passage; Shenstone seems almost to blush as he doggedly insists that he has the right 'to consider himself as a real shepherd' because he really does live in the country (as any visitor was welcome to confirm for himself.) Shenstone's nervousness about this claim comes through again in the truly remarkable parenthesis in which he says that the fact that he chose to retire to the country (unlike 'a real shepherd') 'is not material', as if he fears being accused of having done so purely from literary ambition.

This is the trade-off of the new-modelled ethos poetics: in return for greater latitude in claiming occasional basis for a wide range of purely mental events, the poet must subject himself to scrutiny on ethos, not occasion. The new-modelled elegiac poet is in this sense always a 'persona', as it were – in every social setting, the poet must strive at all times to act like an inspired being (even to the extent of stubbornly living in the country, hoping for visitors as witnesses to one's dramatized solitude). Testimonials backing up epideictic claims no longer attest to the reality of a particular incident, but to the ethos of the poet. Thus it is not surprising that Cowper's first volume of verse on the new pattern was prefaced by a testimonial to his moral character by his religious guide, Mr. Newton. That testimonial replaces the long, occasion-substantiating subtitles of previous generations. The 'dispositions of the [poet's] mind', if sufficiently vetted by clergy or other reliable persons (second-order ethos!) becomes the new ground of belief in lyric narrative; and as ever in the English lyric, belief precedes, grounds, and all but makes superfluous the act of reading the text itself.

Funereal pathos without the corpse; the intra-cranial space as the last, costly refuge from the truth demands of a suspicious audience; abandonment of overt narrative invention to the novel; restriction to a narrow, putatively autobiographical domain; the final obviation of the *habeas corpus* requirement in this retreat from invention to a mutated occasionality; these are the enduring results of the poetics which Gray, Young and Blair pioneered; which Shenstone exemplifies and codified; which Wordsworth was to popularize; and which grounds one major strain of English-language poetry to this day.

7
Conclusion: the Deployment of the New-Modelled Lyric by Wordsworth

One is ashamed to be pleased with the works of one knows not whom.

Henry MacKenzie, *The Man of Feeling*

It is indeed true, that the language of the earliest Poets was … the language of extraordinary occasions …

William Wordsworth, 1802 Appendix, Preface to the
Lyrical Ballads

At the end of the eighteenth century, in the work of William Wordsworth, ethos-occasioned poetics attained the 'Romantic' form in which it finally became the first-person epiphanic narrative. Wordsworth is the poet who brings the new ethos-occasioned poetics to complete hegemony. By showing the tremendous debt Wordsworth's poetry owes to the mid-eighteenth-century innovators, I hope to suggest (in a necessarily brief manner) how the rules and limits of the poetics first deployed by the great mid-eighteenth-century innovators became the predominant (though by no means the only) poetics of most of the nineteenth century.

Like many of Wilde's quips, his remark that Wordsworth himself hid the sermons he found in stones has much more truth than might at first appear. Wordsworth, 'poet of nature', was in fact a master-strategist, a Bonaparte, of the new-modelled lyric, who combined all the mid-eighteenth-century innovations into one overwhelmingly powerful force. In his works, the sort of poem invented by Gray and Young became *the* English lyric poem – the paradigm of modern poetic narrative.

Two seemingly contradictory conclusions appear when one tries

191

to place Wordsworth within the context delineated here: first, the surprisingly familiar content of his 'revolutionary' poetic manifestoes; and second, the completely new tone – of pride and self-assurance – in which he states these familiar theoretical conclusions. But there is not really a contradiction between content and tone; Wordsworth simply synthesizes, publicizes and successfully markets the dispersed ethos-occasioning strategies of an earlier generation of poets who had tried to hide the novelty of their techniques. Wordsworth represents the perfect integration of ethos and occasion; though he rests soundly in the mental-occasion tradition, he brings to it a lifelong commitment to the maintenance of the proper ethos which alone can properly undergird mental-occasion lyrics. Wordsworth was, unquestionably, a great strategist. Wordsworth seems to have thought about the career implications of poetic decisions from an early age – his refusal to engage in the opportunity to exploit the death of a college figure by means of an elegy is a triumph of the aesthetic discipline which characterizes his whole life. Wordsworth's ethos alone is what sets him apart from his models, Gray, Young and Cowper; except for the radically ethos-based grounding of his poems, he is not really the technical innovator which he claimed to be. His emphasis on the interaction of mental event and outer, stimulus-event, summed up in the famous description of the poet as exploiting '... interchange / Of action from within and from without' is not actually new, but a more blunt announcement of what had been more subtly practised by poets since Gray's time. The 'Preface' *to the Lyrical Ballads* is a work of pure ethos, in that its main claim is to daring rather than to any particular technical innovation. The actual rhetorical design of the series of Prefaces to the editions of *Lyrical Ballads,* and especially of the 'Appendix on Poetic Diction' appended to the 1802 edition, is to create the situation Wordsworth projects backwards in time to the Ur-poetry he wishes to reproduce, a time when 'the Poet spake to [others] in the character of a man to be looked up to, a man of genius and authority.' (*Lyrical Ballads*, 761).[1]

The innovation of which Wordsworth makes the most in his dramatization of his method is the adoption of low or common diction. As part of the self-dramatizing rhetoric of the 'Preface', Wordsworth implies that this use of low diction is very daring. It was not. Cowper's practice offered a clear precedent for the successful use of such diction. In fact, the diction of 'Epitaph on a Hare' is actually lower than that of anything Wordsworth wrote.

Cowper actually employs a polysyndeton, covering two stanzas, to list the vegetables preferred by a hare (as discussed above): 'His diet was of wheaten bread, / And milk, and oats, and straw....' This line is echoed in Wordsworth's better-known elegiac polysyndeton, 'Rolled round in Earth's diurnal course, / With rocks, and stones, and trees.' But Wordsworth's polysyndeton of rocks and stones in the context of an elegy for a young woman is not as radical as Cowper's polysyndeton of vegetables in the context of an epitaph for a rabbit.

Wordsworth's real innovation, and it is a very important one, is the presentation of the techniques developed by the mid-eighteenth-century poets in the service of an ethos highlighting the daring and pure sensibility of the poet. This is how Wordsworth benefits from belatedness; since it is actually a well-established poetics he brings to the public, he can afford to play the daring innovator. Actual daring innovators generally cannot afford this; they generally try to hide their innovations, as Gray did with his constant footnoting of his truly new techniques to alleged Classical models. Wordsworth presents a dramatized prose version of his poetic ethos – this is the real 'thesis' of the 'Preface'. Wordsworth again and again hints at a narrative in which he is opposed by (imaginary) conservatives who reject his work for its newness:

> They who have been accustomed to the gaudiness and inane phraseology of many modern writers … will be induced to inquire by what species of courtesy [the *Ballads]* can be permitted to assume that title [of poetry]. (Wordsworth, 743*ff*)

The future-tense rejection narrated in this passage is the single most frequent rhetorical move employed by Wordsworth in the *Preface to the Second Edition.* Wordsworth becomes a hero for deploying devices which have been in existence for generations; but he does so by first becoming a hero in his own narrative of poetic history.

The argument for low-diction poetry, which Wordsworth represents as dangerously radical in the several versions of the 'Preface', rests on Cowper's mid-century practice and theory – specifically Shenstone's theories (which are not necessarily original to him so much as they represent a summary of mid-century commonplaces) about the 'Progress of Poesy', and specifically of elegy. Wordsworth reproduces almost word-for-word the argument about the expansion of poetry from strict occasion to ethos-occasion, as narrated by Shenstone:

> The earliest poets of all nations generally wrote from passion excited by real events; they wrote naturally, and as men: feeling powerfully as they did, their language was daring, and figurative. (Wordsworth, 761)

In the beginning was the occasion – this is the basic dogma of Shenstone's claim about the history of the elegy, and it is one Wordsworth clearly shares, adding only an emphasis on the heroic nature of the first poets ('daring') which is entirely in keeping with his overall ethos-centred strategy. Like Shenstone, Wordsworth imagines elegiac history as expanding away from strict occasionality; but unlike Shenstone, and in keeping with his dramatization of everything involved in literary history, his evolution has a villain: the ambitious poet. His thesis is that since poets in truly occasionally-inspired states tended to speak a lofty language distinct from common speech, other poets, unscrupulously eager to produce emotional effects in the reader ('Poets, and Men ambitious of the fame of Poets') realized they could induce the transports of pleasure in a willing reader simply by mimicking the diction of the truly inspired:

> Poets, and men ambitious of the fame of poets, perceiving the influence of such language, and desirous of producing the same effect, without having the same animating passion ... applied [poetic diction] to feelings and ideas with which they had no natural connection whatever. (Wordsworth, 761)

The reader was willingly coopted into this process because s/he enjoyed it, enjoyed being transported by imitated occasional pathos:

> The Reader or Hearer of this distorted language found himself in a perturbed and unusual state of mind; when affected by the genuine language of passion he had been in a perturbed and unusual state of mind also; in both cases he was willing that his common judgment and understanding should be laid asleep, and he had no instinctive and infallible perception of the true to

make him reject the false; the one served as passport for the other. (Wordsworth, 761)

As a summary of the progress of poetry from antiquity, this is meaningless – but as a history of reader response to occasional claims in lyric narrative in the eighteenth century, it is quite accurate. This feature it shares with Shenstone's 'Prefatory Essay on Elegy'; both are histories of the recent past of this genre, projected into antiquity. When Wordsworth claims that elegiac language has acquired special powers 'because it was [thought to be] the language of extraordinary occasions' (Wordsworth, 762), he is describing the invasion of non-traditional occasions by the diction of the elegy – the same process Shenstone, a much more modest strategist, intended to justify.

Wordsworth is after much more than justification, of course; he is attempting the definitional argument popularized by Quintilian, who cut the Gordian knot of rhetorical ethics by redefining Rhetoric as 'The good man speaking well'. This is essentially Wordsworth's solution as well – pathos must become a function of a prior decision by the reader about the validity of the ethos of the poet. As ethos is the actual setting of the new mental-event occasion, so ethos is the key, the criterion for the right to commemorate such occasions. Wordsworth presents this as a new, daring, radical argument; in fact it is simply the announcement, the codification, the legitimization of the poetics installed *de facto* by the mid-century innovators. Instead of hiding the repertoire of the mid-century poets, Wordsworth co-opts it, points the spotlight at himself using this 'dangerous', 'daring' repertoire, and makes of this 'daring' first-person character the basis of a heroic saga which is the real essence of the 'Preface'.

The devices for which Wordsworth expects to be denounced are those of Young and Gray; for example, after suggesting, in the passage just cited, that he will face stiff opposition for the use of low diction, he mentions his daring in choosing mere peasants as subjects: 'Low and rustic life was generally chosen because in that situation the essential passions of the heart find a better soil in which they can attain their maturity ...' (Wordsworth, 743). 'Whose woods these are I think I know', as Frost might remark; these are Thomas Gray's woods, Thomas Gray's peasants, Thomas Gray's passions provoked by and incarnated in the peasantry, the uncommemorated. Given the size of his debt to Gray's technical innovations in occasioning lyrics, the bluntness of Wordsworth's dislike of Gray constitutes a striking case of anxiety of influence. Wordsworth clearly wants to erase the traces of his debt to Gray by making a display of disdain for the earlier poet. In the 'Preface', Wordsworth calls Gray 'the head of those who, by their reasonings, have attempted to widen the space betwixt prose and metrical composition' and offers a scornful analysis of the diction of 'Sonnet on the Death of Mr. Richard West' as an example. 'Richard West' is one of the most important of the early mental-event occasioned lyrics, and as such a direct ancestor of such important works as the 'Lucy' poems. In fact, those poems employ precisely the same device as 'Richard West': a death which has no effect on the larger world, but has exercised a devastating effect on the inner landscape of the poet's mind, with the inner/outer conflict highlighted ('... but oh, the difference to me').

Wordsworth is often said to have developed or popularized a theory of poetic creation, summarized by the famous phrase about emotion recollected in tranquillity. In a sense, this claim has some basis; not because the theory of creation presented in the 'Preface' is really very new, but because it is presented with the spotlight determinedly on the poet, on Wordsworth. Wordsworth borrows the ethos-refraction device Young employs at the beginning of the 'Night Thoughts' – and not only the device but the very phrasing:

> [I]t is proper that I should mention one ... circumstance which distinguishes these poems from the popular Poetry of the day; it is this, that the feeling therein developed gives importance to the action and situation, and not the action and situation to the feeling. (Wordsworth, 746)

The debt to Young's 'Preface' to the 'Night Thoughts' is clear:

> [This poem] differs from the common mode of poetry, which is, from long narrations to draw short morals. Here, on the contrary, the narrative is short, and the morality arising from it makes the bulk of the poem. (Young, 35)

The argument is the same: moral purpose comes first, and the narrative proceeds from it. The rhetorical structure is the same as well: an antithesis between the new work and the alleged norm.

What is different in Wordsworth's dramatized 'Preface' is propor-
tion; while Young devotes one brief paragraph to this claim of
daring and originality, Wordsworth makes the claim over and over
in the twenty-odd pages of the 'Preface'. As the claim is repeated, a
hierarchy emerges: poetic technique gives way to moral purpose,
and moral purpose is subsumed by the ethos of the poet. The effect
of the 'Preface ...' is cumulative and non-logical; it is created by the
continual repetition of 'I' in the context of 'right' and 'moral
purpose'. The antithesis between Wordsworth's allegedly daring
and moral poetry and the alleged norm is offered the reader again
and again, each time more dramatically, until there is a direct chal-
lenge to the reader to make a choice:

> ... [E]ach of [these poems] has a worthy *purpose.* Not that I mean
> to say, that I always began to write with a distinct purpose
> formally conceived; but I believe that my habits of meditation
> have so formed my feelings, as that my descriptions of such
> objects as strongly excite those feelings, will be found to carry
> along with them a *purpose.* If in this opinion I am mistaken I can
> have little right to the name of a Poet. For all good poetry is the
> spontaneous overflow of powerful feelings ... (Wordsworth, 744)
> [italics in original]

Wordsworth here begins with Young's ethos but again drama-
tizes it, foregrounds it, challenges the reader to accept or deny it.
Young had claimed occasional validity for the 'Night Thoughts'
from the way that its hidden occasion 'imposed' the poem on the
poet. Wordsworth makes the same claim the entire basis of his
ethos, his 'right to the name of poet'. The 'revised' mental event is
no longer a real occasion; the poems which are the product cannot
share in the grounding accorded those considered as the product of
pure ethos. The poet of the mental occasion requires trust above all;
thus Wordsworth here assures the reader that his right to be called
a poet is the product of what he describes as a course of spiritual
discipline: 'habits of meditation' which 'regulated his feelings' until
they could not help but be morally instructive.
Along with Young's technique for claiming mental occasion
Wordsworth borrowed what might be called the 'Lorenzo' device,
which he used to great effect in the 'Lucy' poems. Young's original
innovation in employing Christian names without a clear referent
was based on the idea that the reader, feeling something too real to

mention was hidden behind the false name, would believe the narrative to be true. Young had to resort to this device because his own occasional losses were not great enough to justify 10 000 lines of verse; Wordsworth has the same problem and comes up with the same solution in the 'Lucy' poems. The story of reader response to these poems, with their elusive 'Lucy' corpse, should be a familiar one. Here is a twentieth-century editor's version:

> The question of Lucy's identity, much discussed but never solved, is not very important [!]. She is best thought of either as an imaginary character or as a now unknown early sweetheart of the poet. In any event, the focus of the poems is principally on the mental experiences of the poet-speaker. (Stillinger, 518)

This sort of discussion roughly parallels Croft's investigation of the autobiographical basis of Young's work. First we learn that the question of Lucy's actual identity has been 'much discussed'; then that it 'is not very important', perhaps because it has 'never [been] solved'. The editor then offers a choice of mutually exclusive interpretations: one should either think of Lucy as made-up, or as an early sweetheart – that is, either made-up or not made-up. The familiar tone of warning and avoidance is noticeable here; one simply 'should' do this. The implication is that worrying too much about Lucy's identity would be imprudent.

Lucy's identity is not far to seek; she is of the same family as Young's 'Philander', 'Narcissa', and 'Lorenzo'. Of course, 'Lucy' is a name as determinedly low and ordinary sounding as Young's are Italianate and fanciful; that simply means that Wordsworth is going for the impression of using her real name, not a transparent pseudonym. This 'low' dimension of grief is what is borrowed from Gray in the 'Lucy' poems: the commemoration of a death too low, too ordinary to be noted (i.e. to be checked-up-on.) As if in unconscious acknowledgment of the debt to Gray which he always denied, Wordsworth gives to another poem of the same era a telltale name: 'Lucy *Gray*'. (Wordsworth, 170)

Considered as technical productions, the 'Lucy' poems are simple and familiar; they consist of Young's preface and his character-naming device, plus Gray's peasant-commemoration and use of obscurity of reference, plus Cowper's calculatingly low diction. The most famous of them is a direct descendant of the 'Elegy':

> She dwelt among th' untrodden ways,
>   Beside the springs of Dove,
> A Maid whom there were none to praise
>   And very few to love.
>
> A Violet by a mossy Stone
>   Half-hidden from the Eye!
> – Fair as a star when only one
>   Is shining in the sky!
>
> She *liv'd* unknown, and few could know
>   When Lucy ceas'd to be;
> But she is in her Grave, and oh!
>   The difference to me.
>   (Wordsworth, 163)

The funereal technique is a familiar mix of Young and Gray, with a noticeable emphasis on the untraceable nature of the event commemorated. The profusion of terms indicating obscurity is actually greater in this small poem than in any of Gray's works. The first thing the reader learns is that the narrative cannot be verified; 'She dwelt among untrodden ways.' Confirming the impression of obscurity, line three states directly that the corpse in question cannot be commemorated. Stanza two makes the same point via metaphors; this is Gray's trope, the buried gem, the flower blooming, unseen, in the desert. The final stanza, which derives more from the name-dropping techniques of Young than the pure blurring obscurity-rhetoric of Gray, begins, in a purposely delayed manner, to divulge, or seem to divulge, a bit of the facts of the case: we learn that the 'Maid's' name was 'Lucy' and that the narrator loved her (which was rather strongly implied already). The litotes of line four, 'very few to love' is retroactively lit up by the last line; 'very few' clearly equals 'one' – the 'poet-speaker', as Wordsworth's editor calls this character.

But Wordsworth is not, simply because he borrows their techniques of occasioning poetry, a mere epigone of Gray and Young; he is a great figure, an evolutionary success story – because he realized that he could turn what they hid into a point of pride; that he could foreground the 'I' they snuck in through the back door. As Wordsworth's modern editor says in the passage cited above, 'the focus of the [Lucy] poems is primarily on the mental experiences of the poet-speaker'.

Overwhelming the reader with the whole ethos-apparatus at once; this is what is Napoleonic in Wordsworth, who exploits the entire corpus of literary devices in the same bold, integrated manner that Bonaparte used to move armies. Bonaparte did not waste time on metallurgy or ballistics; instead he grasped the strategic picture and used the artillery developed by technicians in a strategically effective manner. Wordsworth did not invent the poetic components he deploys; those components were developed by Gray, Young, Blair, Cowper *et al*. But Wordsworth places them, for the first time, under a single command. Ethos, Wordsworth realized, was the key, the landscape in which the mental-occasion poem took place; and so everything in Wordsworth's life and work is subsumed to dominating the ethos-landscape. When Wordsworth wrote, 'In truth, my life has been unusually barren of events'[2] he was speaking of the uncanny discipline which caused him to focus on the campaign he was waging in this crucial battle-front, the interior landscape. Wordsworth maintained, in his focus on this inner strategic landscape, an extraordinary restraint; nothing he said or did ever contradicted the emphasis on the ethos of the musing poet. The strategically important flank is the ethos which occasions the work – the life must be arranged in such a way as to be seen to commission or occasion the poems. One of the recurrent conclusions of my analysis of modern verse has been that readers make their decisions about ethos-lyrics based not on their evaluation of the literary worth of the text but on a pre-reading decision to accept or reject the poet's claim to authenticity.

Wordsworth devoted his entire life to the maintenance of the mutual reinforcement of the 'Life' and the 'Works'. He claimed, as noted above, that he could provide chapter and verse – that is, date and location – for every incident narrated in every poem. Late in life (1843) he began doing so in a systematic manner, recounting the time and place each poem had occurred to him to Isabella Fenwick.

From the point of view of poetic occasion, Fenwick's notes are perhaps the most important part of the Wordsworth corpus. They show an extraordinary concern with literal truth, even when it would not seem to affect the reader's response to the poem. A striking case of this is the tale of Vaudracour and Julia in Book IX of *The Prelude*. Although this lovers' tale has no part in the autobiographical case made by the poem, Wordsworth, Fenwick and Wordsworth's editor, Ernest de Selincourt, have all gone to considerable lengths to ground the story in some actual event, as shown in the oddly anxious note Selincourt appends to this part of the poem (*The Prelude* 166–71 and 296–8 ff.)

The instinctive focus of Wordsworth and/or Fenwick, in recording the genesis of each poem, is the moment at which the idea occurred to the poet, not so much the identity of any characters described in it. This is not because these characters are 'fictional'; that would be anathema to Wordsworth's poetics, and on occasion, when the 'character' is someone real, someone important – that is, someone known to the poet – their identities are specified (as in Fenwick's notes to 'Evening Walk', in which the aged Wordsworth, willing now to lose the romantic tinge given the poem by the anonymity of the female character, tells Fenwick 'The young lady to whom this was addressed was my sister' (Wordsworth, 497). But in most cases it is not central, hence not stressed. In most cases, occasion, as recorded by in Isabella Fenwick in the 'IF Notes', means the Pauline moment at which the mental event occurred. Sometimes the Pauline parallel is very strong, as in the notes to Wordsworth's own 'Night Piece' (Wordsworth, 276):

> Composed on the road between Nether Stowey and Alfoxden, extempore. I distinctly recollect the very moment when I was struck, as described 'He looks up at the clouds' &c. (*The Fenwick Notes of William Wordsworth* [ed. J. Curtis] p. 13)

Besides the implication of a sacred ethos in the parallel to the road to Damascus, the mode of composition is an essential part of the occasion: 'extempore'. This is not a mere boast; this is a claim to occasion, an occasion happening at night, on a lonely road, and inside the poet's skull.

When the average reader of the twentieth century imagines a lyric poem, s/he imagines a paradigmatic narrative in which a lone figure, wandering alone in a landscape, experiences an intense 'mental occasion'. Examples are innumerable, but some of the best-known incarnations of this paradigm would be Wordsworth's wanderer, 'lonely as a cloud' coming upon those famous daffodils, and Whitman's 'I', who wanders away from the lecture-hall to escape the intrusive voice of 'the learn'd astronomer' to dominate a less crowded landscape 'in perfect silence'. In this work, I have attempted to explain how this paradigmatic narrator/protagonist of the modern lyric set out on that lonely walk.

Appendix: Johnson's Summary of Contemporary Accounts of Dryden's Funeral

On the Wednesday morning following, being May-day, 1700, under the most excruciating dolours, [Dryden] died ... Lord Halifax sent ... to My Lady [Elizabeth, Dryden's widow] and Mr. Charles [Dryden, his son], that, if they would give him leave to bury Mr. Dryden, he would inter him with a gentleman's private funeral, and afterwards bestow 550 [pounds] on a monument in the Abbey; which, as they had no reason to refuse, they accepted. On the Saturday following the company came; the corpse was put into a velvet hearse, and eighteen mourning coaches filled with company attended; when, just before they began to move, Lord Jeffries, with some of his rakish companions, coming by, in wine, asked whose funeral? On being told, 'What,' cries he, 'Shall Dryden, the greatest honor and ornament of the nation, be buried after this private manner? No, gentlemen, let all that loved Mr. Dryden, and honour his memory, alight and join with me in gaining my Lady's consent to let me have the honour of his interment, which shall be after another manner than this; and I will bestow 1000 [pounds] on a monument in the Abbey for him.' The gentlemen in the coaches, not knowing of the Bishop of Rochester's favour, nor of the lord Halifax's generous design (these two having, out of respect for the family, enjoined Lady Elizabeth and her son to keep their favour concealed to the world, and let it pass for her own expense, etc.), readily came out of the coaches, and attended Lord Jeffries up to the lady's bedside, who was then sick; but she absolutely refusing, he fell on his knees, vowing never to rise till his request was granted. The rest of the company, by his desire, kneeled also; she, being naturally of a timorous disposition, and then under a sudden surprise, fainted away. As soon as she recovered her speech she cried, 'No, no!' 'Enough, Gentlemen,' replied he (rising briskly) 'My Lady is very good; she says, *Go, go!*' She repeated her former words with all her strength; but alas! in vain! her feeble voice was lost in their acclamations of joy; and Lord Jeffries ordered the hearsemen to carry the corpse to Russell's, an undertaker in Cheapside, and leave it there till he sent orders for an embalmment, which, he added, should be after the Royal manner.

His directions were obeyed, the company dispersed, and Lady Elizabeth and Mr. Charles remained inconsolable. Next morning Mr. Charles waited on Lord Halifax, etc. to excuse his mother and himself, by relating the real truth. But neither his Lordship nor the Bishop would admit any plea; especially the latter, who had the Abbey lighted, the ground opened, the choir attending, an anthem already set, and himself waiting for three hours without any corpse to bury. Russell, after three days' expectance of orders for embalmment without receiving any, waits on Lord Jeffries; who, pretending ignorance of the matter, turned it off with an ill-natured jest, saying, that those who observed the orders of a drunken frolic deserved no better; that he remembered nothing at all of it; and that he might do what he pleased with the corpse. On this, Mr. Russell waits on the Lady Elizabeth and Mr. [Charles] Dryden; but alas! it was not in their power to answer. The season was very hot, the deceased had lived high and fast, and, being corpulent and abounding with gross humours, grew very offensive. The undertaker, in short, threatened to bring the corpse home and set it before their door. It cannot be easily imagined what grief, shame and confusion seized this unhappy family. They begged a day's respite, which was granted. Mr. Charles wrote a very handsome letter to Lord Jeffries, who returned it with this cool answer: – 'He knew nothing about the matter, and would be troubled no more about it.' He then addressed the Lord Halifax and the Bishop of Rochester, who were both too justly, though unhappily, incensed to do anything in it.

In this distress, Dr. Garth, a man who entirely loved Mr. Dryden, and was withal a man of generosity and great humanity, sent for the corpse to the college of physicians, in Warwick Lane, and proposed a funeral by subscription … and at last a day, about three weeks after his decease, was appointed for the interment at the Abbey. Dr. Garth pronounced a fine Latin oration over the corpse at the college; but the audience being numerous and the room large, it was requisite the orator should be elevated that he might be heard; but, as it unluckily happened, there was nothing at hand but an old beer-barrel, which the Doctor with much good-nature mounted; and, in the midst of his oration, beating time to the accent with his foot, the head broke in and his feet sunk to the bottom, which occasioned the malicious report of his enemies that he was turned Tub-Preacher: however, he finished the oration with a superior grace, to the loud acclimations of mirth which inspired the mixed, or rather *mob,* auditors.

The procession began to move – a numerous train of coaches attended the hearse – but, Good God! in what disorder can only be expressed by a sixpenny pamphlet soon after published, entitled *Dryden's Funeral.* At last the corpse arrived at the Abbey, which was all unlighted. No organ played, no anthem sung; only two of the singing boys preceded the corpse, who sung an ode of Horace with each a small candle in their hand. The butchers and other mob broke in like a deluge, so that only about eight or ten gentlemen could get admission, and those forced to cut the way with their drawn swords. The coffin, in this disorder, was let down into Chaucer's grave, with as much confusion and as little ceremony as was possible, every one glad to save themselves from the gentle-men's swords or the clubs of the mob....' (Johnson, *Lives*, 145–7)

Notes

1 OCCASIONAL POETICS IN THE EARLY MODERN LYRIC

1. Hunter Davies, *William Wordsworth* (London, 1980).
2. Philip Stewart, *Imitation and Illusion in the French Memoir-Novel, 1700–1750: The Art of Make-Believe* (New Haven: Yale University Press, 1969).
3. Dennis Kay, *Melodious Tears: the English Funeral Elegy from Spenser to Milton* (Oxford: Clarendon Press, 1990).
4. Russell Fraser, *The War against Poetry* (Princeton: Princeton University Press, 1970).
5. Samuel Johnson, 'Johnson's Lives of the English Poets', in Chalmers, *Works of the English Poets from Chaucer to Cowper* (21 vv.).
6. Philip Pinkus, *Grub Street Stripped Bare* (London, 1968).
7. F. W. Hillis, ed. *Portraits by Sir Joshua Reynolds* (New York, 1952).
8. Paul Fry, *The Poet's Calling in the English Ode* (New Haven, 1980).
9. Malcolm Lipking, *The Life of a Poet: Beginning and Ending Poetic Careers* (Chicago, 1981).

2 'PARDON, BLEST SOUL, THE SLOW PAC'D ELEGIES': AMBITION AND OCCASION IN *JUSTA EDOVARDO KING*

1. R. B. Jenkins, *Milton and the Theme of Fame* (The Hague/Paris: Mouton, 1973).
2. *Complete Prose Works of John Milton* (New Haven: Yale University Press, 1953).
3. Eric Smith, *By Mourning Tongues: Studies in English Elegy* (London, 1977).
4. Leo Braudy, *The Frenzy of Renown: Fame and Its History* (New York/Oxford, 1986).
5. Richard Helgerson, *Self-Crowned Laureates* (Berkeley, 1986).
6. Graham Parry, *The Seventeenth Century: the Intellectual and Cultural Context of English Literature, 1603–1700* (London, 1989).
7. John Guillory, *Poetic Authority: Spenser, Milton and Literary History* (New York, 1983).
8. E. M. W. Tillyard, *Milton* (London, 1966).
9. E. P. J. Corbett, introduction, *The Rhetoric and Poetics of Aristotle*, ed. Corbett (New York: Random House, 1984).
10. Don M. Wolfe, *Milton and His England* (New York, 1970).
11. *The Poems of John Milton*, eds John Carey and Alistair Fowler (London: Longmans Green, 1968).
12. *The Poems of Thomas Carew*, ed. Rhodes Dunlap (Oxford: Oxford University Press, 1949).

13. A. N. Wilson, *The Life of John Milton* (New York, 1983).
14. Barbara Johnson, 'Fiction and Grief' *Milton Quarterly* (1984): [p].
15. Dustin Griffin, 'The Beginnings of Modern Authorship: Milton and Dryden'. *Milton Quarterly* 24.1l (1990): [p].
16. *Justa Edovardo King I & II* , ed. Ernest C. Mossner (New York, 1939).

3 CARRION CROWS: OCCASION IN THE BEGINNING AND END OF DRYDEN'S LITERARY LIFE

1. W. H. Auden, ed. *A Choice of Dryden's Verse* (London: Faber and Faber, 1973), p. 9.
2. Arthur L. Cooke, 'Did Dryden Hear the Guns?' *Notes & Queries*, 196 (1951): 204–5.
3. Walter Scott, *The Life of John Dryden* from *Miscellaneous Prose Works of Sir Walter Scott, Bart.* (Edinburgh, 1834; Omaha, NE, 1963).
4. James Osborn, *John Dryden: Some Biographical Facts and Problems* (New York: Columbia University Press, 1940).
5. James A. Winn, *John Dryden and His World* (New Haven/London: Yale University Press (1987).

4 NADIR: THE GENERATION OF NAMUR AND THE FAMINE OF OCCASIONS

1. Felicity Nussbaum and Laura Brown, *New Eighteenth Century: Theory, Politics, English Literature* (New York/London, 1987).
2. Claude Rawson, *Order from Confusion Sprung: Studies in Eighteenth-Century Literature from Swift to Cowper* (London, 1985).
3. Alexander Chalmers, ed., *Works of the English Poets from Chaucer to Cowper*; Vols. 9–18 include Lives of the English Poets by Samuel Johnson (London, 1810).
4. James Boswell, *Boswell's London Journal 1763–1764*, ed. Frederick Pottle (New York, 1950).
5. Maynard Mack, *Alexander Pope: A Life* (New Haven/London, 1985).
6. Eric Rothstein, *Restoration and Eighteenth Century Poetry 1660–1780* (Boston/London: Routledge and Keegan Paul, 1981).
7. Edward Young, 'Conjectures on Original Composition' (1759); reprinted in Edward Young's 'Conjectures on Original Composition' in *England and Germany: A Study in Literary Relations*, ed. M. W. Steinke (New York: F. C. Stechert Co., 1917).

5 'TO DARKNESS AND TO ME': MENTAL EVENT AS POETIC OCCASION

1. Martin Price, 'Sacred to Secular: Thomas Gray and the Cultivation of the Literary' in *Context, Influence and Mid-Eighteenth-Century Poetry* (Los Angeles: Clark Memorial Library, 1990).

2. The *Norton Anthology of English Literature* (Revised) (New York, 1968).
3. *The Correspondence of Thomas Gray* (Oxford, 1935).
4. *Selected Letters* (London: Everyman's Library, 1926).
5. Boswell, James, *Life of Johnson* (London, 1893).
6. Paul Fussell, ed., introduction, *English Augustan Poetry* (New York: Doubleday, 1972).
7. James Boswell, *Boswell in Holland, 1763–1764*, ed. Frederick Pottle (New York: McGraw-Hill, 1952).
8. Roger Lonsdale, ed., *Gray & Collins: Poetical Works* (Oxford: Oxford University Press, 1977).

6 GRAY TO COWPER: CAT TO CAST-AWAY VIA 'NIGHT THOUGHTS'

1. James Sambrook, ed., *William Cowper: the Task and Selected Other Poems* (London: Longman Group UK, 1994).
2. Rachel Trickett, 'Cowper, Wordsworth, and the Animal Fable'. *Review of English Studies* (l983): 471–80.
3. *The Poems of William* Cowper, eds J. H. Baird and Charles Ryskamp Vol. 1: 1748–1782 (Oxford: Clarendon Press, 1980).
4. *Poetry of the Landscape and the Night*, ed. Peake, Charles (London, 1967).
5. *Edward Young: Night Thoughts*, ed. Stephen Cornford (Cambridge: Cambridge University Press, 1989).
6. Harold Forster, *Edward Young: the Poet of the 'Night Thoughts', 1683–1765* (Norfolk, 1987).

7 CONCLUSION: THE DEPLOYMENT OF THE NEW-MODELLED LYRIC BY WORDSWORTH

1 James Butler and Karen Green, eds, *Lyrical Ballads and Other Poems 1797–1800 by William Wordsworth* (Ithaca: Cornell University Press, 1992).
2. William Wordsworth, *letter* of April 9, 1801.

Bibliography

Aristotle. *The Rhetoric and Poetics of Aristotle*. Trans. Ingram Bywater. Ed. E. P. J. Corbett. New York, 1984.

Bate, W. J. *The Burden of the Past and the English Poet*. Cambridge, Mass., 1970.

Blair, Hugh. *Critical Dissertation on the Poems of Ossian the Son of Fingal, with an Appendix containing a Variety of Undoubted Testimonials Establishing their Authenticity*. London, 1765.

—— *Lectures on Rhetoric and Belles Lettres*. 2 vols. London, 1783.

Bloom, Harold. *A Map of Misreading*. New York: Oxford University Press, 1975.

—— *The Anxiety of Influence: a Theory of Poetry*. New York, 1973.

Boswell, James *Boswell in Holland, 1763–1764*. Ed. Frederick A. Pottle. New York: McGraw-Hill, 1952.

—— *Boswell's London Journal 1762–1763*. Ed. F. C. Pottle. New York: Heinemann, 1950.

—— *Boswell on the Grand Tour*. Ed. Frederick A Pottle.

—— *Life of Johnson*. London, 1791. London, 1893.

Bowra, C. M. *From Virgil to Milton*. London, 1945.

Braudy, Leo. *The Frenzy of Renown: Fame and Its History*. New York, 1986.

Broadus, E. K. *The Laureateship: a Study of the Office of Poet Laureate in England …* Oxford, 1921.

Broich, Ulrich. *The Eighteenth-Century Mock-Heroic Poem*. Tr. D. H. Wilson. Cambridge, 1990.

Brown, Cedric C., *John Milton: a Literary Life*. Basingstoke & London 1995.

——, 'Mending and Bending the Occasional Text: collegiate elegies and the case of "Lycidas"' in *Texts and Cultural Change in Early Modern England*, eds Cedric C. Brown and Arthur F. Marotti. Basingstoke & London 1997.

Butt, John, and Geoffrey Carnall. *The Mid-Eighteenth Century*. Oxford, 1979.

Chalmers, Alexander F. S. A., ed. *Works of the English Poets from Chaucer to Cowper*. 18 vols. (vols. 9–18 including *Lives of the English Poets* by Samuel Johnson). London, 1810.

Clark, Donald *John Milton and St. Paul's School*. New York 1948.

Clark, George. *The Seventeenth Century*. London, 1929.

Clayton, Thomas, Ed. *Cavalier Poets: Selected Poems*. Oxford 1978.

Cleveland, John. *The Poems of John Cleveland*. Eds Brian Morris and Eleanor Withington. Oxford, 1967.

Coleridge, Samuel Taylor. *Biographica Literaria*. Ed. George Watson. New York, 1971.

—— *Selected Poetry and Prose of Coleridge*. Ed. Donald Stauffer. New York, 1951.

Cooke, Arthur L. 'Did Dryden Hear the Guns?' *Notes & Queries* 196 (12 May, 1951): 204–5.

Cowper, William *The Poems of William Cowper* (v. 1) Eds John H. Baird and Charles Ryskamp Oxford 1980.

—— *William Cowper: The Task and Other Poems* Ed. James Sambrook London 1994.

Curtis, Jared (ed.) *The Fenwick Notes of William Wordsworth*. Wiltshire 1993.

Curtius, Ernst. *European Literature and the Latin Middle Ages*. Tr. W. R. Trask. New York, 1963.

Davies, Hunter. *William Wordsworth*. London, 1980.

Donne, John *The Elegies and the Songs and Sonnets of John Donne*. Ed. Helen Gardner Oxford Oxford University Press 1978.

Doughty, Oswald. *Forgotten Lyrics of the Eighteenth Century*. London, 1924.

Downie, J. A. *The Succession of the State: Literature and Politics, 1678–1750*. Basingstoke and London 1994.

Dryden, John. *The Works of John Dryden*. Eds E. N. Hooker and H. T. Swedenborg, University of California Press Berkeley and Los Angeles 1956.

Eade, J. C. *Aristotle Anatomised: The 'Poetics' in England 1764–1781*. Frankfurt, 1988.

Edwards, Michael. *Poetry and Possibility*. Basingstoke, 1988.

Ferguson, Frances. *Wordsworth: Language as Counterspirit*. New Haven, 1977.

Fish, Stanley. *Self-Consuming Artifacts: the Experience of Seventeenth-Century Literature* Berkeley/Los Angeles 1972.

Forster, Harold. *Edward Young: the Poet of the 'Night Thoughts,' 1683–1765*. Norfolk, 1987.

Fraser, Russell. *The War against Poetry*. Princeton: Princeton University Press, 1970.

Fromm, Harold. *Academic Capitalism and Literary Value*. Athens, Georgia, 1991.

Fry, Paul. *The Reach of Criticism: Method and Perception in Literary Theory*. New Haven, 1983.

—— *The Poet's Calling in the English Ode*. New Haven, 1980.

Frye, Northrop. *The Critical Path: an Essay on the Critical Context of Literary Criticism*. Bloomington, Indiana, 1971.

Fussell, Paul, ed. *English Augustan Poetry*. New York: Doubleday, 1972.

Fussell, Paul. *The Rhetorical World of Augustan Humanism: Ethics and Imagery from Swift to Burke*. London, 1964.

Garrison, James D. *Dryden and the Tradition of Panegyric*. Berkeley and Los Angeles 1975.

Gilman, Ernest B. *Iconoclasm and Poetry in the English Reformation*. Chicago, 1986.

Gittings, Clare *Death, Burial and the Individual in Early Modern England*. London, 1984.

Gray, Thomas *Gray & Collins: Poetical Works* Ed. Roger Lonsdale Oxford 1977.

Green, F. C. *Literary Ideas in Eighteenth-Century France and England*. New York, 1966.

Greer, Germaine *et al*. *Kissing the Rod: an Anthology of Seventeenth-Century Women's Verse*. New York, 1988.

Griffin, Dustin H. *Literary Patronage in England, 1650–1800*. Cambridge 1996.

—— *Regaining Paradise: Milton and the Eighteenth Century*. Cambridge 1995.

Guilhamet, Leon *The Sincere Ideal: Studies on Sincerity in Eighteenth-Century English Literature*. Montreal, 1974.

Guillory, John. *Poetic Authority: Spenser, Milton and Literary History*. New York, 1983.

Hawkins, Harriet *Poetic Freedom and Poetic Truth: Chaucer, Shakespeare, Marlowe, Milton*. Oxford, 1976.

Hayley, William. *An Essay on Epic Poetry*. London 1782. Gainesville, Florida, 1968.

Haywood, Ian. *The Making of History: a Study of the Literary Forgeries of James MacPherson and Thomas Chatterton in Relation to Eighteenth-Century Ideas of History and Fiction*. Cranbury, New Jersey, 1986.

Hazlitt, William. *Lectures on the English Poets*. London, 1910.

Helgerson, Richard *Self-Crowned Laureates*. Berkeley, 1986.

Hill, Christopher. *The Experience of Defeat: Milton and Some Contemporaries*. New York, 1985.

Hillis, F. W., ed. *Portraits by Sir Joshua Reynolds*. New York, 1952.

Hillis Miller, J. *Fiction and Repetition*. Oxford, 1982.

Hilson, J. C., M. M. B. Jones, and J. R. Watson, eds *Augustan Worlds: New Essays in Eighteenth-Century Literature*. New York: Barnes & Noble Books, 1978.

Hopkins, Kenneth *The Poets Laureate*. London, 1954.

Hutching, Bill. *The Poetry of William Cowper*. London, 1983.

Hutton, Ronald *The Restoration: a Political and Religious History of England and Wales, 1658–1667*. Oxford, 1985.

Jacobus, Mary *Tradition and Experiment in Wordsworth's Lyrical Ballads (1798)*. Oxford Clarendon Press 1976.

Janowitz, Anne. *England's Ruins: Poetic Purpose and the National Landscape*. Cambridge, MA, 1990.

Jenkins, R. B. *Milton and the Theme of Fame*. The Hague: Mouton, 1973.

Johnson, Barbara 'Fiction and Grief …' *Milton Quarterly* 1988.

Johnson, Samuel *Lives of the English Poets: a Selection*. Ed. John Wain. London: Dent, 1975.

—— *Journey to the Western Islands of Scotland. 1775*. London, 1970.

—— *Selected Writings*. Ed. Katharine Rogers. New York, 1981.

Jose, Nicholas *Ideas of the Restoration in English Literature, 1660–1671* Cambridge (MA), 1984

Jump, John D. *The Ode*. London, 1974.

Justa Edovardo King. Cambridge, 1638. Ed. E. C. Mossner. New York, 1939.

Kay, Dennis. *Melodious Tears: the English Funeral Elegy from Spenser to Milton*. Oxford: Clarendon Press, 1990.

Krieger, Murray. *Poetic Presence and Illusion*. Baltimore, 1979.

Laing, Malcolm. *The Poems of James MacPherson*. 2 vols. Edinburgh, 1805.

Lipking, Malcolm. *The Life of the Poet: Beginning and Ending Poetic Careers*. Chicago, 1981.

Lonsdale, Roger. 'The Poetry of Thomas Gray: Versions of the Self'. Chatterton Lecture for 1973, London, 1973.

Lytton-Sells, Arthur. *Thomas Gray, His Life and Works*. London, 1980.

Mack, Maynard. *Alexander Pope: A Life.* New Haven: Yale University Press, 1985.

MacKenzie, Henry. *The Man of Feeling.* Edinburgh, 1771. Oxford, 1987.

MacPherson, James. *Fingal, an Ancient Epic Poem in Six Books, Together with several other Poems, composed by Ossian the son of Fingal. Translated from the Galic Language, by James MacPherson.* London, 1762.

—— *Fragments of Ancient Poetry, Collected in the Highlands of Scotland, and Translated from the Gaelic or Erse Language.* Edinburgh, 1760.

Milton, John. *Complete Prose Works of John Milton.* New Haven: Yale University Press 1953.

—— *Areopagitica and Other Prose Works.* London 1955.

—— *Milton's 'Lycidas': the Tradition and the Poem.* Ed. C. A. Patrides. New York, 1961.

Miner, Earl *The Restoration Mode from Milton to Dryden.* Princeton 1974.

Moore, Cecil A. *Backgrounds of English Literature, 1700–1760.* Minneapolis 1953.

Morley, Edith (ed.) *Hurd's Letters on Chivalry and Romance, with the Third Elizabethan Dialogue.* 1762. London, 1911.

Morris, David. 'Virgilian Attitudes in Pope's "Windsor Forest"'. *TSLL* 15 (1973).

Newey, Vincent. *Cowper's Poetry: a Critical Study and Reassessment.* London, 1982.

—— *Centring the Self: Subjectivity, Society and Reading from Thomas Gray to Thomas Hardy.* Aldershot 1995.

Nichols, John, ed. *Illustrations of the Literary History of the Eighteenth Century.* 8 vols. New York, 1966.

Nizan, Paul. *Aden, Arabie.* Trans. Joan Pinkham. New York, 1987.

Nussbaum, Felicity and Laura Brown, eds. *The New Eighteenth Century: Theory, Politics, English Literature.* New York, 1987.

Osborn, James. *John Dryden: Some Biographical Facts and Problems.* New York: Columbia University Press, 1940.

Parker, William Riley *Milton: a Biography* (ed., Gordon Campbell) Oxford 1996 v. 1.

Patterson, Annabel *Censorship and Interpretation: the Conditions of Writing and Reading in Early Modern England.* Madison, 1984.

Peake, Charles, ed. *Poetry of the Landscape and the Night.* London, 1967.

Percy, Thomas. *Reliques of Ancient English Poetry.* London, 1765.

Pigman, G. W. *Grief and English Renaissance Elegy.* Cambridge, 1985.

Pinkus, Philip. *Grub Street Stripped Bare.* London, 1968.

Pittock, Joan. *The Ascendancy of Taste: the Achievement of Joseph and Thomas Warton.* London, 1973.

Pope, Alexander. *Selected Poetry and Prose.* Ed. Aubrey Williams. New York, 1969.

—— *The Poems of Alexander Pope.* Ed. John Butt. New York, 1963.

Postlethwaite, Norman and Gordon Campbell, eds. 'Edward King, Milton's "Lycidas": Poems and Documents' *Milton Quarterly* v. 28, No. 4 December 1994.

Prior, Mary. *Women in English Society, 1500–1800.* London, 1985.

Quintana, Ricardo, and Alvin Whitley, eds. *English Poetry of the Mid and Late Eighteenth Century.* New York, 1963.

Rader, Ralph. 'The Dramatic Monologue and Related Lyric Forms'. *Critical Inquiry* 3:l (Autumn, 1976).

Rawson, Claude. *Order from Confusion Sprung: Studies in Eighteenth-Century Literature from Swift to Cowper.* London, 1985.

Reed, A. L. *The Background of Gray's Elegy.* New York, 1924.

Ricks, Christopher *The Force of Poetry.* Oxford, 1984.

Rogers, W. E. *The Three Genres and the Interpretation of Lyric.* Princeton, 1980.

Rothstein, Eric. *Restoration and Eighteenth-Century Poetry, 1660–1780.* Boston: Routledge and Kegan Paul, 1981.

Russo, John Paul *Alexander Pope: Tradition and Identity.* Cambridge (MA), 1972.

Rzepka, Charles J. *The Self as Mind: Vision and Identity in Wordsworth, Coleridge, and Keats.* Cambridge (MA), 1986.

Sacks, Peter M. *The English Elegy: Studies in the Genre from Spenser to Yeats.* Baltimore, 1985.

Sambrook, James. *The Eighteenth Century: The Intellectual and Cultural Context of English Literature, 1700–1789.* London, 1986.

Saunders, J. W. *The Profession of English Letters.* London, 1964.

Schiffhorst, Gerald J. *John Milton.* New York, 1990.

Scodel, Joshua. *The English Poetic Epitaph: Commemoration and Conflict from Jonson to Wordsworth.* Ithaca, NY, 1991.

Scott, Walter. *Life of John Dryden.* Omaha, NE, 1963. From *Miscellaneous Prose Works of Sir Walter Scott, Bart.* Edinburgh, 1834.

Showalter, English. *The Evolution of the French Novel, 1641–1782.* Princeton, New Jersey, 1972.

Sitter, John *Literary Loneliness in Mid-Eighteenth-Century England.* Ithaca, 1982.

Sloane, Thomas O. *Donne, Milton, and the End of Humanist Rhetoric.* Berkeley/Los Angeles 1985.

Smart, J. S. *James MacPherson: an Episode in Literature.* London, 1905.

Smith, Adam. *Lectures on Rhetoric and Belles Lettres.* Ed. J. C. Bryce. Indianapolis, 1985.

Smith, Eric. *By Mourning Tongues: Studies in English Elegy.* London, 1977.

Spacks, P. M. *The Poetry of Vision: Five Eighteenth-Century Poets.* Cambridge, MA, 1967.

Steinke, M. W., ed. *Edward Young's 'Conjectures on Original Composition' in England and Germany: a Study in Literary Relations.* New York: F. C. Stechert Co., 1917.

Stewart, Philip. *Imitation and Illusion in the French Memoir-Novel, 1700–1750: The Art of Make-Believe.* New Haven: Yale University Press, 1969.

Stillinger, Jack, ed. *Selected Poems and Prefaces of William Wordsworth.* Boston Houghton Mifflin 1965.

Stone, P. E. K. *The Art of Poetry, 1750–1820.* London, 1967.

Sylvester, Richard S. *English Seventeenth-Century Verse.* 2 vols. New York, 1968.

Thomas, K. V. *Man and the Natural World: a History of the Modern Sensibility.* New York, 1983.

Toynbee, Paget, and Leonard Whibley, eds. *Correspondence of Thomas Gray.* Oxford, 1935.

Trickett, Rachel. 'Cowper, Wordsworth, and the Animal Fable.' *Review of English Studies* (1983).

Trilling, Lionel. *Sincerity and Authenticity: Six Lectures.* New York, 1980.

Trowbridge, Hoyt. *From Dryden to Jane Austen: Essays on English Critics and Writers, 1660–1818.* Albuquerque, New Mexico, 1977.

Tuve, Rosemond. *Elizabethan and Metaphysical Imagery....* Chicago, 1947.

Wain, John. *Samuel Johnson: a Biography.* New York, 1974.

Warton, Thomas. *History of English Poetry.* London, 1774.

Watson, J. R., ed. *Pre-Romanticism in English Poetry of the Eighteenth Century: The Poetic Art and Significance of Thomson, Gray, Collins, Goldsmith, Cowper and Crabbe.* London, 1989.

Watt, Ian. *The Rise of the Novel.* London, 1960.

Weinbrot, Howard D., and Martin Price. *Context, Influence, and Mid-Eighteenth-Century Poetry.* Los Angeles, 1990.

Wellek, Rene. *The Rise of English Literary History.* Chapel Hill, North Carolina, 1941.

Wicker, C. *Edward Young and the Fear of Death: a Study in Romantic Melancholy.* Albuquerque, 1952.

Wilde, Oscar. 'The Decay of Lying.' *Literary Criticism of Oscar Wilde.* Ed. Stanley Weintraub. Lincoln, Nebraska, 1968.

Williams, R. *The Country and the City.* London, 1973.

Williamson, George. *Seventeenth-Century Contexts.* London, 1960.

Wilson, A. N. *The Life of John Milton.* New York, 1983.

Winn, James A. *John Dryden and His World.* New Haven: Yale University Press, 1987.

Wolfe, Don. *Milton and His England.* New York, 1970.

Wordsworth, William *Lyrical Ballads and Other Poems 1797–1800* Ed. James Butler and Karen Green Ithaca (NY) Cornell University Press 1992.

—— *The Prelude, or Growth of a Poet's Mind.* Ed. Ernest de Selincourt Oxford: Oxford University Press, 1949.

Wright, G. T. 'Stillness and the Argument of Gray's "Elegy"'. *Modern Philology* 74 (1977).

—— *The Poet in the Poem.* Berkeley, 1960.

Young, Edward *Night Thoughts* Ed. Stephen Cornford. Cambridge: Cambridge University Press, 1989.

—— *Conjectures on Original Composition* (see Steinke, M. W. [ed.]).

Index

Addison, Joseph, 95, 96
  'The Campaign': style, 99–100
ambition, literary, 12
  of Milton, 2, 18–20, 21, 50, 52–3
  in Namur era, 90–1, 95
  and occasionality, 3, 4, 19–20
  and writer's block, 7, 27–9
  see also careers; ethics
animal elegies, 156–61
Anne, Queen: and preferment,
  90–1
Anson, George, 149
aporia
  as trope: in Cowper, 154–6; in
  Young, 167, 181
  in writers' careers, *see* delay
  under Dryden; Milton
Aristotle, 2, 22, 23, 134
attribution: and response, 128–9
  Gray parody, 127–8, 129–30, 137
Auden, W. H., 56
'authority': in invention, 13
autobiographical truth, 16, 17
  in Milton: 'Lycidas', 35
  in Shenstone, 188–90
  in Wordsworth, 5, 16–17, 200–1
  in Young, 167, 168, 172–7, 179–83

Bate, W. J., 13
Beaumont, Joseph, 40–1
Birch, Thomas, 80
Blackmore, Sir Richard, 93, 115
Blair, Robert: 'The Grave', 32, 123,
  125–6, 165, 188
Blenheim, battle of, 87, 96
Bloom, Harold, 13
Boileau, Nicolas: and Prior, 111–15
booksellers: and memorial
  volumes, 6–7, 95–6, *see also* Curll
Boswell, James, 90–1, 128
  and Gray, 122, 127–8, 129–30
  'sensitive' ethos, 184
Boyne: victory, 103

Braudy, Leo, 20
Bredvold, L., 59, 67
Briggs, Sampson, 48
Broich, Ulrich, 93
Brown, Cedric C., 26, 49, 50, 51, 61
Brown, Laura, 87
Brown, Tom, 87, 95, 106
  on Dryden's funeral, 82–3, 85
Buckinghamshire, Duke of (John
  Sheffield), 106–7, 116–17
Busby, Richard, 96, 97

Campbell, Gordon, 12, 34, 35
Cana miracle, Milton on, 24, 25, 26,
  48
careers: of poets, 15–16, 56–7
  in Namur era, 90–2, 100;
  example: Edmund Smith, 96–9
  via memorial volumes, 1, 4, 7, 17,
  33, 36–8, 55
  Wordsworth, 2, 192
Carew, Thomas: elegies on Mary
  Villiers, 29–32, 45, 64
Chalmers, Alexander F. S. A., 6,
  135, 156
Chatterton, Thomas, 93, 181
Chaucer, grave of: and Dryden's
  burial, 80, 81, 204
Chichikov, Pavel Ivanovich (in
  Dead Souls), 124, 126
Churchill, Charles, 106
Cibber, Colley, 118–20
Clark, Donald L., 21
Cleveland, John, 4, 41–6, 55
competition(s), 15, 17
  Cleveland on, 41–6
  in Namur era, 87, 106–7; as
  'Session of Poets', 116–21
  in rhetorical training, 23, 24,
  25–6; and writer's block, 7, 21,
  27–9
  via memorial volumes, 1, 17, 33,
  36–8, 55